To Rikki

From Manny (Chicago).

(I hope this is useful to you).

CROWNING ELEGANCE

A Kosher Culinary Experience

Arie Crown Hebrew Day School

Copyright © 2004
by
Arie Crown Hebrew Day School

1st Printing   2004   5,000 copies

ISBN: 0-9760243-0-6
LCCN: 2004095507

WIMMER
COOKBOOKS
ConsolidatedGraphics
800.548.2537
wimmerco.com

Contents:

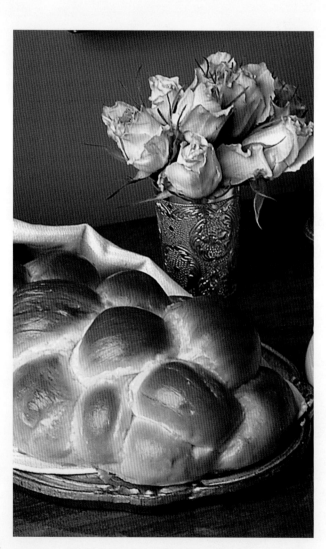

Forward

With our own busy lives and families, we know the joys and challenges of cooking. For everyday dinners for our large families, company-filled Shabbos meals or extravagant Yom Tov feasts, there is nothing as valuable as a variety filled cookbook with time-tested, clear, detailed, organized, and most important, delicious recipes. *Crowning Elegance* is this cookbook. Created exclusively by parents of Arie Crown Hebrew Day School, from recipes, photographs, food design and tasting parties, *Crowning Elegance* represents a unique compilation of extraordinary dishes. Moroccan Chickpea and Lentil Soup, Syrian Fila with Cheese, and Ashkenazic Kokosh cake…sound tempting? *Crowning Elegance* features American, Asian, French, Israeli, Italian, Mexican, Moroccan, Persian, Syrian and traditional European-Jewish recipes, displayed in the casually chic settings that today's home makers and at-home chefs prize. With close to three hundred recipes and one-hundred and eighty color photographs, *Crowning Elegance* has something for everyone.

Creating this cookbook was an adventure all its own. Central to the selection process were our formal 'blind' tasting parties. The cooks and tasters didn't know whose recipe they were cooking and rating. Recipes needed to meet not only the approval of the editors and the tasting-party chef, but the approval of seventy-five percent of the tasters. In addition, for even greater ease of use, the multitude of varied and savory recipes have been categorized by level of difficulty of their entire cooking process, and the "average" chef's preparation time. We've also included wine suggestions and a medley of menus to suit a wide range of occasions.

Similar to the inexhaustible re-testing of the recipes, the myriad of color photographs embedded throughout *Crowning Elegance* are aimed at assisting you in your own creations. Unlike many cookbooks, we didn't alter the food in any way for the photography, rendering it inedible. These delicious dishes are truly replicable in all aspects in your own kitchen.

Crowning Elegance has been a labor of love for us and the extended Arie Crown family. Lending their heirloom dishes, opening their homes for photo shoots, preparing dishes, reading, editing and eating, the Arie Crown parents have truly committed themselves to every aspect of this endeavor. We give you a creation inspired by love of family and food, community and tradition. We hope it brings you joy.

Valerie Kanter and Mandy Bachrach

About Arie Crown Hebrew Day School

In 1947, a group of parents shared a vision of an educational institute where the Jewish children of Chicago could receive the highest quality education in a warm and caring environment. Arie Crown Hebrew Day School was born. Through the years our school has grown while remaining true to its founders' original vision, continuing to strive for academic excellence while fostering a love for one's fellow man and a desire to help the community.

Arie Crown Hebrew Day School boasts a highly qualified, professional, creative and caring faculty who are dedicated to the growth and needs of each child. Their warmth, dedication and devotion creates a unique environment that provides the proper direction for our children's education. In Arie Crown, our tradition is to encourage proper middos and mitzvah observance through discussion, practice and example. Our students are encouraged to express their creativities and talents, allowing them to develop a strong, positive, self-esteem and a positive feeling about learning.

We believe that we must weave the values of Torah Judaism into the texture of living Jewish law, and encourage our students to live their lives with dignity. We are proud of our many graduates who have gone from Arie Crown's classrooms into the world armed with the strengths and values of our traditions. To find out more about our school, please call the school office at (847) 982-9191 to schedule an appointment with our administration.

A Letter from the Editor

Crowning Elegance's success is due to the dedication and commitment of the parent body of Arie Crown Hebrew Day School. Masterfully handling all aspects of the process, including cooking, baking, timing, tasting, opening their homes, photo styling, and photography, they helped make *Crowning Elegance* both a magnificent and a user-friendly cookbook.

A special thank you to my right hand person, my assistant editor, Mandy Bachrach, without whose daily diligence, energy and creativity this cookbook would not have been completed. Thank you to Jay Friedman of Satin Photo Studio Inc., for his patience and artistic talents and to Miri Rosenwasser of Tres Joli Designs, for her expert vision and exquisite taste that helped bring beauty to these pages.

Most importantly, I would like to thank my family and the families of my assistants for their tremendous support and encouragement over these past 3 years. From mid-night cooking to late night tasting parties from schlepping in the snow for photo shoots to never ending "Mommy's editing the cookbook." They have endured all too much take out food and tuna for dinner on paper plates while I worked on other people's recipes. Thank You!!

Valerie Kanter
Editor in Chief

CROWNING ELEGANCE would like to extend a special thank you to our photographer, *Jay Friedman*, for his undying patience, enthusiasm, creativity and generosity. The perfect photographs that surround this book reflect the love and dedication with which they were taken.

JAY FRIEDMAN is an award winning photographer specializing in food photography, portraiture and wedding photography. Jay's photography studio, Satin Photo Studio, Inc., is located in Skokie, Illinois. With over twenty years of experience, Jay integrates photography and food with a unique style and great attention to detail. Through his work, he has been able to merge his creative talents, appreciation for fine food, dedication to his family and his ongoing support for quality Jewish education. Jay and his wife live in Chicago with their two children.

SPONSORS

CROWNING ELEGANCE gratefully acknowledges our sponsors, whose generosity and belief in this project have made our cookbook a reality.

BATYA AND BINYOMIN KLEIN   ALBERT MILTON KANTER FOUNDATION

OMNICARE CHARITABLE FOUNDATION   DEBRA AND SHABSAI WOLFE

JO AND JONAH BRUCK   ROBERT AND DEBBIE HARTMAN

BRIAN AND MICHELLE LEVINSON AND FAMILY   JOYCE AND DENNIS RUBEN AND FAMILY

THE WEINSCHNEIDER FAMILY   FLORA AND MARTY WEISS

DONNA AND YIGAL YAHAV AND FAMILY

The editors wish to thank the professional volunteers with whom we worked side by side. Their loving insights and contributions make CROWNING ELEGANCE a truly special book.

Residential interior designer MIRI ROSENWASSER brings a flair for European charm to her imaginative food designs and exquisite table settings. Growing up in Israel in a traditional Moroccan home, under the tutelage of a mom whose catering drew high-profile raves, she absorbed a passion for refined cuisine and stylish presentation and an inspiration for sharing those gifts with her community. Whether designing an entire home, an individual room, or special party, Miri blends high style with Old World sensibility. She and her husband, David, are the proud, grateful parents of six children. Miri is the founder of Tres Joli Designs in Chicago.

SARELLE WEINER is a pastry artist trained in the creation of gourmet and custom made theme creations. She has been professionally trained by world renowned Gold Medal cake sculptor, Roland Winebeckler and the nationally acclaimed cake designer, Colette Peters of New York, as well as others. Sarelle's custom cakes and confections are spectacular gourmet quality works of art which reflect her exquisite expressions, spanning the range of elegant and whimsical. Sarelle's online portfolio from her designs for Edible Gems by Sarelle can be viewed at www.gemsbysarelle.com. Sarelle is the source for the finest, most beautiful cakes in Chicagoland, where she lives with her husband and seven children.

Crowning Elegance thanks all those who graciously opened their homes to our tasting parties and photo-shoots. Words cannot express our gratitude for the use of your homes, dishes, time and privacy. The beauty that surrounds your daily life surrounds this book.

Hosts for Tasting Parties:

Bill and Valerie Kanter
Elly and Mandy Bachrach
Ben and Eva Weinschneider
Alan and Connie Kadish

Hosts for Photo-Shoots:

Miri Rosenwasser
Leah Shapiro
Gitti Berk
Connie Kadish
Eva Weinschneider

Crowning Elegance gratefully acknowledges the chefs and tasters who prepared for the photo-shoots and tested all the recipes. Your time, support, comments and appetites, ensure that each and every recipe is tantalizing, delicious and accurate.

Chefs for Photo-Shoots:

Tamar Abell	Missy Kost	Andy Shandalov
Mandy Bachrach	Sharon Matten	Noemy Skidelsky
Eleanor Birnbaum	Miriam Mendelsberg	Mimi Stein
Michelle Bulgatz	Ellie Merzel	Julie Steinberg
Gitta Domsky	Rochie Porush	Chani Turk
Alexa Friedman	Dina Romanoff	Voie Weinfeld
Connie Kadish	Miri Rosenwasser	Eva Weinschneider
Valerie Kanter	Terri Rosenwasser	Sharon Wishner
Bill Kanter	Shani Schultz	

Chefs for Tasting Parties:

Tamar Abell
Pnina Arsers
Shani Aryeh
Shulamis Ashkanazy
Zevi Ashkanazy
Ora Azose
Mandy Bachrach
Naomi Bayever
Renee Birn
Eleanor Birnbaum
Michelle Bulgatz
Gitta Domsky
Tami Drapkin
Elana Dubovick
Cheryl Fishman
Alexa Friedman

Haskel Garfinkel
Rochel Garfinkel
Jodi Gershman
Leslie Goldmeier
Adina Greenberg
Ronit Gutnicki
Shaina Hunt
Roz Isaacs
Jenny Jacobson
Connie Kadish
Bill Kanter
Valerie Kanter
Missy Kost
Galya Lapson
Esther Mashiach
Margaret Matanky

Sharon Matten
Miriam Mendelsberg
Ellie Merzel
Heidi Meyerowitz
Tamar Miller
Jenny Nadoff
Rochie Porush
Dina Romanoff
Miri Rosenwasser
Terri Rosenwasser
Michelle Rubin
Jean Sadoff
Shani Schultz
Rusie Schwartz
Huvie Shabat
Andy Shandalov

Leah Shapiro
Davida Siegal
Sharon Siegal
Erica Simon
Noemy Skidelsky
Mimi Stein
Julie Steinberg
Linda Stone
Tema Taxer
Sarelle Weiner
Voie Weinfeld
Eva Weinschneider
Tanya Weissman
Wendy Wilens
Donna Yahav

Tasters:

David and Tamar Abell
Michael and Pnina Arsers
Moshe David and Shani Aryeh
Zevi and Shulamis Ashkanazy
Yaakov and Orah Azose
Elly and Mandy Bachrach
Wayne and Naomi Bayever
Juli Bell
Irv and Eleanor Birnbaum
Joe and Michelle Bulgatz
Zave and Gitta Domsky
Elana Dubovick
Adam and Cheryl Fishman
Colin and Alexa Friedman

Jay Friedman
Hal and Rochel Garfinkel
Haskel and Shani Garfinkel
Alan and Jodi Gershman
Shaya and Leslie Goldmeier
Kevin and Adina Greenberg
Abie and Ronit Gutnicki
Yosef and Shaina Hunt
Dean and Roz Isaacs
Joel and Jenny Jacobson
Alan and Connie Kadish
Bill and Valerie Kanter
Sue Klein
Jerold and Melissa Kost

Dovid and Galya Lapson
Randi Loskove
Margaret Matanky
Alan and Sharon Matten
Shelly and Miriam Mendelsberg
David and Ellie Merzel
Gavin and Heidi Meyerowitz
Jonathan and Tamar Miller
David and Rochie Porush
Dina Romanoff
David and Miri Rosenwasser
Michelle Rubin
Marty and Shani Schultz
Chaim and Rusie Schwartz

Jerry and Jean Sadoff
Zev and Andy Shandalov
Leah and Hillel Shapiro
Michael and Davida Siegal
Jeremy and Erica Simon
Neil and Mimi Stein
Mark and Julie Steinberg
Steve and Linda Stone
Lance and Tema Taxer
Moshe and Chani Turk
Heschel and Sarelle Weiner
Avrum and Voie Weinfeld
Ben and Eva Weinschneider
Yigal and Donna Yahav

Crowning Elegance thanks all the cooks who contributed their treasured and original recipes to this book. We regret that we were unable to include all the recipes. We hope that we have not inadvertently overlooked any contributors.

Recipe Contributors:

Adina Aaron
Tamar Abell
Elka Abramchik
Ellen Abramowitz
Debbie Alexander
Robin Alford
Esther Appel
Pnina Arsers
Shani Aryeh
Shulamis Ashkanazy
Orah Azose
Mandy Bachrach
Debbie Bajtner
Naomi Bayever
Hannah Bekritsky
Roberta Berger
Gita Berk
Rivka Leah Bernath
Rachelle Bernstein
Eleanor Birnbaum
Chaya Esther Brand
David Brand
Bluma Broner
Sarita Brooks
Michelle Bulgatz
Debbie Cash
Gitta Domsky
Elana Dubovick
Donna Elfman
Joseph Lev Fabisoff
Ruti Rachel Fabisoff
Rachel Feit
Abigail Felt

Akiva Felt
Ilene Finkel
Pessie Finn
Cheryl Fishman
Alexa Friedman
Phyllis Garden
Jodi Gershman
Lori Gerson
Sharon Gertz
Esther Goldman
Fraydelle Goldson
Barbara Goldstein
Chana Goldstein
Riki Greenberg
Devorah Greenfield
Ronit Gutnicki
Heather Haggler
Deborah Hirsch
Shayna Hunt
Jenny Jacobson
Rachel Jakofsky
Connie Kadish
Bill Kanter
Valerie Kanter
Janet Katz
Linda Kirshner
Malka Kleiman
Soosan Kohananoo
Sarah Malka Krinsky
Michelle Kushner
Galya Lapson
Gittel Leichtman
Roni Lichtman

Malka Loterstein
Rachelle Marcus
Meryl Mark
Esther Mashiach
Lee Matanky
Margaret Matanky
Sharon Matten
Louise Mayefsky
Miriam Mendelsberg
Doreen Mermelstein
Ellie Merzel
Faye Meyers
Miriam Meyers
Lori Meystel
Rachel Montrose
Lorraine Mosery
Victoria Mosery
Jenny Nadoff
Yehudit Nathan
Sheila Ozmina
Debbie Peikes
Chana Polatsek
Bob Polisky
Norma Pollack
Shana Polsky
Esther Porush
Rochie Porush
Tina Pressburger
Karen Reiffman
Dina Romanoff
Ellen Romanoff
Miri Rosenwasser
Terri Rosenwasser

Jean Sadoff
Inger Saphire-Bernstein
Susan Schrek-Greer
Shani Schultz
Shana Schuman
Mimi Seleski
Tanni Seruya
Huvi Shabbat
Andy Shandalov
Leah Shapiro
Phyllis Shapiro
Marsha Sheinfeld
Marci Siebzener
Erica Simon
Noemy Skidelsky
Amy Stark
Lev Stark
Julie Steinberg
Linda Stone
Roz Sugarman
Tema Taxer
Brooke Warso
Sarelle Weiner
Voie Weinfeld
Debbie Weingrow
Eva Weinschneider
Lorye Weiss
Wendy Wilens
Isabella Wiznitser
Libby Wolf
Becky Zimmerman
Sarah Zimmerman

Loaned Us Their Beautiful Things:

BBj Fine Linen Rental	Valerie Kanter	Mimi Stein
Miri Rosenwasser	Mandy Bachrach	Debby Wolfe
Leah Shapiro	Denise Friedman	Eva Gertzfeld
Eva Weinschneider	Connie Kadish	Terri Rosenwasser
Gitti Berk	Sandy Kanter	Israela Dackman
	Devorah Weinfeld	

Flowers Donated and Provided by:

A Gentle Wind	Valerie Kanter
Blooming Gardens	Mandy Bachrach
Gitti Berk	Miri Rosenwasser

Photographer:

Jay Friedman of Satin Photo Studio, Inc.

Food Designers:

Miri Rosenwasser of Tres Joli Designs
Mandy Bachrach
Valerie Kanter

Cake Decorating Adviser:

Sarelle Weiner of Edible Jems

Wine Adviser:

Connie Kadish

Proofreaders:

Evie Pearlman of ImagiCom Media Services, Inc.
Denice Friedman
Mandy Bachrach
Gitta Domsky

Marketing and Advertising Committee:

Molly Cohen	Chaya Tova Hartman	Andrea Polster
Shani Garfinkle	Wendy Malkin	Michelle Rubin
Lori Gerson	Yocheved Neuman	Miki Schreiber

Editor in Chief:

Valerie Kanter

Assistant Editor:

Mandy Bachrach

Treasurer:

Jodi Gershman

Special Thank You:

ACHDS SCHOOL BOARD	**ACHDS PTA**	**OFFICE STAFF**
Gary Hoberman	Debbie Peikes	Delores Lindenbaum
Jordan Klein	Eleanor Birnbaum	Yocheved Goldwag
Michael Klein	Sue Klein	Bruchie Levy
Jeffery Schwartz	Randi Loskove	Rabbi Lester
	Louise Mayefsky	

Cooks Notes:

As a rule it is best to cook and bake using the freshest ingredients one can find.

For fruits and vegetables, purchase those in season, free of blemishes and bruises, preferably organic. Farmers markets and green grocers are closer to the source and usually carry better quality produce than supermarkets. Wash all fruits and vegetables well before using.

Get to know your local butcher or fishmonger. Clue them in on which cuts of meat or types of fish you prefer. Butchers are usually accommodating to put something aside for regular customers; this ensures you'll get the best of what's available. All meats, poultry and fish must be rinsed and patted dry with paper towels prior to using or freezing. Do not leave these ingredients at room temperature unnecessarily, keep refrigerated until actively ready to prepare or cook.

Use fresh, large eggs for all recipes. For baking all ingredients should be at room temperature, unless the recipe specifies otherwise. Yeast should be at room temperature when preparing breads and yeast doughs.

When handling hot peppers use caution. Wear disposable gloves and keep hands away from eyes. Wash hands thoroughly with soap and water after touching.

For recipes that call for good quality chocolate, purchase the best quality you can afford for exquisite results. Many of the cakes, desserts, pies, cookies and bars are parve. If they are listed as only dairy they may have been attempted parve with unsatisfactory results, hence kept dairy as originally submitted.

Preparation time is an average. Each individual cooks at a different pace with many factors contributing to the results, from the size of ones kitchen to the ingredients being readily available. Use these preparation times as ballpark figures, as each chef cooks a little faster, or slower than his neighbor.

Cook with love for your task at hand, your results will be visually more enjoyable and a pure pleasure to taste.

TAKING CHALLAH:

The name Challah comes from the biblical commandment to give a portion of dough, Challah, to the Kohen, priest in the Temple. Because the Temple is no longer standing today, we take the portion of dough and burn it.

Challah is only taken when enough dough is prepared. When baking any bread, using between 7¾ to 11¾ cups of flour, Challah should be taken without saying a blessing. When using 12 or more cups of flour the Challah should be taken with a blessing. The blessing 'להפריש חלה מן העסה'..., '...lehafrish challah min ha esah' is said. A small portion of dough is then removed from the main batch of dough. The Challah is then burned and disposed of.

The blessing of Challah can be said in the merit of others. When reciting the blessing, keep the names of those you hold in your prayers in your thoughts.

SIX STRAND BRAIDED CHALLAH:

Divide dough into 6 logs. Lay logs next to each other and pinch ends together at the top. Arrange logs with 3 on each side and a space in the middle (photo 1).

Grasp left outermost log with right hand and right outermost log with left hand (photo 2).

Bring left log over log in left hand to outer right then bring right log to center so that it overlaps the log that was just moved to the right (photo 3).

From now on their will always be a log that extends away from the other 5.

Grasp log, closest to extended log and bring to opposite side (photo 4).

Bring extended log to center space (photo 5).

Repeat, alternating sides, (photo 6) until logs are finished.

Pinch ends together to finish braid (photo 7).

The dough will rise and the finished product will be a beautiful golden challah (photo 8).

Classic Challah

PARVE   YIELD 7 (1-POUND) LOAVES

As its name states this is a "classic" in flavor and texture. This recipe makes 7 (1-pound) loaves, great for a large crowd or to freeze and have on hand. Traditional braiding calls for forming the braids using 3 logs. To try your hand at a more elaborate braid, see page 16 for instructions on how to form a braid using 6 logs.

DOUGH
4 cups warm water
3 tablespoons active dry yeast
13 cups white bread flour
1 cup sugar

2 eggs
1 cup canola oil
2 teaspoons salt

TOPPING
2 egg whites, beaten

DOUGH: In a very large bowl combine water and yeast. Let rest until yeast dissolves, about 5 minutes. Add remainder of ingredients and knead by hand until dough becomes smooth and elastic, about 10 minutes. Cover with a clean kitchen towel and let rise until double in size, about 1 hour.

Punch down and knead for about 5 minutes. Cover and let rise for an additional hour.

Prepare 4 parchment lined (15x10-inch) jelly-roll pans, or 7 greased loaf pans.

Preheat oven to 350°F/180°F.

For 7 (1-pound) braids, divide dough into 7 sections, each section into thirds, then form into logs then braid. Place 1 or 2 braids on each pan. Cover with a clean kitchen towel and let rise for 30 minutes.

TOPPING: Using a pastry brush, brush challahs with beaten egg whites. Bake for 30 minutes. Place on wire racks to cool.

Preparation Time: 30 minutes
Rising Time: 2 hours 30 minutes
Cook Time: 30 minutes in 2 batches, 1 hour total
Experience Level: Intermediate

Wine decanters can be crafted from many materials. Striking silver, hand blown glass or earthenware can be formed into whimsical or traditional shaped vessels. Fill your favorite decanter with your choice of dinner wine to bring to the table and delight your guests. Use a funnel to pour your leftover wine into the original bottle for storage after your meal.

Sweet Honey Challah

PARVE   **YIELD 2 LOAVES**

This challah is sweet with the perfect texture. It is important to make enough because everyone always wants seconds and thirds.

DOUGH
1 cup water
4 tablespoons oil
2 tablespoons honey
2 eggs

4 cups white pastry flour
1½ teaspoons salt
4 teaspoons sugar
2½ teaspoons active dry yeast

TOPPING
2 to 3 tablespoons honey

2 to 3 tablespoons sesame seeds

DOUGH: Place all ingredients for dough in bread machine container according to manufacturer's recommendation for 2-pound dough cycle.

Prepare a (15x10-inch) parchment lined jelly-roll pan.

When dough cycle is complete, turn dough out onto a lightly floured work surface. Divide dough in half. Divide each half into thirds. Roll each section into a log. Form logs into 2 braids and place on prepared cookie sheet. Cover with a clean kitchen towel and let rise 30 minutes to 1 hour.

Preheat oven to 350°F/180°C.

After dough has risen drizzle honey over challahs. Sprinkle with sesame seeds.

Bake for 23 minutes or until lightly browned. Remove from oven and place on wire racks to cool.

Preparation Time: 10 minutes
Rising Time: 30 minutes to 1 hour
Cook Time: 23 minutes
Experience Level: Beginner

Seven Grain Challah

PARVE   YIELD 2 LOAVES

When making a healthier challah, this sweet and moist version is the way to go. It is an excellent alternative to the traditional white wheat challah.

1 cup bulgur wheat
1½ cups boiling water
4½ teaspoons active dry yeast
½ cup warm water
6 tablespoons canola oil
⅓ to ½ cup honey

2 teaspoons salt, optional
2 eggs, beaten
2 cups whole wheat pastry flour
½ cup soy flour
3 cups white bread flour

Place bulgur wheat in the bowl of a mixer fitted with a dough hook. Pour boiling water over bulgur wheat. Set aside.

In a small bowl dissolve yeast in warm water, about 5 minutes.

When bulgur has cooled to lukewarm, add yeast mixture, oil, honey, salt, eggs, whole wheat pastry flour and soy flour. Mix on medium speed for 2 minutes. Slowly add white flour, ½ cup at a time until incorporated.

Cover with a clean kitchen towel and let rise 30 minutes.

Punch down dough and let rise until doubled in size, about 30 minutes.

Preheat oven to 375°F/190°C.

Prepare 2 (15x10-inch) parchment lined jelly-roll pans.

Divide dough in half. Divide each half into 3 sections. Roll sections into logs. Braid using 3 sections for each braid. Place on prepared pans and bake for 20 to 30 minutes. Transfer to wire racks to cool.

Preparation Time: 1 hour
Rising Time: 1 hour
Cook Time: 30 minutes
Experience Level: Beginner

Caramelized Onion Braids

PARVE   YIELD 2 LOAVES

This bread has an attractive braided presentation. The slightly sweet soft dough is a good balance with a filling that has a light onion flavor. To form even braids, begin braiding in center, braiding out towards each end.

FILLING
¼ cup margarine

2 medium onions, finely chopped

1 tablespoon sesame seeds

1 teaspoon garlic salt

1 teaspoon paprika

DOUGH
¾ cup warm water

2¼ teaspoons active dry yeast

4 to 4½ cups white bread flour, divided

½ cup non-dairy creamer

¼ cup sugar

¼ cup margarine, softened

1 egg

1½ teaspoons salt

TOPPING
1 egg, beaten

2 to 3 tablespoons sesame seeds, optional

FILLING: In a small skillet over medium heat, melt margarine. Add onions and cook until soft and tender. Add sesame seeds, garlic salt and paprika. Mix, remove from heat and allow to cool completely.

DOUGH: In the bowl of a mixer fitted with a dough hook, place warm water and yeast, let mixture rest until yeast dissolves, about 5 minutes. Add 2 cups of the flour, non-dairy creamer, sugar, margarine, egg and salt. Beat at low speed until blended. Add remaining 2 cups flour, beating at medium speed to form a soft dough. If dough is sticky, add additional flour. Cover with plastic wrap and allow to rise 1 hour.

On a lightly floured work surface, roll out dough to form a (18x12-inch) rectangle. With a pizza wheel or a sharp knife cut dough lengthwise into 3 (18x4-inch) strips. Cut in half widthwise so you have 6 (9x4-inch) strips. Spread about 2 tablespoons of filling on each strip, leaving a ½-inch border around the edges. Bring lengthwise edges of each strip together to enclose filling. Pinch edges and ends to seal.

Prepare 2 (15x10-inch) parchment lined jelly-roll pans.

On prepared pan braid 3 logs together, pinch ends to seal. Repeat with remaining 3 logs for a second braid. Cover with a clean kitchen towel and let rise 1 hour or until doubled in size.

Preheat oven to 350°F/180°C.

TOPPING: Using a pastry brush, brush loaves with beaten egg. Sprinkle with sesame seeds. Bake for 27 minutes or until golden brown. Transfer to wire racks to cool.

Preparation Time: 30 minutes
Rising Time: 2 hours
Cook Time: 27 minutes
Experience Level: Intermediate

HONEY OAT BREAD

PARVE   YIELD 2 LOAVES

This bread is a winner in every aspect. It has a wonderfully sweet flavor and is fantastic for sandwiches. Requiring only a minimal amount of work, it will quickly become a frequent request in your home.

DOUGH

1¾ cups warm water, divided

1 tablespoon active dry yeast

¾ cup quick cooking oats

⅓ cup honey

3 tablespoons canola or vegetable oil

2½ teaspoons salt

5 cups white bread flour

1 teaspoon canola oil

TOPPING

1 egg, beaten

3 tablespoons quick cooking oats

DOUGH: In a large bowl, combine ¼ cup warm water with yeast. Let stand until yeast is dissolved, about 5 minutes. With a large spoon, stir in remaining 1½ cups water, oats, honey, oil and salt. Gradually knead in flour until a soft dough is formed. Place teaspoon oil in bowl and turn dough to coat. Cover with a clean kitchen towel and let rise until doubled, about 1 hour.

Prepare 2 greased (8½x4½-inch) loaf pans.

Punch down dough and divide in half. Shape into loaves and place into prepared loaf pans. Cover and let rise until doubled, approximately 20 minutes.

Preheat oven to 350°F/180°C.

TOPPING: Using a pastry brush, brush egg over tops of loaves. Evenly sprinkle oats over each loaf.

Place pans side by side and bake about 40 minutes. Transfer to wire rack to cool.

Preparation Time: 30 minutes
Rising Time: 1 hour 20 minutes
Cook Time: 40 minutes
Experience Level: Beginner

Raisin Herb Bread

PARVE   **YIELD 2 LOAVES**

Rosemary beautifully compliments the golden raisins to create a loaf that is both savory and sweet.

DOUGH

6½ cups white bread flour, divided

4½ teaspoons active dry yeast

2½ cups rice milk or non-dairy creamer

3 tablespoons sugar

2 tablespoons margarine

2 teaspoons salt

1 egg yolk

1½ cups golden raisins

4 teaspoons dried rosemary, crushed

1 teaspoon canola oil

TOPPING

1 egg white

1 tablespoon rice milk or non-dairy creamer

DOUGH: In the bowl of a mixer fitted with a dough hook, combine 3 cups of the flour with the yeast. In a medium saucepan over a medium low flame, heat rice milk, sugar, margarine and salt. Stir with a wooden spoon until warm (about 120°F/55°C) and margarine almost melts. Add milk mixture and egg yolk to flour mixture. Beat on low speed for 30 seconds, until combined. Scrape down sides of bowl with a rubber spatula as needed. Beat at high speed for 3 minutes. On low speed, stir in rosemary and raisins. Add remaining flour ½ cup at a time, mixing at medium speed until incorporated. Beat for 6 minutes at medium speed to make a soft and elastic dough. Place oil in bowl, place dough in bowl, turn dough to coat. Cover with a clean kitchen towel and allow to rise for 40 minutes to 1 hour, or until doubled in size.

Lightly grease 2 (9x5x3-inch) loaf pans. Punch down dough and divide in half. Form dough into the shape of a loaf and place in prepared pans. Cover and let rise for 30 to 40 minutes or until doubled in size.

TOPPING: Preheat oven to 375°F/190°C.

In a small bowl combine egg white and rice milk. Using a pastry brush, gently brush egg wash over tops of loaves. With a serrated knife, carefully make a shallow cut down the length of each loaf.

Bake for 30 minutes. Loosely cover loaves with aluminum foil and bake an additional 10 minutes. Bread should sound hollow when tapped on bottom. Loosen breads from pans immediately and cool on wire racks.

Preparation Time: 25 minutes
Rising Time: 1 hour 30 minutes
Cook Time: 40 minutes
Experience Level: Intermediate

Magnificent Crown Herb Bread

PARVE   **YIELD 1 LOAF**

This bread lives up to its name. It tastes magnificent, light and full of flavor. Its shape is beautiful, as a crown. This is the bread to choose for Purim or Sheva Brachos or any special event. Once you get the hang of it, this is an easy recipe to prepare.

¾ cup margarine
1 tablespoon garlic powder
2 tablespoons minced, dried onion flakes
2 tablespoons dried parsley flakes

1 (2-pound) recipe Basic Rolls (page 36) right out of the bread machine or purchased prepared frozen dough defrosted overnight in the refrigerator

In a large skillet over medium heat, melt margarine. Add garlic powder and onion flakes. Sauté for about 3 minutes until spices cook. Turn off heat, add parsley flakes and mix. Cut dough into about 14 pieces. Place pieces of dough in skillet and let soak into margarine mixture. Flip dough pieces and move margarine mixture around to ensure dough is coated on all sides.

In an ungreased tube pan, place pieces of dough in single file, side by side in a circle around pan. Do not stack dough on top of each other, squeeze them in if necessary. Pour remaining margarine mixture evenly over top of dough. Cover with a clean kitchen towel and let rise 3 to 4 hours.

Prepare oven by placing aluminum foil as a liner over lower rack to catch any drips. Preheat oven to 325°F/160°C. Place dough on middle rack. Bake for 30 to 35 minutes or until golden. Bread will puff up and look like a big mushroom.

Let cool in pan at room temperature. When removing from pan, place 2 pieces of aluminum foil, about 18 inches long, on counter side by side. Turn bread over onto foil, puffed up part face down. Cut 1 or 2 pieces of foil, 18-inches long and place on bottom part of bread (side that was in tube pan) to secure bread. Use 2 other pieces of foil to wrap puffed up part. Bread can be frozen at this point.

When ready to serve, remove top foil only in order to see the puffed up part. Keep bottom foil in place to keep bread secure.

Preparation Time: 20 minutes
Rising Time: 3 to 4 hours
Cook Time: 40 minutes
Experience Level: Intermediate

French Baguettes

PARVE   YIELD 3 LOAVES

A classic daily bread similar to Italian bread with a nice crisp crust. An excellent choice for dipping and to accompany your favorite soup or stew.

DOUGH

1¾ cups water   2 teaspoons salt
3½ cups white bread flour   2 teaspoons active dry yeast
¼ cup whole wheat flour

TOPPING

1 egg white, beaten   1 tablespoon sesame seeds

DOUGH: Place dough ingredients in bread machine container according to manufacturer's recommendations for 2 pound dough cycle.

Lightly grease a baguette pan or line a (15x10-inch) jelly-roll pan with parchment paper.

When dough cycle is complete, turn dough out onto lightly floured work surface. Divide dough into 3 sections. Roll each piece of dough into a baguette the length of pan. Cover with a clean kitchen towel and let rise for 1 hour.

Preheat oven to 425°F/220°C.

TOPPING: Using a pastry brush, lightly brush unbaked baguettes with beaten egg white and sprinkle with sesame seeds. Using a sharp serrated knife, diagonally slash 3 or 4 cuts ½-inch deep across baguettes.

Spray or splash about ¼ cup of cold water into the hot oven to create steam. Immediately place bread into oven. Bake for approximately 20 minutes. Baguettes will have a light golden color and crisp crust.

Remove from oven and place on cooling racks. Let cool 20 minutes before slicing.

Preparation Time: 10 minutes
Rising Time: 1 hour
Cook Time: 20 minutes
Experience Level: Beginner

Whole Wheat Baguettes

PARVE   YIELD 3 LOAVES

A rich whole grain flavor that nicely complements a simple weeknight meal.

DOUGH

1½ cups warm water

1 cup whole wheat flour

3 cups white bread flour

1½ teaspoons fine sea salt or table salt

2 teaspoons active dry yeast

TOPPING

2 tablespoons olive oil

2 tablespoons zatar, optional

DOUGH: Place dough ingredients into container of bread machine according to manufacturer's recommendation for 2 pound dough cycle.

Prepare a lightly greased baguette pan or a parchment lined (15x10-inch) jelly-roll pan.

When dough cycle is complete, turn dough out onto a lightly floured work surface. Divide dough into 3 equal pieces. Roll and stretch each piece of dough into a log about 15-inches long. Place on prepared pan. Cover with a clean kitchen towel and let rise about 45 minutes.

Preheat oven to 450°F/230°C.

Using a serrated knife, diagonally score 4 cuts into the top of the baguettes about ⅛-inch deep.

TOPPING: Using a pastry brush, lightly brush baguettes with olive oil and sprinkle with zatar.

Spray or splash about ¼ cup of cold water into the hot oven to create steam. Immediately place baguettes in oven. Bake for 12 minutes or until baguettes sound hollow when tapped on bottom. Baguettes will have a nice crisp crust. Transfer to wire racks and let cool.

Preparation Time: 15 minutes
Rising Time: 45 minutes
Cook Time: 12 minutes
Experience Level: Beginner

When morning's light streams in through the windows be prepared to start your day. Plan ahead and you will have wonderful treats to anticipate as you snuggle under the covers for a few more solitary moments.

FRENCH BAGUETTES WITH OLIVES

PARVE   YIELD 2 LOAVES

This is not a traditional French bread. The savory olives and rosemary give a delicious change of pace to these baguettes. Even those who normally do not enjoy olives will like this bread.

DOUGH

4½ teaspoons active dry yeast
1½ cups warm water
4½ to 5 cups bread flour, divided
1¾ teaspoons salt

1 (6-ounce) jar pitted kalamata or black olives, drained, coarsely chopped
2 teaspoons chopped fresh rosemary
½ teaspoon canola oil

TOPPING

¼ cup cool water

¼ teaspoon salt

DOUGH: In the bowl of a mixer fitted with a dough hook, stir together yeast and warm water. Let mixture rest until yeast dissolves, about 5 minutes. On medium speed, mix in 2 cups of flour and the salt to form a paste. Cover with a clean kitchen towel and let rise for 20 minutes to make a frothy sponge. Add olives, rosemary and 2½ cups of the flour to the sponge and combine to make a soft dough.

Turn dough out onto a lightly floured work surface and knead until smooth and elastic, about 10 minutes. Add flour as necessary to prevent sticking.

Place oil in a large bowl. Add dough and turn to coat. Cover with a clean kitchen towel and allow to rise until almost doubled in size, about 45 minutes.

Prepare a greased baguette pan or parchment lined jelly-roll pan.

Punch down dough. On a lightly floured work surface, divide dough in half. With a rolling pin, roll each half into a 17x6-inch rectangle, 15x6-inch if using jelly-roll pan. On the length roll up jelly-roll style. Tuck ends under to form a long skinny loaf. Place loaves 3-inches apart on prepared pan. Cover baguettes with a clean kitchen towel and let rise for 45 minutes.

Heat oven to 425°F/220°C.

TOPPING: In a small bowl combine cool water and salt. Using a pastry brush, gently brush water mixture over the unbaked bread. Using a sharp serrated knife, cut 5 diagonal cuts about ½-inch deep across the tops of each baguette.

Bake for 30 minutes or until crust forms and is golden browned. Let cool on wire racks.

Preparation Time: 25 minutes
Rising Time: 1 hour 55 minutes
Cook Time: 30 minutes
Experience Level: Intermediate

CRESCENT ROLLS

PARVE   YIELD 24 ROLLS

DOUGH

¾ cup warm water

4¼ teaspoons yeast

½ teaspoon sugar

¼ cup margarine

½ cup sugar

½ teaspoon salt

2 eggs

4 cups white unbleached flour

TOPPING

4 tablespoons margarine, softened

DOUGH: In a small bowl, combine water, yeast and sugar. Let stand until yeast is dissolved, about 5 minutes.

In the bowl of a mixer fitted with a whisk, cream margarine and sugar. Add salt and eggs. Slowly add flour and mix on medium speed for 5 minutes until combined. Add yeast mixture and mix for an additional minute. Cover with a clean kitchen towel and let rise for 1½ hours.

Prepare 2 (15x10-inch) parchment lined jelly-roll pans.

On a lightly floured work surface, divide dough in half. Roll each half into a circle. Spread tops evenly with margarine. With a pizza wheel or a sharp knife cut each circle into 12 triangles.

Beginning with the wide end, roll up each triangle, rolling towards the point. Curve each into a crescent shape and place on pans 3-inches apart. Cover with a clean kitchen towel and let rise for 1 hour.

Preheat oven to 400°F/200°C.

Bake for 12 to 15 minutes or until golden.

Preparation Time: 35 minutes
Rising Time: 2 hours 30 minutes
Cook Time: 12 to 15 minutes
Experience Level: Beginner

*F*OCACCIA

PARVE SERVES 8

Savory and full of texture, this is the type of bread that can turn a simple soup or salad into a delicious and filling meal.

DOUGH
1⅛ cups water
2 tablespoons olive oil
2¼ cups white bread flour
1 cup whole wheat flour

2 teaspoons coarse salt
1 teaspoon dried basil
1 tablespoon active dry yeast

TOPPING
2 tablespoons olive oil
½ teaspoon dried leaf thyme
½ teaspoon dried basil

1 teaspoon coarse salt
4 ice cubes

DOUGH: Place dough ingredients into container of bread machine according to manufacturer's recommendation for 2 pound dough cycle.

Prepare a parchment lined (15x10-inch) jelly-roll pan.

When dough cycle is complete remove dough from machine. Stretch and pull, roll if necessary until dough fits onto full size of prepared pan. Take all ten fingers and poke indentations all over dough. Cover with a clean kitchen towel and let rise for 20 to 40 minutes.

Preheat oven to 425°F/220°C.

Place one oven rack in center of oven. Place another oven rack at top level. Put an empty baking tray on top level.

TOPPING: Uncover dough and repoke indentations. Using a pastry brush, brush dough with olive oil. In a small bowl combine thyme, basil and salt. Sprinkle evenly on top of dough.

Place ice cubes in tray on top level of oven, this creates steam and gives bread a nice crust. Immediately place bread on center rack. Bake for 15 minutes.

Transfer to cooling rack. Let cool 5 minutes. Cut into squares.

Preparation Time: 10 minutes
Rising Time: 20 to 40 minutes
Cook Time: 15 minutes
Experience Level: Beginner

BREAD MACHINE RYE BREAD

PARVE   YIELD 1½ POUND LOAF OR 2 POUND LOAF

This bread has a light rye flavor that is delicious warm, right out of the machine. Since there are no eggs in this recipe, it's the perfect one for setting on a timer to be ready at dinnertime.

1½ POUND LOAF
1 cup plus 2 tablespoons water
1½ tablespoons canola oil
2⅔ cups white bread flour
⅓ cup wheat germ
⅓ cup rye flour
3 tablespoons sugar
1½ teaspoons salt
1 teaspoon active dry yeast

2 POUND LOAF
1½ cups plus 1 tablespoon water
2 tablespoons canola oil
3½ cups white bread flour
½ cup wheat germ
½ cup rye flour
¼ cup sugar
2 teaspoons salt
1½ teaspoons active dry yeast

Place ingredients for the size loaf desired in bread machine container according to manufacturer's recommendations. Set baking cycle for appropriate size. When cycle is completed transfer to wire rack to cool.

Preparation Time: 5 minutes
Experience Level: Beginner

OASIS NAN BREAD

PARVE   YIELD 8 FLAT BREADS

This is an impressive middle eastern rustic bread with an awesome flavor. Straight out of the oven by itself, or dipped in a good quality olive oil, this is a flat-bread that will soon become one of your favorites. As the bread bakes, the centers puff up, then fall when the baking process is complete.

DOUGH
1¼ cups warm water
2¾ to 3 cups bread flour, more if it's a
  humid day, less if it's not

½ tablespoon salt
1 teaspoon active dry yeast

TOPPING
1½ tablespoons coarse salt

3 scallions, trimmed and chopped

DOUGH: Place dough ingredients in bread machine container according to manufacturer's recommendation for a 1 pound dough cycle.

Place oven rack in center of oven. Place a pizza stone or an inverted baking sheet in the oven to preheat. Preheat oven to 500°F/250°C.

When dough cycle is complete, remove dough and let rest on a lightly floured work surface for one minute. Lightly flour hands. Divide dough into 8 equal sections. Working with one section at a time, flatten dough into ⅛-inch thickness by pulling and stretching dough with hands. Place on a floured baking sheet. Sprinkle dough lightly with water. Prick bread all over with fingertips, (photo 1) then a fork, (photo 2) to make deep closely spaced rows of indentations. Lift dough and drape over hands stretching to create a rough oval shape approximately 5x9-inches.

TOPPING: Drape dough over rolling pin. Sprinkle dough with coarse salt and scallions (photo 3). When two or three sections of dough are draped over rolling pin, sprinkle inside of oven with water, this ensures a crisp crust. Lift rolling pin and roll dough onto pizza stone or inverted pan in oven.

Bake for 6 to 8 minutes until tops begin to color slightly. Carefully remove the breads with a spatula, leaving the stone in the oven for the next batch. Let cool on cooling rack for 5 minutes. Wrap in a towel to keep warm until ready to serve.

Prep Time: 30 minutes
Cook Time: 6 to 8 minutes in 3 batches, approximate total 18 to 24 minutes
Experience Level: Intermediate

Basic Rolls

This is a simple white bread roll which compliments any filling nicely. An excellent choice for the Pulled Chicken Sandwiches on page 186 and Sloppy Joes on page 149 as well as your basic tuna sandwich.

1 POUND–16 ROLLS	2 POUND–24 ROLLS
1 cup warm water	1¼ cups warm water
1 teaspoon lemon juice	1 teaspoon lemon juice
2 tablespoons canola oil	¼ cup canola oil
2 tablespoons non-dairy creamer	3 tablespoons non-dairy creamer
2 tablespoons sugar	3½ tablespoons sugar
3¼ cups bread flour	5 cups bread flour
1 teaspoon salt	2½ teaspoons salt
2¼ teaspoons active dry yeast	4 teaspoons active dry yeast

Place all ingredients in bread machine container according to manufacturer's recommendations for the dough cycle of either the 1 or 2 pound recipe.

Prepare 2 or 4 (15x10-inch) parchment lined jelly-roll pans.

When cycle is complete, place dough on a lightly floured work surface.

For the 1 pound cycle, divide dough into quarters, then divide each quarter into 4 sections, for a total of 16 pieces.

For the 2 pound cycle, divide dough into quarters, then divide each quarter into 8 sections, for a total of 24 pieces.

Place on prepared pans no more then 8 rolls per pan.

Cover with a clean kitchen towel and allow to rise for 30 minutes or until doubled in size.

Preheat oven to 350°F/180°C. Bake for 25 minutes or until tops are golden. Transfer to wire racks to cool.

Preparation Time: 10 minutes
Rising Time: 30 minutes
Cook Time: 25 minutes in 2 batches, 50 minutes total
Experience Level: Beginner

CARAWAY TWISTS

PARVE   YIELD 32 TWISTS

DOUGH

1½ cups warm water

2½ teaspoons active dry yeast

1 teaspoon sugar

1 teaspoon caraway seeds, crushed

1 teaspoon salt

4 cups white bread flour, divided

1 teaspoon canola oil

TOPPING

1 tablespoon baking soda

½ cup warm water

1 tablespoon coarse salt

DOUGH: In the bowl of a mixer fitted with a dough hook, combine water, yeast and sugar. Let stand until yeast dissolves, about 5 minutes. Add caraway seeds, salt and 2 cups of the bread flour to the yeast mixture. Beat, beginning on low, then medium speed until ingredients are combined. Scrape sides of bowl as needed with a rubber spatula. Gradually add 1½ cups flour. Beat on medium high speed for approximately 6 minutes until smooth and elastic. Add enough of the remaining ½ cup flour to keep dough from sticking to the sides of the bowl.

With hands, shape dough into a ball. Add canola oil to bottom of bowl. Place dough in bowl and turn to coat. Cover with a clean kitchen towel and let rise for 30 minutes or until double in size.

Preheat oven to 400°F/200°C. Prepare 2 parchment lined (15x10-inch) jelly-roll pans.

TOPPING: In a shallow bowl, whisk baking soda and water until dissolved.

On a lightly floured work surface, punch down dough and divide into quarters. Working with one quarter at a time, cut dough into 8 pieces. Roll each piece into a 5-inch rope. Dip ropes into baking soda mixture to coat. Twist dough once, to form a spiral. Place on prepared jelly-roll pan, 1-inch apart. Press ends against pan to prevent twists from uncurling.

Sprinkle twists with course salt. Bake for 16 to 18 minutes. Rotate pans halfway through baking. Transfer to wire racks to cool.

Preparation Time: 35 minutes

Rising Time: 30 minutes

Cook Time: 16 to 18 minutes

Experience Level: Beginner

Italian Herb Knots

PARVE   **YIELD 16 ROLLS**

An herb enhanced, flavorful bread tied into little knots. They will soon become your staple bread for company.

DOUGH

1½ cups water

4 tablespoons olive oil

1 tablespoon honey

4 cups white bread flour

4 tablespoons dried minced onion

1 tablespoon dried, fresh or frozen chopped
chives

1½ teaspoons garlic powder

1½ teaspoons oregano

2 teaspoons salt

2½ teaspoons active dry yeast

TOPPING

2 tablespoons olive oil

3 teaspoons garlic powder, oregano or zatar,
optional

DOUGH: Place all ingredients in bread machine container according to manufacturer's recommendation for large dough cycle.

Prepare 2 parchment lined (15x10-inch) jelly-roll pans.

When dough cycle is complete, turn dough out onto a lightly floured work surface. Form dough into a long log approximately 1-inch in diameter. Cut into 16 sections. Shape each section into logs about 6 to 8-inches long. Form logs into knots. Place knots onto prepared pans, leaving a 2-inch space between knots.

Cover with a clean kitchen towel and let rise for 30 minutes.

Preheat oven to 425°F/220°C.

TOPPING: Using a pastry brush, gently brush knots with olive oil. Sprinkle with any of the above listed herbs and seasonings.

Bake for 12 to 15 minutes or until bottoms begin to brown. Tops will not change color.

Preparation Time: 15 minutes
Rising Time: 30 minutes
Cook Time: 12 to 15 minutes
Experience Level: Intermediate

NEAPOLITAN PRETZEL RINGS WITH FENNEL SEEDS

MEAT   YIELD 24 PRETZELS

This is an Italian version of the soft pretzels that are sold on the streets of Manhattan. Children love them cut in half, as one would cut a bagel, and filled with cream cheese.

DOUGH

1¼ cups warm water
2¼ teaspoons active dry yeast
½ teaspoon sugar
¼ cup virgin olive oil

1½ teaspoons coarse salt
2 tablespoons fennel seeds
3 cups white bread flour
1 teaspoon olive oil

TOPPING

1 egg, beaten
1 tablespoon water

4 tablespoons sesame seeds
3 tablespoons coarse salt

DOUGH: In the bowl of a mixer fitted with a dough hook, combine water, yeast and sugar. Let stand 5 minutes until yeast is dissolved.

With a wooden spoon, stir in olive oil, salt and fennel seeds. Add flour and mix on medium speed for 2 minutes, scraping sides of bowl as necessary to incorporate. Remove and knead by hand for 1 minute, then another 2 minutes with mixer on low until dough is smooth and elastic. Pour teaspoon of olive oil on bottom of bowl. Place dough in bowl. Turn to coat. Cover with a clean kitchen towel, let rise 2 hours or until double in size.

Prepare 3 (15x10-inch) parchment lined jelly-roll pans.

Lightly flour work surface and hands. Cut dough into quarters, each quarter in half, each half into thirds. Roll each into a 5-inch log, form a ring and attach by overlapping ends. Place on prepared jelly-roll pans 2-inches apart. Cover with a clean kitchen towel. Let rise 30 minutes to 1 hour.

Preheat oven to 350°F/180°C.

TOPPING: In a small bowl combine beaten egg and water.

In another small bowl combine sesame seeds and salt.

Using a pastry brush, brush rings with egg mixture. Sprinkle sesame and salt mixture over each ring.

Bake for 30 to 35 minutes until light golden brown.

Preparation Time: 30 minutes
Rising Time: 2 hours 30 minutes to 3 hours
Cook Time: 30 minutes in two batches, total 1 hour
Experience Level: Intermediate

KAAK

PARVE   YIELD 36 PRETZELS

The flavors and texture of this traditional Syrian pretzel cannot be duplicated. Perfect for after a fast with some orange juice, or Shabbos afternoon with some tea.

½ cup water	¾ teaspoon cumin
½ teaspoon sugar	6 tablespoons margarine, melted
1⅛ teaspoons active dry yeast	¼ cup oil
2 cups flour	2 tablespoons anise seeds
1½ tablespoons semolina	1 egg, beaten with 1 tablespoon water
1½ teaspoons coarse salt	½ cup sesame seeds

In a small bowl combine water, sugar and yeast. Set aside for 10 minutes.

In the bowl of a mixer fitted with a flat beater, combine flour, semolina, salt and cumin. Add margarine and oil. Beat on medium speed until combined. Add yeast mixture and anise seeds, beat on medium high speed for about 5 minutes until dough is soft and elastic. Using hands form dough into a ball. Cover and let rise at room temperature for 1 hour.

Preheat oven to 400°F/200°C.

Prepare 2 parchment lined (15x10-inch) jelly-roll pans.

Place beaten egg with water in a small bowl. Have sesame seeds ready in a small bowl.

Working with about 1½ teaspoons of dough at a time roll into a 4-inch log. Bring ends together. Press to seal and form a ring. Dip ring in egg mixture then in sesame seed mixture, on one or both sides. Place on prepared jelly-roll pan. Continue with remaining dough. Once one pan is full, place in oven and bake for about 10 minutes or until lightly browned. Repeat filling second pan until all are baked at 400°F/200°C.

Place kaak all on one pan when first baking is completed. Lower oven temperature to 250°F/120°C. Bake for an additional 40 minutes.

Kaak can be stored in an airtight container at room temperature for 1 week, or in the freezer for about 3 months.

Preparation Time: 1 hour
Rising Time: 1 hour
Cook Time: 1 hour
Experience Level: Intermediate

*D*epression Glass

was manufactured in a

rainbow assortment of colors

that allow it to fit into anyone's

decorating scheme. Use as

accent pieces to brighten your

home and your spirit.

*R*OSEMARY *S*ALT *B*READSTICKS

PARVE   YIELD 48 BREADSTICKS

A wonderful companion to soup or salad, these breadsticks are crunchy on the outside but light and airy on the inside. Don't be shy experimenting with toppings. Poppy seeds, sesame seeds, crushed garlic, minced onion, zatar, the sky's the limit for your imagination and your taste buds! A compliment to any buffet table.

DOUGH

½ cup warm water	1½ teaspoons dried rosemary, crushed
2¼ teaspoons active dry yeast	¾ teaspoon coarse salt
½ teaspoon sugar	2 cups white bread flour
½ cup olive oil	

TOPPING

1 egg, beaten	1½ teaspoons salt

DOUGH: In the bowl of a mixer fitted with a whisk attachment, combine water, yeast and sugar. Let stand 5 minutes until yeast is dissolved. With mixer on low speed, gradually add oil, rosemary, salt and one cup of flour into yeast mixture. Scrape sides of bowl with a rubber spatula when necessary. Increase mixer speed to medium and continue beating for 2 minutes. Using a wooden spoon stir in remaining cup of flour until a dough is formed. Knead by hand for 2 to 3 minutes until dough is smooth and elastic. Cover with a clean kitchen towel and allow to rise for 2 hours or until doubled in size.

Prepare 2 (15x10-inch) parchment lined jelly-roll pans.

Preheat oven to 350°F/180°C.

Turn dough out onto a lightly floured work surface. Divide dough into quarters. Work with one section at a time, keep remaining dough covered. Cut first section into 12 pieces. Roll each piece into a 10-inch long rope. Place ropes onto prepared pans 1-inch apart. Repeat with remaining 3 sections of dough.

TOPPING: Using a pastry brush, gently brush egg over unbaked breadsticks. Evenly sprinkle salt over breadsticks.

Bake for 15 to 20 minutes or until crisp and golden. Transfer to wire racks to cool.

Preparation Time: 35 minutes
Cook Time: 15 to 20 minutes
Experience Level: Beginner

Pepper Sticks

PARVE   YIELD 48 STICKS

DOUGH

⅔ cup water
1 tablespoon canola oil
2 cups white bread flour
½ teaspoon sugar

¾ teaspoon pepper
½ teaspoon salt
1 teaspoon active dry yeast

TOPPING

1 egg white, beaten
1 tablespoon water

⅓ cup sesame seeds

DOUGH: Place dough ingredients into container of bread machine according to manufacturer's recommendation for a 1 pound dough cycle.

When dough cycle is complete, remove from machine, cover container with a clean kitchen towel and let stand 10 minutes.

Preheat oven to 400°F/200°C.

Turn dough out onto a lightly floured work surface. Cut in half. Using a rolling pin, roll each half into a 12x8-inch rectangle. Using a pizza wheel or a sharp knife, cut dough into ½x8-inch strips. Do not separate.

Prepare 2 (15x10-inch) parchment lined jelly-roll pans.

TOPPING: Combine egg white with water in a small bowl. Using a pastry brush, brush dough with egg white mixture. Sprinkle with sesame seeds.

This part can be a little messy. Lift strips up one at a time, twist into a spiral and place ½-inch apart on prepared pans.

Bake 10 minutes or until golden brown. Cool on a wire rack.

Preparation Time: 20 minutes
Cook Time: 10 minutes
Experience Level: Intermediate

Paprika and Cayenne Breadsticks

PARVE   YIELD 64 BREADSTICKS

Crunchy breadsticks with a big kick of spice, this is no ordinary breadstick.

DOUGH

2 teaspoons active dry yeast
2 cups warm water, divided
1½ tablespoons honey
5 tablespoons olive oil
5¾ cups white bread flour

⅓ cup whole wheat flour
4 teaspoons coarse salt
2 teaspoons paprika
1 teaspoon cayenne pepper
1 teaspoon olive oil

TOPPING

1 teaspoon salt
1 teaspoon garlic powder
½ teaspoon black pepper
½ teaspoon onion powder

½ teaspoon cayenne pepper
½ teaspoon dried oregano
½ teaspoon dried leaf thyme
2 teaspoons olive oil

DOUGH: In a medium sized bowl mix yeast and ¼ cup of the water. Let rest until yeast dissolves, about 5 minutes.

In a small bowl combine honey and oil, stir into dissolved yeast mixture. Set aside.

In a large bowl combine flours, salt, paprika and cayenne. Pour yeast and oil mixture over flour mixture and add remaining 1¾ cups water. Using hands, knead to form a dough. Transfer to a lightly floured work surface and knead dough for about 5 minutes until soft and elastic.

Pour a teaspoon of olive oil into the large bowl. Place dough into bowl turning to coat. Cover with a clean kitchen towel and let rise for 1½ hours.

Prepare 3 (15x10-inch) parchment lined jelly-roll pans.

Divide dough into 4 sections, cover 3 of the sections with a clean kitchen towel. Roll remaining section into a log. Cut log into 16 pieces. Roll each piece into thin sticks about 12 to 14-inches long. Place 1-inch apart on prepared pans. Repeat with remaining 3 sections. Cover and let rise for 30 minutes.

Preheat oven to 425°F/220°C.

TOPPING: Combine topping herbs, spices and seasonings in a small bowl. Using a pastry brush, baste breadsticks with olive oil and sprinkle with spice combination. Bake breadsticks for 10 to 12 minutes.

Preparation Time: 30 minutes
Rising Time: 2 hours
Cook Time: 10 minutes in 3 batches 30 minutes total
Experience Level: Intermediate

Oven Baked Apple French Toast

DAIRY   **SERVES 10**

A great breakfast food to be prepared in just a few minutes the night before and placed in the oven upon rising. The aroma of cinnamon and brown sugar will fill your home beckoning late risers to start the day with this indulgent sweet treat.

1 cup packed brown sugar
½ cup butter, melted
3 teaspoons cinnamon, divided
3 tart apples peeled, cored and thinly sliced
    into 16 sections

1 loaf French or Italian bread, cut into 1-inch
    slices
6 eggs
1½ cups milk
1 tablespoon vanilla

In a (9x13x2-inch) pan preferably not glass or ceramic, combine brown sugar, butter and 1 teaspoon of the cinnamon. Add apples to the pan and toss to coat. Spread the apples evenly over bottom of pan. Arrange bread slices on top of apples. In a large bowl, mix eggs, milk, vanilla and remaining cinnamon until well combined. Pour over bread, soaking bread completely. Cover with aluminum foil and refrigerate for 4 to 24 hours.

Preheat oven to 375°F/190C°.

Keep pan covered with aluminum foil. Bake for 40 minutes. Remove aluminum foil and bake an additional 5 minutes. Remove from oven and let stand 5 minutes. Serve warm.

Preparation Time: 10 minutes
Chill Time: 4 to 24 hours
Cook Time: 45 minutes
Experience Level: Beginner

*C*HEESE *C*RACKERS

DAIRY   SERVES 10

*O*nce *you have made these it'll be hard to go back to store bought. They are super easy to make and kids love rolling out the dough and cutting out the shapes.*

DOUGH

1 cup unbleached white flour
1 cup finely grated sharp Cheddar cheese
½ teaspoon paprika
¼ teaspoon garlic powder
¼ teaspoon black pepper
¼ teaspoon onion powder
¼ to ½ teaspoon cayenne pepper

¼ teaspoon dried oregano
¼ teaspoon dried thyme
1 teaspoon coarse salt
½ teaspoon dry mustard powder
4 tablespoons cold unsalted butter, cut into ½-inch pieces
2 tablespoons cold water

TOPPING

1 egg white, beaten

DOUGH: In a large mixing bowl combine flour, cheese, herbs and spices. Add butter, using fingers or a pastry blender. Knead until mixture resembles coarse crumbs. Add cold water and knead until a smooth dough is formed. Shape dough into a flat disk, cover with plastic wrap, and refrigerate for 30 minutes to 1 hour.

Preheat oven to 375°F/190°C. Prepare 2 (15x10-inch) parchment lined jelly-roll pans.

Place dough on a lightly floured work surface. Flour rolling pin. Roll dough to a scant ⅛ of an inch thickness, the thinner the better. Using a 1-inch heart, star, draidel, etc. cookie-cutter, cut shapes out of dough or cut into 1-inch squares with a sharp knife and place on prepared cookie sheet.

TOPPING: Using a pastry brush, brush dough with beaten egg white just before placing into oven. Poke a fork into the crackers as one would a pie shell. Bake until crisp, about 10 minutes. Transfer to wire racks to cool.

Preparation Time: 30 minutes
Cook Time: 10 minutes in 3 batches approximately 30 minutes
Chill Time: 30 minutes to 1 hour
Experience Level: Beginner

Pumpkin Rolls with Streusel Filling

PARVE   **YIELD 16 ROLLS**

A sweet and warmly colored roll reveals a delicious surprise in the center. This will soon become an anticipated Thanksgiving tradition for your family.

DOUGH
½ cup non-dairy creamer
½ cup water
¼ cup margarine
¼ cup sugar
¾ teaspoon salt

4½ to 5 cups flour, divided
2¼ teaspoons active dry yeast
1 egg, beaten
½ cup canned pumpkin
1 teaspoon canola oil

FILLING
⅔ cup chopped hazelnuts
⅓ cup packed brown sugar
⅓ cup flour

¼ cup coarsely chopped dried apricots
⅓ cup margarine, melted

DOUGH: In a medium sized saucepan heat non-dairy creamer, water, margarine, sugar and salt until just warm and margarine almost melts. In the bowl of a mixer fitted with a flat beater, combine 1½ cups of the flour with the yeast. Add the margarine mixture to the dry mixture along with the egg. Beat on medium speed for 30 seconds constantly scraping sides of bowl with a spatula. Switch mixer speed to high and continue beating for 3 minutes. Stir in canned pumpkin. With a wooden spoon, stir in as much flour as necessary to create a soft, elastic, workable dough.

Turn dough onto a lightly floured work surface. Knead in as much flour as necessary to make a stiff dough that is smooth and elastic. Shape the dough into a ball. Place oil into bowl, add dough and turn once to coat. Cover bowl with plastic wrap and refrigerate overnight.

Punch down dough and place on a lightly floured surface. Divide dough in half. Cover and let rest for 10 minutes.

FILLING: In a medium mixing bowl, combine hazelnuts, brown sugar, flour and apricots. Add melted margarine and mix to combine.

Prepare 2 (15x10-inch) parchment lined jelly-roll pans.

Divide each half of dough into 8 sections. Flatten each section into a 3½-inch disk. Place one disk in the palm of your hand. Spoon a generous tablespoon of filling in the center of the disk. Pull dough up and over filling, shaping into a ball. Pinch edges to seal. Repeat with remaining disks and filling.

Place rolls pinched side down on prepared baking pans. Cover and let rise until nearly doubled in size, about 40 minutes.

Preheat oven to 375°F/190°C.

Bake rolls 12 to 14 minutes or until golden brown. Immediately remove rolls from pans. Cool on wire rack.

Rolls can be made a day ahead and stored in an airtight container or prepared several weeks in advance and frozen. To reheat frozen rolls, wrap in foil and place in a 375°F/190°C oven for 20 minutes or until heated through.

Preparation Time: 40 minutes
Rising Time: 50 minutes
Cook Time: 12 to 14 minutes
Experience Level: Intermediate

SOUPS

DRIED MUSHROOMS AND WILD RICE SOUP

MEAT   SERVES 6

This soup contains dried mushrooms which have an intense, earthy flavor. Serve with crusty bread.

2½ ounces assorted dried mushrooms
3 cups boiling water
4 tablespoons olive oil, divided
4 medium ribs celery, chopped
1 medium onion, chopped
20 ounces fresh white mushrooms, sliced
6 cups fresh chicken stock

2 tablespoons soy sauce
1 teaspoon dried leaf thyme
½ teaspoon black pepper
½ cup cream sherry
1 cup wild rice, prepared according to
    package directions

Place dried mushrooms in a medium bowl. Pour boiling water over dried mushrooms, set aside.

In a large skillet over a medium-high flame, heat 2 tablespoons olive oil. Add celery and onion. Cook for 10 minutes, stirring occasionally until vegetables are tender and brown. Transfer vegetables to a 4-quart stock pot.

Add remaining 2 tablespoons olive oil to skillet. Add fresh mushrooms and cook for 10 minutes, stirring occasionally. Add mushrooms to vegetables in stock pot.

Drain dried mushrooms that have been rehydrated and coarsely chop. Add to vegetables in stock pot. Stir in chicken stock, soy sauce, thyme and pepper. Bring to a boil over medium-high heat. Stir in cream sherry. Simmer for 25 minutes.

To serve, place a generous amount of wild rice in each bowl. Ladle soup over rice.

Preparation Time: 20 minutes
Cook Time: 1 hour
Experience Level: Beginner

ROASTED ASPARAGUS SOUP

MEAT   SERVES 6

2 bunches scallions
1½ pounds asparagus, trimmed, cut into
    2 to 3-inch pieces
1 medium onion, cut into thin wedges
2 tablespoons olive oil
2 (14-ounce) cans chicken broth

¼ teaspoon coarse salt
¼ teaspoon black pepper
½ cup non-dairy creamer
1 tablespoon snipped fresh dill
Fresh dill sprigs, optional garnish

Preheat oven to 450°F/230°C.

Trim root ends of scallions. Cut white and green parts into 1-inch pieces. Reserve green parts.

In a large roasting pan arrange the white parts of scallions, asparagus and onion wedges in an even layer. Drizzle with olive oil. Roast uncovered until vegetables are charred and tender, about 15 to 20 minutes.

In the work bowl of a food processor or blender, place half the vegetables with ½ a can of broth. Process until smooth. Transfer to an 8-quart stock pot. Repeat with remaining vegetables.

Add remaining broth, salt and pepper to stock pot. Stir to combine and place over medium flame until heated. Mix in non-dairy creamer and dill.

To serve, ladle into bowls and top with reserved scallion tops. Garnish with fresh dill sprigs if desired.

Preparation Time: 20 minutes
Cook Time: 30 minutes
Experience Level: Intermediate

ONION SOUP

MEAT   SERVES 4 TO 6

A simple soup to prepare, this soup is thick and creamy. Slide slices of French bread under broiler for a minute or two to toast and place in each bowl after ladling soup or garnish with croutons.

6 cups beef broth or 1½ tablespoons beef
    bouillon dissolved in 6 cups water
3 tablespoons margarine
4 medium sweet yellow onions, halved and
    thinly sliced

½ teaspoon pepper
1 tablespoon paprika
2 bay leaves
1 generous teaspoon salt
½ cup flour

In a 4-quart stock pot over medium-high flame, heat beef broth until simmering.

In a large skillet over medium heat, melt margarine and add sliced onions. Sauté onions for at least 20 minutes. Add pepper, paprika, bay leaves, salt and flour to onions. Cover and cook for 5 minutes. Gradually stir hot beef broth into onion mixture. Lower flame, cover and simmer for 1 hour. Remove bay leaves before serving.

Preparation Time: 30 minutes
Cook Time: 1 hour 30 minutes
Experience Level: Beginner

Split Pea Soup

MEAT   SERVES 8 TO 10

Corned beef adds an abundance of flavor to this simple and delicious soup. The vegetables may be chopped in the food processor to simplify the preparation.

1 (16-ounce) bag dried split peas
2 medium onions, chopped
3 medium carrots, chopped
2 medium ribs celery, chopped
¼ pound sliced corned beef, torn into
    ¼-inch pieces

12 cups water
2 tablespoons salt
½ teaspoon white pepper
Scant ⅛ teaspoon red pepper flakes, optional
2 tablespoons lemon juice
½ teaspoon dried basil

In an 8-quart stock pot over medium-high flame, combine split peas, onions, carrots, celery, corned beef, water, salt, pepper, red pepper, lemon juice and basil. Bring to a boil, lower flame and simmer partially covered for 2 hours, stirring occasionally. Adjust seasonings if necessary.

Preparation Time: 10 to 20 minutes
Cook Time: 2 hours
Experience Level: Beginner

Chickpea Lentil Soup

MEAT   SERVES 12

Cumin lends an authentic flavor to this hearty Moroccan soup. Serve complete turkey necks in soup for a satisfying meal.

- 16 cups water
- 1 large onion, grated
- 2 ribs celery, chopped
- 6 turkey necks
- 2 (15-ounce) cans chickpeas, drained and slightly mashed
- ¾ cup dried black lentils, presoaked for 15 minutes in boiling water
- ¼ cup dried orange lentils or dried yellow split peas
- 4 tablespoons chicken soup flavoring, divided
- 3 tablespoons vegetable oil
- 1 teaspoon white pepper
- ½ teaspoon turmeric
- 1 tablespoon garlic powder
- 1 tablespoon cumin
- 8 sprigs cilantro, chopped or 5 sprigs fresh parsley chopped

Place water in an 8-quart stock pot over high heat. Bring to a boil. Add onion, celery, turkey necks, chickpeas, lentils, 3 tablespoons chicken soup flavoring, oil, white pepper, and turmeric. Lower heat. Simmer for 1 hour, stirring occasionally to prevent lentils from sticking to bottom of pot.

After first hour of cooking add garlic powder and 1 tablespoon chicken soup flavoring or to taste. Simmer for another hour, stirring occasionally. Stir cumin and cilantro or parsley into soup just before serving.

Preparation Time: 15 minutes
Cook Time: 2 hours
Experience Level: Beginner

ROOT VEGETABLE SOUP

MEAT   SERVES 10

4 medium leeks, diced, white and light
   green part only

¼ cup olive oil

3 large potatoes, peeled and diced

1 medium-large celery root, peeled and
   diced

1 large sweet potato, peeled and diced

1 pound parsnips, peeled and diced

1 pound carrots, peeled and diced

3 small turnips or rutabagas, peeled and
   diced

3 cloves garlic, minced

2 teaspoons salt

1 teaspoon white pepper

2 tablespoons fresh or 1 tablespoon dried
   sage or thyme

8 cups fresh chicken stock

2 cups soy milk

In an 8-quart stock pot over medium-heat, sauté leeks in olive oil until tender. Add potatoes, celery root, sweet potatoes, parsnips, carrots, turnips or rutabagas and garlic and sauté for 3 to 5 minutes.

Add salt, white pepper and sage or thyme. Pour in chicken stock. Raise heat and bring to a boil. Lower flame, cover and let simmer for about 1 hour, until vegetables are tender.

Carefully pour soup into blender or food processor and purée soup in batches. Return soup to pot and add soy milk. Adjust seasonings to taste. Heat gently, do not bring to a boil.

Preparation Time: 30 minutes
Cook Time: 1 hour 15 minutes
Experience Level: Beginner

TURKEY CHOWDER

MEAT   SERVES 10

Be prepared to offer second helpings of this soup. You may find yourself making turkey just so you can have the leftovers for this crowd pleasing recipe.

STOCK

1 roasted turkey carcass, meat removed
1 large onion, quartered
2 ribs celery
1 teaspoon fresh rubbed sage

1 teaspoon allspice
2 teaspoons poultry seasoning
8 cups chicken broth
1 cup non-dairy creamer

SOUP

2 tablespoons sweet unsalted margarine
1 large onion, chopped
4 medium sweet potatoes, peeled and cut
　　into ½-inch chunks

10 ounces frozen, canned or fresh corn kernels
3 to 4 cups diced, cooked turkey
Salt and black pepper to taste
Chives or scallions, chopped for garnish

STOCK: Break carcass into pieces to fit in an 8-quart stock pot. Place over medium-high heat. Add onion, celery, sage, allspice, poultry seasoning, chicken broth and non-dairy creamer. Bring to a boil, reduce heat and simmer, covered, for about 2 hours. Strain stock into a large pot.

SOUP: In an 8-quart stock pot over medium heat, melt margarine. Add onion and sweet potatoes. Cook, stirring until onions are transparent, about 10 minutes. Raise heat to high, add stock and bring to a boil. Reduce heat, cover and simmer until sweet potatoes mash easily, about 20 minutes. Mash potatoes coarsely with a fork. Add corn and turkey. Season to taste with salt and pepper. Cook through until turkey is heated.

Garnish individual servings with chives or scallions.

Preparation Time: 1 hour
Cook Time: 2 hours 30 minutes
Experience Level: Intermediate

61

PERSIAN MEATBALL SOUP

MEAT   SERVES 8 TO 10

MEATBALLS

1½ pounds ground beef, bison or chicken
2 medium onions, minced finely or grated
1 egg, beaten
⅓ cup chopped fresh parsley

½ teaspoon salt
½ teaspoon ground cinnamon
¼ teaspoon turmeric
⅛ teaspoon black pepper

SOUP

8 cups chicken stock
3 medium carrots, sliced
3 medium boiling potatoes, peeled and
    quartered
1 to 2 teaspoons cumin or more to taste
½ to 1 teaspoon turmeric or more to taste or
    for a more intense golden color

1 to 2 pinches cayenne pepper or red
    pepper flakes
4 cups cooked white rice
1½ cups cooked chickpeas, or
    1 (15-ounce) can, drained, optional

MEATBALLS: In a medium bowl combine ground beef, onions, beaten egg, parsley, salt, cinnamon, turmeric and black pepper. Cover with plastic wrap and refrigerate for 1 to 2 hours.

About 30 minutes before preparing the soup, remove meatball mixture from refrigerator. Wet hands and form meatball mixture into approximately 24 1-inch balls.

SOUP: In an 8-quart stock pot over a high flame place the stock, carrots and potatoes. Bring to a boil. Cover, reduce heat to low, simmer for 30 minutes. Add cumin, turmeric and cayenne.

Bring soup to a boil, add meatballs, cover, reduce heat, and simmer for 30 minutes.

To serve place ⅓ to ½ cup rice in center of soup bowl. Ladle soup and 2 to 3 meatballs on top of rice. Garnish with chickpeas if desired.

Preparation Time: 30 minutes
Chill Time: 1 to 2 hours
Cook Time: 1 hour
Experience Level: Beginner

Hearty Vegetable Soup

MEAT   SERVES 8

This thick and varied soup can be a complete meal. Browning the meat gives this soup a rich flavor, which blends well with the abundant assortment of vegetables. The delicious aroma is guaranteed to peak the interest of hungry family members before it has completed cooking.

½ pound ground beef
1 medium onion, coarsely chopped
1 clove garlic, minced
7 cups water
1 (14½-ounce) can unsalted whole
  tomatoes, drained

½ cup barley
1 medium rib celery, coarsely chopped
2 medium carrots, coarsely chopped
2 beef bouillon cubes
½ teaspoon dried basil
1 (9-ounce) package frozen mixed vegetables

In 4-quart stockpot over medium-high heat, brown ground beef until no longer pink. Add onion and garlic. Cook until wilted and soft, about 10 minutes. Drain off fat. Turn down heat. Stir in water, drained tomatoes, barley, celery, carrots, beef bouillon, and basil. Cover and bring to a boil. Simmer for 50 to 60 minutes, stirring occasionally. Add mixed vegetables and cook until tender, about 10 minutes.

Preparation Time: 20 minutes
Cook Time: 1 hour 20 minutes
Experience Level: Beginner

Sweet Potato Soup

PARVE   SERVES 10

1 tablespoon olive oil
2 large yellow onions, chopped
4 cloves garlic, crushed
4 medium sweet potatoes, peeled and cubed
8 cups water
3 tablespoons chicken soup flavoring

4 medium carrots, sliced
½ cup minced fresh parsley
2 teaspoons salt
½ to 1 teaspoon black pepper
Fresh minced parsley for garnish

In an 8-quart stock pot over medium flame, heat oil. Add onions and garlic. Sauté for about 10 minutes.

Add sweet potatoes, water, chicken soup flavoring, carrots, parsley, salt and pepper. Raise heat and bring to a boil. Reduce heat and simmer covered for 1½ to 2 hours.

Let cool about 5 minutes. Carefully pour soup into a food processor or blender and purée until smooth or use an immersion blender. Return soup to stock pot, reheat before serving.

Serve garnished with minced fresh parsley.

Preparation Time: 15 minutes
Cook Time: 2 hours
Experience Level: Beginner

Moroccan Couscous Soup

MEAT   SERVES 8 TO 10

This soup is authentic in its Moroccan roots, from the chickpeas to the cuts of meat. A healthy serving of this soup will make you think of the beautiful Moroccan villages of yesteryear.

- 2 tablespoons olive oil
- 2 onions, chopped
- 1 pound short ribs
- 1 (15-ounce) can chickpeas, rinsed and drained
- 3 medium zucchini, sliced
- 1 head green cabbage, cut into thirds
- ½ small butternut squash, peeled, seeded and cubed
- 3 medium carrots, cut into 1-inch slices
- 2 chicken legs and thighs
- 10 cups water
- 1 teaspoon turmeric
- 5 tablespoons chicken soup flavoring
- Salt and white pepper to taste
- 1 (10-ounce) package couscous

In an 8-quart stock pot over medium-high flame, heat oil, add onions and sauté until translucent. Add short ribs. Turn until browned. Add chickpeas, zucchini, cabbage, squash, carrots, chicken, water, turmeric, chicken soup flavoring, salt and white pepper to taste. Bring to a boil over high heat. Cover and reduce heat to a simmer. Simmer for 3 to 4 hours. Taste and adjust salt and pepper before serving.

Prepare couscous according to package directions.

For a hearty soup course, place a few tablespoons of couscous in each bowl. Ladle broth with vegetables, meat and chicken on top of couscous.

As a main course, place all of the couscous on a large serving platter and spoon vegetables, meat and chicken on top. You may use the broth as a starter on its own, with a simple garnish of some fresh parsley or cilantro.

Preparation Time: 15 minutes
Cook Time: 4 hours
Experience Level: Beginner

GAZPACHO

PARVE   SERVES 8

Refreshing on a summer day, this soup is a colorful beginning to any meal. Make the most of summer's bounty by using fresh garden tomatoes.

1 medium cucumber, coarsely chopped
1 medium green bell pepper, coarsely chopped
1 medium onion, coarsely chopped
6 medium tomatoes, peeled and coarsely chopped
2 to 4 large cloves garlic

Juice of ½ medium lemon
⅛ cup olive oil
½ teaspoon chili powder
½ teaspoon dried basil
1 tablespoon salt
19 ounces tomato juice

Place ½ of ingredients in blender or food processor and purée. Repeat until all has been processed. Place in a bowl or covered container, refrigerate and allow flavors to mingle for at least 6 hours. Serve chilled.

Preparation Time: 10 minutes
Chill Time: 6 hours
Experience Level: Beginner

JERUSALEM ARTICHOKE SOUP

DAIRY OR PARVE   SERVES 8 TO 10

Contrary to what the name implies this vegetable is not an artichoke. It is a variety of sunflower, with a lumpy brown skinned tuber that often resembles a ginger root. The name Jerusalem is derived from the Italian word for sunflower, girasole.

3 pounds Jerusalem artichokes, peeled and sliced
¾ cup butter or margarine
4 medium onions, thinly sliced
2 ripe pears peeled, cored and cut into chunks

4 cups water
4 cups milk or soy milk
Salt and freshly ground black pepper to taste
Pinch of sugar
1 tomato, peeled, seeded, julienned, optional

In an 8-quart stock pot over medium heat, sauté Jerusalem artichokes in butter until soft, about 7 minutes. Add onions and sauté for an additional 5 minutes or until soft.

Add pears and water to stock pot. Raise heat and bring to a boil. Reduce heat and simmer for 30 minutes.

Carefully purée soup in batches in a food processor until smooth or use an immersion blender. Return soup to stockpot, add milk and season to taste with salt, pepper and sugar. Let cool.

Refrigerate at least 6 hours or up to 24 hours.

Heat gently, stirring occasionally, do not bring to a boil. To serve, garnish with julienne strips of tomato and a sprinkle of pepper.

Preparation Time: 45 minutes
Cook Time: 45 minutes
Chill Time: 6 to 24 hours
Experience Level: Beginner

CELERY AND GARLIC SOUP

DAIRY OR PARVE   **SERVES 6**

When the cupboards are bare and you are in the mood for a deliciously satisfying soup, this is one that requires just the basic kitchen staples.

1 tablespoon canola oil
3 scallions, green and white parts, chopped
1 head garlic, peeled
5 ribs celery, sliced
1 large potato, diced
3 cups milk or rice milk

3 cups water, divided
2 teaspoons parve chicken soup flavoring
1 teaspoon dried parsley
½ teaspoon salt
⅛ teaspoon black pepper

In a 4-quart stock pot over medium flame, heat oil. Sauté scallions until soft, about 3 to 5 minutes. Add garlic, celery, potatoes, milk, 1 cup water and chicken soup flavoring. Cover, lower flame and simmer until vegetables are tender, about 20 minutes.

Purée soup in food processor or blender until smooth. Return soup to stock pot, add remaining 2 cups water, parsley, salt and pepper. Cook for an additional 30 minutes over low flame. Serve hot.

Preparation Time: 20 minutes
Cook Time: 55 minutes
Experience Level: Beginner

CREAMY YELLOW PEPPER SOUP

DAIRY   **SERVES 4 TO 6**

GARNISH

8 ounces plain yogurt, not nonfat

1 teaspoon fennel seeds, crushed

SOUP

2 tablespoons olive oil

1½ pounds yellow bell peppers, about 5 to 7, seeded and coarsely chopped

2 medium shallots, chopped

¾ teaspoon ground cardamom

2⅔ cups water

2 tablespoons parve chicken soup flavoring

2 tablespoons apple cider vinegar

GARNISH: In a small bowl, combine yogurt with fennel seeds. Cover and let stand at room temperature for 30 minutes to allow flavors to mingle.

SOUP: In a 4-quart stock pot over medium flame, heat oil. Add peppers, shallots and cardamom, stirring occasionally. Cook for 15 minutes until peppers begin to soften. Add water, chicken soup flavoring and vinegar. Raise flame and bring soup to a boil. Lower heat, cover and let simmer for 5 minutes.

Remove from heat and allow to cool for 10 minutes.

Purée soup in batches in a food processor or blender until smooth. Return soup to stock pot and cook over medium heat until heated through.

Soup may be served warm or chilled. Garnish with dollop of yogurt.

Preparation Time: 40 minutes
Cook Time: 25 minutes
Experience Level: Beginner

ROASTED RED OR YELLOW PEPPER SOUP

DAIRY OR PARVE   **SERVES 6**

When making this soup, keep in mind the beautiful presentation that is possible when doubling the recipe. It is worth making it twice, once with red peppers and once with yellow peppers and don't forget a dollop of sour cream. Use 2 ladles at once to pour into a bowl, for simply stunning colors and an impressed, "How did you do that?!" reaction from friends and family.

1 tablespoon olive oil

4 tablespoons butter or margarine

6 medium yellow or red bell peppers, seeded and thinly sliced

3 medium shallots, peeled and thinly sliced

1 clove garlic, peeled and thinly sliced

1 medium pear, peeled and thinly sliced

4 cups vegetable or chicken stock

2 medium roasted yellow or red peppers, peeled, seeded and thinly sliced see page 108 for roasting directions

Dash of cayenne pepper

Salt and freshly ground white pepper

¼ cup heavy cream or original flavor soy milk

Sour cream or non-dairy sour cream for garnish, optional

In a 4-quart stock pot over medium flame, heat oil and margarine. Add sliced peppers, shallots, garlic and pear, cooking until tender, about 5 minutes.

Add stock, roasted peppers, cayenne, salt and pepper to taste. Bring to a boil and simmer covered for 30 minutes.

Purée soup in batches in a food processor or blender. Pour through a strainer and discard shredded pepper skins. Return soup to stock pot. Add heavy cream or soy milk and reheat over low flame.

Preparation Time: 20 minutes
Cook Time: 40 minutes
Experience Level: Beginner

FISHERMAN'S CATCH CHOWDER

DAIRY   SERVES 6

The combination of rich, creamy broth and tender fish is just delightful. Serve with hearty bread for a wholesome meal.

2 tablespoons butter
1 medium onion, chopped
2 ribs celery, chopped
3 medium carrots, peeled and sliced into
    ½-inch pieces
¼ cup finely chopped fresh parsley
½ teaspoon dried crushed rosemary leaves
1 (14½-ounce) can whole tomatoes
2 cups dry white wine

1 teaspoon salt
1 cup water
3 tablespoons flour
3 tablespoons butter
½ pound salmon fillet cut into 1-inch pieces
½ pound halibut fillet cut into 1-inch pieces
½ pound whitefish fillet cut into 1-inch pieces
⅓ cup light cream

In an 8-quart stock pot over a medium heat, melt butter. Add onion, celery, carrots, parsley and rosemary. Sauté for about 15 minutes.

Add whole tomatoes, wine, salt and water. Bring to a boil, cover and simmer for 5 minutes.

In a small bowl make a roux by kneading flour and butter for about 1 minute. Add to soup mixture and simmer until thickened.

Add fish and cream. Simmer on low heat just until fish is cooked, about 8 to 10 minutes.

Preparation Time: 20 minutes
Cook Time: 30 minutes
Experience Level: Beginner

DAIRY VEGETABLE SOUP

DAIRY   SERVES 6

A delightfully creamy soup with beautiful color. A wonderful introductory course when breaking a fast or for any light meal.

4 cups vegetable stock
3 slender carrots, sliced
1 small leek, white and green parts, sliced
4 cups frozen chopped spinach
    or broccoli, approximately
      2 (10-ounce) packages
¾ cup frozen peas

½ cup whipping cream
2 eggs
⅛ teaspoon curry
⅛ teaspoon salt
⅛ teaspoon allspice
Black pepper to taste

In a 4-quart stock pot over medium-high heat, bring stock to a boil. Add carrots and leek. Cook for 20 minutes. Add spinach and peas. Cook for 10 minutes. Turn off heat.

If a finer consistency soup is desired, purée soup in batches, and return to stock pot.

In a small bowl mix whipping cream, eggs, curry, salt, allspice and black pepper. Remove ¼ cup of soup from stock pot and slowly whisk it into cream and egg mixture. Whisk all into soup and reheat, taking care not to boil.

Preparation Time: 15 minutes
Cook Time: 30 minutes
Experience Level: Beginner

Cheese Topped Broccoli and Potato Soup

DAIRY   SERVES 6

3 tablespoons butter
1 large onion, diced
3 cloves garlic, chopped
1½ pounds chopped frozen broccoli
3 cups clear vegetable broth
4 cups milk, divided

½ cup flour
½ to ¾ teaspoon salt
1 to 2 teaspoons white pepper
6 medium potatoes, boiled, peeled and cubed
9 ounces shredded or cut up Cheddar cheese
2 tablespoons flour

In a 4-quart stock pot over medium heat, melt butter. Sauté onion, garlic and broccoli until just tender. Add broth and reduce heat to low.

In a small bowl stir 1 cup of the milk with flour until smooth. Slowly add mixture to stockpot, stirring over low heat until soup thickens. Add remaining 3 cups milk, salt, pepper and potatoes. Cook for about 30 minutes.

Toss cheese with 2 tablespoons flour, sprinkle onto soup. Cook until cheese begins to melt.

Preparation Time: 30 minutes
Cook Time: 1 hour
Experience Level: Beginner

SALADS

Mixed Greens with Portobello Mushrooms and Honey Glazed Almonds

PARVE   **SERVES 8**

Portobello mushrooms can grow up to 6-inches in diameter. They have a concentrated and earthy flavor with a dense meaty texture. A sweet and sour vinaigrette nicely compliments sautéed mushrooms in this delightful salad.

SALAD
2 tablespoons olive oil

3 to 4 Portobello mushroom caps, cut into ½-inch pieces

Salt and pepper to taste

6 ounces mixed salad greens, coarsely torn (about 3 cups)

3 cups fresh baby spinach leaves, stems discarded

1 cup cherry tomatoes, halved

1 cup honey glazed almonds

DRESSING
½ cup canola oil

¼ cup white vinegar

¼ cup ketchup

1 clove garlic, minced

¼ cup sugar

¼ teaspoon mustard powder

¼ teaspoon paprika

¼ teaspoon salt

SALAD: In a large skillet over medium flame heat oil. Add mushrooms and cook until meaty and fragrant, about 7 minutes. Season with salt and pepper. Set aside.

DRESSING: In a jar combine oil, vinegar, ketchup, garlic, sugar, mustard powder, paprika and salt. Cover and shake well.

In a large bowl combine mixed salad greens and baby spinach. Add cherry tomatoes, honey glazed almonds and cooked mushrooms. Pour dressing over salad. Toss.

Preparation Time: 15 minutes
Cook Time: 7 minutes
Experience Level: Beginner

Five Color Summer Salad

PARVE   SERVES 8

White wine vinegar lends a pleasantly pungent flavor to black olives and sun-dried tomatoes, while cashews and sunflower seeds add a welcome crunch.

SALAD

1 medium head romaine lettuce, coarsely torn (about 6 cups)

½ medium yellow bell pepper, coarsely chopped

½ medium orange bell pepper, coarsely chopped

2 medium ribs celery, finely chopped

2 small scallions, finely chopped

1½ cups pitted black olives, halved

4 tablespoons marinated, sun-dried tomatoes with oil, chopped

DRESSING

⅓ cup white wine vinegar

¼ cup olive oil

2 tablespoons garlic oil

1 teaspoon dried basil

½ teaspoon garlic powder

½ teaspoon salt

½ teaspoon black pepper

GARNISH

⅓ cup salted chopped or whole cashews

¼ cup raw sunflower seeds

SALAD: Place lettuce in a large salad bowl. Add peppers, celery, scallions, olives and sun-dried tomatoes.

DRESSING and GARNISH: In a small bowl combine vinegar, oils, basil, garlic powder, salt and pepper. Immediately before serving pour over salad. Toss. Sprinkle cashews and sunflower seeds over salad.

Preparation Time: 20 minutes
Experience Level: Beginner

Spinach, Orange and Pomegranate Salad

PARVE   SERVES 8

Choose pomegranates that are heavy for their size and have a bright fresh color and blemish free skin. Each tiny seed has a sparkling sweet and tart flavor and is rich in potassium and vitamin C.

Here is a beautiful, crisp autumn salad dressed with honey and red wine vinegar. Sure to become one of your Rosh Hashanah favorites.

SALAD
- 1 medium pomegranate
- 2 bunches fresh spinach leaves, coarsely torn, stems discarded (about 8 cups)
- 2 navel oranges, peeled, pith removed, segments halved
- ½ small red onion, thinly sliced

DRESSING
- ¼ cup olive oil
- ¼ cup red wine vinegar
- 2 teaspoons honey
- ¼ teaspoon salt
- ¼ teaspoon black pepper

SALAD: Slice pomegranate in quarters and remove seeds, set aside. Place spinach in a large salad bowl. Add oranges, red onions and pomegranate seeds.

DRESSING: In a small bowl or jar combine olive oil, red wine vinegar, honey, salt and pepper.

Drizzle salad with vinegar mixture and toss to coat. Serve immediately.

Preparation Time: 20 minutes
Experience Level: Beginner

Mango Relish

PARVE   SERVES 6

A refreshing addition to a summer picnic or barbecue, this relish can be used as an introduction, side or finish to a meal.

- 3 ripe mangoes, peeled and cubed
- 1 pint strawberries, hulled and sliced
- 2 teaspoons brown sugar
- Juice from 1 medium lime
- ¾ teaspoon finely chopped fresh ginger
- 1 lime, thinly sliced

In a medium serving bowl place mangoes and strawberries. Set aside.

In a small bowl combine brown sugar, lime juice and ginger. Add to mangoes and strawberries and toss. Place lime slices on salad as a garnish.

Preparation Time: 10 minutes
Experience Level: Beginner

Mango Papaya and Avocado Salad

PARVE   SERVES 6

This salad is from a South African native. In South Africa as well as on our continent the best season for these fruits is during the late summer.

SALAD

2 mangoes, peeled and thinly sliced

2 medium avocados, peeled and thinly sliced (pits kept with sliced avocado until serving)

1 ripe papaya, seeded, peeled and thinly sliced

1 cup sugared almonds, pecans or cashews, see recipe below

DRESSING

½ cup canola oil or vegetable oil

½ cup white wine vinegar

2 tablespoons honey

½ teaspoon mustard powder

¼ cup brown sugar or more to taste

SALAD: On a round serving platter, arrange mangoes, avocados and papaya in spoke fashion. Sprinkle with nuts.

DRESSING: In a blender place oil, vinegar, honey, mustard powder and brown sugar. Blend to combine. Refrigerate until ready to serve. At serving time, pour dressing over salad.

Preparation Time: 20 minutes
Experience Level: Beginner

Sugared Almonds

PARVE   SERVES 12

1¾ cups sugar, divided

1 cup almonds

Prepare a 12-inch piece of parchment paper on counter, to place nuts on when completed.

Heat a large skillet over medium flame. In hot skillet place 1 cup of the sugar, stirring constantly with a wooden spoon until sugar becomes a light brown liquid. Place nuts in skillet, stirring to coat with liquid. Add remainder of sugar, mixing well to coat almonds. Once almonds are covered with sugar, quickly turn out in a single layer onto prepared parchment paper. Let cool 20 minutes before eating or using for garnish.

Preparation Time: 20 minutes
Cook Time: 20 minutes
Experience Level: Intermediate

CARAMELIZED APPLE AND SAUTÉED MUSHROOM SALAD

PARVE   **SERVES 6**

Caramelized apples add a nice twist to this lettuce based salad. Their sweet flavor is nicely offset by garlic and herbs.

DRESSING

3 cups apple cider
1 cup apple cider vinegar
Salt and pepper to taste

½ teaspoon allspice
¼ cup olive oil
2 small scallions, green and white parts, finely chopped

CARAMELIZED APPLES

2 tablespoons margarine
2 McIntosh apples, cored and sliced in 16ths

¼ cup sugar
3 tablespoons lemon juice
Black pepper

SALAD

2 medium cloves garlic, thinly sliced
½ pound fresh wild mushrooms, cut into large chunks
2 medium Granny Smith apples
Salt and pepper to taste

8 ounces mixed salad greens (about 4 cups)
4 medium scallions, green and white parts, coarsely chopped
1 tablespoon chopped fresh tarragon
1 tablespoon chopped fresh thyme

DRESSING: In a medium saucepan over high heat, combine apple cider and vinegar. Let simmer until reduced to ¾ cup, about 15 minutes. Remove from heat and let cool.

Transfer to a blender. Add salt, pepper and allspice. While slowly pouring olive oil through chute, purée until emulsified. Add scallions and set dressing aside.

CARAMELIZED APPLES: In a medium skillet over high heat, melt margarine. Add apple slices and cook for 3 minutes. Flip onto other side and sprinkle with sugar and lemon juice. Cook for an additional 3 minutes until apples are tender and caramel forms. Transfer apples to a lined pan and lightly sprinkle with pepper. Let cool.

SALAD: In a large skillet over medium flame heat oil. Add garlic and cook for 1 minute. Add mushrooms and cook until golden, about 5 minutes. Season with salt and pepper.

Transfer to a large serving bowl. Thinly slice green apples, using a mandolin if possible. Discard any seeds and place in serving bowl. Add caramelized apples, mixed salad greens, scallions, tarragon, thyme and ½ of the dressing. Toss. Taste and adjust seasonings with salt, pepper and additional dressing.

Preparation Time: 20 minutes
Cook Time: 30 minutes
Experience Level: Intermediate

Chickpea Salad with Sun-Dried Tomatoes

PARVE   SERVES 8

CHICKPEA MIXTURE
1 (1-pound 13-ounce) can chickpeas,
 drained and rinsed
1 (15-ounce) carton vegetable broth or scant
 2 cups fresh vegetable broth

2 medium cloves garlic, minced
3 tablespoons chopped fresh parsley
2 sprigs fresh thyme
½ teaspoon black pepper

MARINADE
2 tablespoons apple cider vinegar
1 teaspoon lemon juice
½ teaspoon coarse salt

1 teaspoon white pepper
2 medium cloves garlic, minced
6 tablespoons olive oil

SALAD
½ cup sun-dried cherry or grape tomatoes
 marinated in oil, drained

1 (10-ounce) package European-style
 lettuce, bib, radicchio, romaine

CHICKPEA MIXTURE: In a small saucepan over medium heat, place chickpeas and vegetable broth. Bring to a slow boil. Add garlic, parsley, thyme and pepper. Lower heat and boil uncovered for about 20 minutes until most of broth has evaporated. Cool to room temperature. Remove sprigs of thyme.

MARINADE: In a small bowl whisk together vinegar, lemon juice, salt, pepper, garlic and olive oil. Pour over chickpeas and toss to coat. Cover and refrigerate 6 to 12 hours.

Remove chickpeas from marinade with a slotted spoon and place in serving bowl. When ready to serve add tomatoes and lettuce, toss gently.

Preparation Time: 20 minutes
Cook Time: 20 minutes
Chill Time: 6 to 12 hours
Experience Level: Beginner

A graceful sugar bowl with its lid removed lends itself to a petite floral arrangement. Place a small arrangement beside hand towels or slide a name card among the flowers to use as an elegant place card at each table setting.

JICAMA AND CARROT SALAD

PARVE   SERVES 6

Jicama is a bulbous root vegetable with white, crunchy flesh and a sweet nutty flavor. Peel the thin skin just before using.

SALAD

1 small jicama, peeled and julienned

2 carrots, peeled and julienned

½ pound baby spinach leaves, stems discarded

1 pint cherry or grape tomatoes, halved

DRESSING

4 tablespoons brown sugar

3 tablespoons soy sauce

3 tablespoons peanut oil

6 to 8 basil leaves, finely shredded

SALAD: In a medium salad bowl toss jicama, carrots, spinach and cherry tomato halves.

DRESSING: In a jar combine brown sugar, soy sauce, peanut oil and basil. Shake well.

Pour dressing over vegetables. Toss and serve.

Preparation Time: 20 minutes
Experience Level: Beginner

FAVA BEAN AND CHICKPEA SALAD

PARVE   SERVES 10

The fava bean is a tan rather flat bean which is very popular in Mediterranean and Middle Eastern dishes.

SALAD

1 (15-ounce) can fava beans, drained and rinsed

1 (15-ounce) can chickpeas, drained and rinsed

6 scallions, green and white parts thinly sliced

1 bunch curly leaf parsley, chopped

DRESSING

Juice of 3 medium lemons

2 tablespoons olive oil

3 medium cloves garlic, crushed

1 teaspoon coarse salt

2 to 3 teaspoons cumin, to taste

½ teaspoon crushed red pepper flakes, optional

½ teaspoon white pepper

SALAD: In a medium salad bowl combine fava beans, chickpeas, scallions and parsley.

DRESSING: In a small bowl combine lemon juice, oil, garlic, salt, cumin, crushed red pepper flakes and white pepper. Mix well.

Pour dressing over salad. Toss to coat. Refrigerate for at least 30 minutes before serving.

Preparation Time: 10 minutes
Chill Time: 30 minutes
Experience Level: Beginner

CHICKPEA AND PEPPER SALAD

PARVE   SERVES 10

The longer this salad marinates the more flavorful it becomes.

SALAD
1 (15-ounce) can chickpeas, drained
1 (12-ounce) can whole kernel corn, drained
3 ribs celery, thinly sliced

1 medium green bell pepper, diced
1 medium red bell pepper, diced
1 medium yellow onion, finely chopped

DRESSING
1 heaping teaspoon flour
½ cup sugar

1 teaspoon prepared yellow mustard
½ cup apple cider vinegar

SALAD: In a medium salad bowl combine chickpeas, corn, celery, green pepper, red pepper and onion.

DRESSING: In a small saucepan over medium heat, combine flour, sugar and mustard. Gradually add vinegar. Bring to a boil. Reduce heat and stir constantly until mixture becomes thick and turns translucent and golden, about 10 minutes.

Pour hot dressing over salad and toss to coat. Cover and refrigerate for at least 2 hours.

Preparation Time: 20 minutes
Cook Time: 10 minutes
Chill Time: 2 hours
Experience Level: Intermediate

Sparkling Kumquat Salad

PARVE   SERVES 10

Kumquats are both sweet and tart. Combined with sparkling grape juice kumquats create a tangy dressing. Here they top a colorful lettuce based salad containing sliced kumquats, fennel and pomegranate seeds.

VINAIGRETTE

²/₃ cup kumquats, seeded and coarsely chopped

1 cup sparkling white grape juice

½ cup canola oil

2 medium shallots, quartered

½ teaspoon salt

¼ teaspoon black pepper

¼ teaspoon ground coriander or freshly ground cardamom seeds

SALAD

⅓ cup walnut pieces, toasted

⅓ cup pomegranate seeds

2 tablespoons fresh fennel tops, snipped

24 ounces mixed salad greens (about 12 cups)

1 medium fennel bulb, trimmed and thinly sliced

½ cup kumquats, seeded and thinly sliced

¼ teaspoon salt

⅛ teaspoon freshly ground black pepper

VINAIGRETTE: In the bowl of a small food processor or blender, place kumquats, grape juice, oil, shallots, salt, pepper and coriander. Process until nearly smooth.

SALAD: In a small bowl combine walnuts, pomegranate seeds, fennel tops and 3 tablespoons of the vinaigrette, set aside.

In a large salad bowl combine salad greens, sliced fennel, kumquats, salt and pepper. Drizzle with remaining vinaigrette. Toss gently to coat. Sprinkle with walnut mixture.

Preparation Time: 30 minutes
Experience Level: Beginner

Mango Salad

PARVE   SERVES 6

This is a beautiful salad that takes advantage of summer's colorful market finds. Choose mangoes that are streaked with a bright rose or peach color and are slightly soft.

CARAMELIZED NUTS

1 cup sugar

1 cup slivered or whole almonds or whole pecans

DRESSING

¼ cup mayonnaise
¼ cup canola oil
¼ cup honey

2 tablespoons apple cider vinegar or salad vinegar
1 tablespoon prepared yellow mustard

SALAD

8 ounces mixed salad greens, romaine, bib, red leaf lettuce (about 4 cups)
1 medium mango, peeled and diced
1 medium avocado, diced

1 medium red bell pepper, diced
¼ cup black raisins
½ cup caramelized nuts

CARAMELIZED NUTS: Prepare a large sheet of greased wax or parchment paper to turn nuts onto when completed.

Heat large skillet over medium heat. Add sugar, watching carefully and stirring constantly. When sugar melts continue stirring constantly until it turns yellow. Add nuts and mix to coat. Spill nuts carefully onto prepared paper. When cool, break into chunks and store in an airtight container until ready to use. This salad uses half of this recipe of nuts.

DRESSING: Combine all ingredients in a jar. Cover and chill until ready to use.

SALAD: In a salad bowl combine mixed salad greens, mango, avocado, red pepper and raisins. Immediately before serving pour dressing over salad. Toss and add nuts.

Preparation Time: 20 minutes, 10 if nuts were completed in advance.
Cook Time: 10 minutes
Experience Level: Intermediate

Mediterranean Pasta Salad

PARVE   **SERVES 6**

Cumin and coriander add a Moroccan twist to this pasta salad. The ingredients are available year round, making it easy to make as often as you desire.

DRESSING

2 teaspoons ground cumin
2 teaspoons ground coriander
⅓ cup olive oil
3 medium cloves garlic, minced
1 tablespoon grated fresh ginger

¼ cup plus 1 tablespoon red wine vinegar
2 tablespoons fresh squeezed lemon juice
1½ teaspoons salt
¼ teaspoon cayenne pepper

SALAD

1 pound bow tie pasta
2 cups fresh or frozen broccoli florets
1 (15-ounce) can chickpeas, drained
40 kalamata olives, drained and pitted, brine reserved

½ cup oven-dried cherry tomatoes, marinated in olive oil, see recipe page 92 or ½ cup sun-dried cherry tomatoes, rehydrated in ¾ cup hot water

DRESSING: In a small skillet heat cumin and coriander over medium heat. Stir constantly until the spices smell aromatic but are not yet brown, about 30 seconds.

Carefully add oil to skillet, heat until hot but not smoking, about 2 minutes. Stir in garlic and ginger. Remove from heat. Let cool for at least 10 minutes or up to 3 hours at room temperature.

Whisk vinegar, lemon juice, salt and cayenne pepper into spice mixture. Set aside so flavors can mingle while salad is being prepared.

SALAD: In a large saucepan cook pasta for 3 minutes less than package directions, add broccoli to pasta. Continue cooking over high heat, about 3 minutes. Pour pasta and broccoli into a colander. Drain and rinse well with cold water.

In a large serving bowl toss pasta with dressing, chickpeas, olives and sun-dried tomatoes.

Preparation Time: 15 minutes
Cook Time: 15 minutes
Experience Level: Beginner

Taco Salad

PARVE   SERVES 8

SALAD
10 ounces mixed salad greens, romaine, iceberg, bib lettuce, coarsely torn (about 5 cups)
1 medium orange bell pepper, coarsely chopped

1 medium yellow bell pepper, coarsely chopped
2 firm avocados, diced
¾ cup small cherry tomatoes
1½ cups taco chips, coarsely broken

DRESSING
¾ cup mayonnaise
2½ tablespoons ketchup

Scant ½ cup salsa
¼ teaspoon chili powder

SALAD: In a medium salad bowl combine salad greens, peppers, avocado and tomatoes.

DRESSING: In a medium bowl combine mayonnaise, ketchup, salsa and chili powder. Mix well. Refrigerate until ready to serve.

When ready to serve, pour dressing over salad. Toss to coat. Add taco chips and lightly toss.

Preparation Time: 10 minutes
Experience Level: Beginner

Tossed Beet Salad

PARVE   SERVES 8

2 (15-ounce) cans sliced beets, drained
2 (12-ounce) cans whole kernel corn, drained
1 (30-ounce) can Mandarin orange segments, drained

4 tablespoons chopped fresh cilantro
4 medium cloves garlic, finely chopped
2 tablespoons fresh lemon juice
½ teaspoon cumin
Salt and pepper to taste

In a medium salad bowl combine beets, corn, Mandarin oranges, cilantro, garlic, lemon juice, cumin, salt and pepper. Refrigerate for 1 hour. Toss before serving.

Preparation Time: 10 minutes
Experience Level: Beginner

Oven-Dried Cherry Tomatoes

PARVE

Oven-dried tomatoes will soon become your basic refrigerator condiment. Add them to salads and pizza or give chicken, fish and pasta dishes a savory awakening. You can even use them for stuffing vegetables. Replace the fresh basil with other fresh herbs such as tarragon, thyme and oregano if desired and be sure to use a parve oven when preparing this recipe, so you may use the tomatoes in any type of cooking.

2 pints cherry or grape tomatoes, halved
1 tablespoon coarse salt
¼ cup white vinegar

1½ cups olive oil
5 fresh basil leaves

Preheat oven to 200°F/93°C.

On a parchment lined jelly-roll pan place tomatoes cut side up, in a single layer. Sprinkle with salt. Bake in oven for 3 to 5 hours or longer if necessary. Tomatoes will have a dried shriveled appearance. Check every 30 minutes after 3 hours. Some may be ready before others.

Prepare a small bowl with vinegar and a small empty jar.

As tomatoes become completely dry, remove from oven and immediately place in bowl of vinegar for 5 seconds. Remove and place in jar. Layer tomatoes in jar with basil leaves. Cover tomatoes and basil completely with olive oil. Close jar tightly and refrigerate. Will stay fresh in refrigerator for months covered in oil.

Preparation Time: 10 minutes
Cook Time: 3 to 5 hours
Experience Level: Beginner

PASTRAMI SALAD

MEAT   SERVES 6

SALAD
1 tablespoon canola oil
⅓ pound sliced pastrami, cut into strips
1 (10-ounce) bag baby leaf spinach, stems discarded

8 ounces white mushrooms, sliced
½ medium red onion, thinly sliced

GARLIC DRESSING
3 tablespoons rice milk, or non-dairy creamer
2 tablespoons white vinegar

2 medium cloves garlic, minced
½ cup mayonnaise
Salt and black pepper to taste

SALAD: In a medium skillet over medium-low flame, heat oil. Add pastrami and fry until pastrami becomes crispy, about 10 to 15 minutes. Remove with a slotted spoon, set aside.

In a medium salad bowl toss spinach, mushrooms and onions.

GARLIC DRESSING: In the bowl of a blender place the rice milk, vinegar, garlic, mayonnaise, salt and pepper. Blend until combined. Refrigerate until ready to serve.

When ready to serve pour dressing over salad and toss well. Sprinkle pastrami over salad.

Preparation Time: 15 minutes
Cook Time: 10 to 15 minutes
Experience Level: Beginner

STIR-FRIED SALAD ON RADICCHIO SPOONS

MEAT   SERVES 8

GARNISH

¼ cup peanut or vegetable oil   8 cloves garlic, thinly sliced

STIR-FRIED VEAL

2 pounds ground veal   4 tablespoons red wine vinegar
1 teaspoon dried chili flakes   4 tablespoons soy sauce
6 cloves garlic, chopped, divided   ½ cup beef broth, fresh or canned
2 inches fresh ginger, peeled, finely   1 bunch cilantro, stems set aside for garnish
   chopped, divided   4 medium scallions, thinly sliced

VINAIGRETTE

4 tablespoons olive oil   ½ teaspoon salt
4 tablespoons red wine vinegar   Pepper to taste
½ teaspoon Dijon mustard

SALAD

2 bunches fresh spinach leaves, stems   24 radicchio leaves
   discarded, julienned (about 8 cups)

GARNISH: In a small skillet over medium-high flame, heat peanut oil. Fry sliced garlic until golden brown. Remove garlic with a slotted spoon and set aside. Reserve oil.

STIR-FRIED VEAL: In a medium bowl, combine ground veal, chili flakes, half of the chopped garlic and half of the ginger.

Heat a wok or large skillet over high flame. Heat reserved oil, add veal mixture and stir-fry, browning veal, for about 5 to 10 minutes. When veal is brown, add remaining half of chopped garlic and remaining half of ginger. Stir-fry an additional 3 minutes. Add vinegar, soy sauce and beef broth. Boil mixture and reduce heat until liquid begins to coat veal, about 10 minutes. Remove from heat. Add cilantro and scallions. Toss to mix thoroughly.

VINAIGRETTE: In a small bowl combine olive oil, vinegar, mustard and salt. Mix with a fork or whisk until vinaigrette is blended. Add pepper to taste.

SALAD: Place spinach in a medium bowl. Toss with vinaigrette to coat.

To serve, place 3 radicchio leaves on edge of each salad plate. Fill with dressed spinach and spoon small amounts of stir-fried veal over spinach. Garnish with cilantro stems and fried garlic slices.

Preparation Time: 45 minutes
Cook Time: 25 minutes
Experience Level: Intermediate

Asian Chicken Salad

MEAT   SERVES 6

DRESSING

3 tablespoons rice vinegar

2 tablespoons soy sauce

2 tablespoons mayonnaise

2 tablespoons vegetable or canola oil

2 tablespoons sesame oil

1 teaspoon mustard powder

SALAD

8 ounces watercress

1 pound napa cabbage, sliced crosswise

12 ounces cooked, boneless, skinless, chicken breasts, cut into ½-inch pieces

½ cup packaged rice noodles

DRESSING: In a large salad bowl combine rice vinegar, soy sauce, mayonnaise, vegetable oil, sesame oil and mustard powder. Mix with a whisk until smooth.

SALAD: Add watercress, cabbage and chicken to dressing. Toss to coat. Sprinkle with rice noodles.

Preparation Time: 10 minutes
Experience Level: Beginner

SZECHUAN CHICKEN SALAD

MEAT   SERVES 10

The Szechuan school of Chinese cuisine is known for its hot, spicy dishes. Chili oil infuses heat to the dressing and marinade for this salad. If an extra kick of spice is desired enhance the flavor with red pepper flakes.

MARINADE AND DRESSING

6 tablespoons rice vinegar	6 tablespoons sugar
4 tablespoons sesame oil	6 cloves garlic, minced
2 tablespoons chili oil	6 tablespoons soy sauce

SALAD

2 whole chicken breasts pounded thin, or breaded and fried chicken breasts	3 cups spring mix
	1 cup grape tomatoes
1 medium head romaine lettuce, coarsely torn (about 6 cups)	2 scallions, white and tender green parts, diagonally sliced

MARINADE and DRESSING: In a medium saucepan, over medium heat, combine rice vinegar, sesame oil, chili oil, sugar, garlic and soy sauce. Bring mixture to a boil, stirring occasionally. Lower heat. Let simmer for about 5 minutes. Remove from heat and let cool. Reserve half of mixture for dressing.

Place raw chicken breasts in a ziploc bag with the remaining mixture, close bag and marinate in refrigerator for 4 to 6 hours.

Remove chicken from marinade. Discard marinade.

Grill chicken over medium heat for 4 to 6 minutes on each side. Let cool. Slice chicken breasts diagonally into ¾-inch strips.

SALAD: On a large platter layer romaine, spring mix, tomatoes and chicken. Garnish with scallions. Immediately before serving drizzle reserved dressing over salad.

Preparation Time: 30 minutes, 20 if using prepared fried chicken breasts
Cook Time: 15 minutes, 5 if using prepared fried chicken breasts
Chill Time: 4 to 6 hours, 20 minutes if using prepared fried chicken breasts
Experience Level: Beginner

Barbecued Chicken Salad

MEAT   SERVES 6 TO 8

Serve a crusty bread along with this salad for a delicious meal. You'll find yourself wiping the plate clean, not missing a drop of the tangy dressing.

4 boneless, skinless, chicken breasts,
   pounded thin
½ cup prepared barbecue sauce
2 tablespoons canola oil, divided
½ pound corned beef or pastrami or beef fry
2 medium cloves garlic, chopped
¼ cup apple cider vinegar

1 tablespoon teriyaki sauce
½ teaspoon hot pepper sauce
2 tablespoons sugar
½ teaspoon salt
½ teaspoon black pepper
16 ounces mixed salad greens
   (about 8 cups)

Preheat barbecue grill or broiler.

Baste chicken on both sides with barbecue sauce. Grill chicken on barbecue grill or in broiler for 5 to 7 minutes on each side, until no longer pink.

In a medium skillet over medium flame, heat 1 tablespoon of oil. Add corned beef and cook, stirring until brown and crispy. Remove with a slotted spoon to a paper towel and crumble carefully while hot. Chill in refrigerator.

In same skillet over medium heat, add remaining tablespoon of oil and garlic, stir for 30 seconds. Add vinegar, teriyaki sauce, hot pepper sauce and sugar, stirring to combine. Bring to a boil. Lower heat and simmer for 5 minutes stirring occasionally. Add salt and pepper. Stir to combine. Transfer to a bowl, cover and chill.

Slice chicken into ½-inch strips. Place greens in a large salad bowl. Toss with chicken strips, dressing and crumbled corned beef. Salad can be eaten room temperature or cold.

Preparation Time: 10 minutes
Cook Time: 15 minutes
Experience Level: Beginner

WARM CHICKEN WITH ASPARAGUS AND SPINACH SALAD

MEAT   SERVES 8

The optimum season for fresh asparagus is from February through June. Select slender spears, which are bright green and have tight tips.

6 teaspoons olive oil, divided

1 pound fresh asparagus, trimmed and cut into 1½-inch pieces

1 large shallot, thinly sliced

2 tablespoons water

6 ounces fresh baby spinach

1 pound boneless skinless chicken breasts, pounded thin, cut into ½-inch strips

½ teaspoon salt, divided

¼ teaspoon coarsely ground black pepper, divided

1 tablespoon balsamic vinegar

1 tablespoon lemon juice

½ teaspoon Dijon mustard

¼ teaspoon sugar

In a large skillet over medium high flame, heat 2 teaspoons of oil. Add asparagus and shallot slices, stirring occasionally. Cook until golden, about 5 minutes. Lower heat to medium. Cover skillet and cook an additional 5 minutes or until asparagus are tender. Do not overcook.

Arrange spinach in the center of a large serving platter. Spoon asparagus over spinach.

In same skillet over medium high heat, add 1 teaspoon of oil. Add chicken and season with ¼ teaspoon salt and ⅛ teaspoon pepper. Cook chicken strips turning all the pieces once, until centers are no longer pink, about 5 minutes. Arrange chicken strips over asparagus.

In a small bowl combine vinegar, lemon juice, mustard, sugar, 3 teaspoons of oil, ¼ teaspoon salt and ⅛ teaspoon of pepper. Mix with a fork or wire whisk until blended. Heat skillet over high heat, add contents of small bowl to hot skillet for 30 seconds, stirring constantly. Remove from heat. Drizzle over chicken and vegetables. Serve immediately.

Preparation Time: 20 minutes
Cook Time: 15 minutes
Experience Level: Intermediate

Tangy Salad with Snow Peas and Tomatoes

PARVE   SERVES 6

SALAD

14 ounces Italian mixed lettuce greens
(about 5 cups)

DRESSING

1 clove garlic, minced

1 tablespoon sugar

½ cup canola oil

½ teaspoon soy sauce

8 ounces small cherry tomatoes

1 cup snow peas

1 teaspoon white vinegar

1 teaspoon black pepper

1 teaspoon mustard powder

SALAD: Place mixed lettuce greens in a medium salad bowl. Add cherry tomatoes and snow peas.

DRESSING: In a small jar combine garlic, sugar, canola oil, soy sauce, vinegar, black pepper and mustard powder. Cover jar. Shake to combine ingredients. Pour dressing over salad. Toss well. Add croutons and toss again.

Preparation Time: 5 minutes
Experience Level: Beginner

Tossed Salad with Swiss Cheese Dressing

DAIRY   SERVES 6

The unusual combination of Swiss and cottage cheeses create a creamy dressing, which nicely coats a basic tossed salad.

SALAD

1 medium head romaine lettuce, shredded
(about 4 cups)

8 ounces fresh white mushrooms, sliced

½ pound cherry tomatoes, halved

1 cup salad croutons

DRESSING

1 medium clove garlic

1 slice Swiss cheese

⅔ cup olive oil

1 teaspoon salt

3 teaspoons sugar

¼ cup white vinegar

3 tablespoons cottage cheese

SALAD: In a medium salad bowl combine lettuce, mushrooms and tomatoes.

DRESSING: In a blender place garlic, Swiss cheese, olive oil, salt, sugar, vinegar and cottage cheese. Blend until smooth. Pour dressing over salad, toss to coat. Add croutons. Serve immediately.

Preparation Time: 15 minutes
Experience Level: Beginner

BABY ROMAINE AND WATERCRESS SALAD WITH CHEESE GARNISH

DAIRY   SERVES 8

Cheese adds to the beautiful presentation of this salad. With mini cookie cutters you can easily customize the salad to suit your occasion. Create hearts for Sheva Brachos, draidels for Chanuka, flowers for Shavuos, or anything your imagination desires.

SALAD
1 bunch watercress

2 heads baby romaine lettuce coarsely torn
   (about 4 cups)

3 canned pear halves, each cut into 16 pieces

CHEESE GARNISH
4 ounces mascarpone or cream cheese

1 teaspoon finely minced fresh dill

1 teaspoon finely minced fresh parsley

1 teaspoon finely minced fresh rosemary

1 teaspoon finely minced fresh tarragon

DRESSING
¼ cup olive oil

2 tablespoons walnut oil or olive oil

3 tablespoons white wine vinegar

1 small shallot, finely chopped

1 small clove garlic, minced

¼ teaspoon mustard powder

Salt and pepper to taste

GARNISH
¼ cup salad croutons

¼ cup toasted walnuts, coarsely chopped

⅛ cup imitation bacon bits

SALAD: In a large salad bowl place watercress, baby romaine and pears. Toss.

CHEESE GARNISH: Place cheese between two sheets of waxed paper. Roll with rolling pin to ¼-inch thickness, remove waxed paper. Using a sharp knife cut cheese into 1-inch triangles or use small cookie cutters. On a sheet of waxed paper, combine dill, parsley, rosemary and tarragon. Place one side of cut out cheese into herbs to coat. Refrigerate until serving.

DRESSING: In a jar combine olive oil, walnut oil, white wine vinegar, shallot, garlic, mustard powder, salt and pepper to taste. Close lid and shake until well blended. Toss dressing with salad. Add garnishes, place cheese on salad herb side up.

Preparation Time: 30 minutes
Experience Level: Intermediate

GARLIC CROUTONS

PARVE OR DAIRY   SERVES 8

3 tablespoons margarine or butter
3 tablespoons olive oil
4 cloves garlic, minced

½ loaf French bread, sliced and cut into
½-inch cubes

Preheat oven to 350°F/180°C.

In a large skillet over medium heat, melt margarine. Add oil and garlic, mix to combine. Add bread cubes and stir until coated with oil mixture. Place on a (15x10-inch) jelly-roll pan in a single layer. Bake until lightly browned and crisp, about 20 minutes. Let cool before using as a garnish.

Preparation Time: 10 minutes
Cook Time: 30 minutes
Experience Level: Beginner

DILL SALAD DRESSING

PARVE   SERVES 6

*O*ur garlic croutons go really well with this dressing. Combine romaine lettuce, tomatoes, croutons *and this dressing for a salad that is a sure hit. Adding chunks of smoked turkey adds substance and turns a simple salad into a light meal.*

¼ cup olive oil
6 tablespoons mayonnaise
2 teaspoons sugar
2 medium cloves garlic
2 teaspoons lemon juice

2 scallions chopped
2 sprigs fresh parsley
2 sprigs fresh dill
Salt and pepper to taste

In the bowl of a blender place olive oil, mayonnaise, sugar, garlic, lemon juice, scallions, parsley, dill, salt and pepper. Process until smooth. Place dressing in an airtight container and refrigerate until ready to serve.

Preparation Time: 5 minutes
Experience Level: Beginner

APPETIZERS

STUFFED MINI SWEET PEPPERS

PARVE   **SERVES 12**

This beautiful and delicious recipe was created as an appetizer for a Sheva Brachos. Additional bell peppers were roasted and heart shapes were cut out using mini cookie cutters and placed between each pepper. What a stunning presentation!

RICE
2¾ cups vegetable stock
1 cup brown rice
¼ cup wild rice

1 bay leaf
½ teaspoon coarse salt

ROASTED PEPPERS FOR VEGETABLE MIXTURE, SAUCE AND GARNISH
1 large red bell pepper, divided, optional additional pepper for garnish

1 large yellow bell pepper, divided

VEGETABLE MIXTURE AND PEPPERS FOR STUFFING
3 tablespoons olive oil
1 medium shallot, chopped
3 cloves garlic, finely chopped
2 ribs celery, finely chopped
4 large white mushrooms, chopped
½ cup fresh spinach, coarsely chopped, may substitute frozen

½ cup vegetable stock
2 teaspoons soy sauce
Salt and pepper to taste
1½ pounds mini, sweet, assorted colored peppers
¾ cup vegetable stock

SAUCE
½ cup vegetable stock
½ teaspoon garlic powder

½ teaspoon salt
½ teaspoon pepper

RICE: In a medium saucepan over high flame, combine stock, brown rice, wild rice, bay leaf and coarse salt. When stock reaches a boil, cover and lower heat to a simmer. Cook for 45 minutes or until water is absorbed. Remove from heat and discard bay leaf.

ROASTED PEPPERS FOR VEGETABLE MIXTURE, SAUCE and OPTIONAL GARNISH: While rice is cooking, wash and dry peppers. Place red pepper directly over a high flame turning frequently with tongs until pepper is blackened on all sides and begins to soften, about 5 minutes per side. Place in a bowl and cover securely with plastic wrap. Let stand 5 minutes. Scrape off all charred skin and seeds using a blunt edged knife. Do not rinse with water or valuable flavors will be lost. Repeat with yellow pepper. Coarsely chop peppers for vegetable mixture and sauce. Do not chop red pepper for garnish. Set aside.

VEGETABLE MIXTURE: In a large skillet over medium flame, heat oil. Add shallots and sauté about 2 minutes. Add garlic and celery, sauté for 4 minutes. Add mushrooms and sauté 2 minutes. Add spinach, stock, soy sauce and half of chopped roasted peppers. Season with salt and pepper to taste. Boil, uncovered until liquid is absorbed, about 5 minutes.

Mix vegetables into rice, combining well. Adjust seasonings.

Preheat oven to 350°F/180°C.

TO STUFF: Wash and dry mini peppers. Cut off tops about ¼-inch from the top of each pepper. Remove and discard seeds and tops. Using a small spoon, stuff peppers with vegetable rice mixture. In a glass or ceramic ovenproof dish, lay peppers down, overlapping if necessary. Add vegetable stock. Cover tightly with aluminum foil and bake for 30 minutes or until peppers can be easily pierced with a fork.

SAUCE: In the bowl of a blender or food processor, place the remaining chopped red and yellow peppers, stock, garlic powder, salt and pepper. Blend until smooth. Pour into a small saucepan and place over medium heat. Stir constantly and cook for about 5 minutes. Taste and adjust seasonings.

TO SERVE: Place 3 stuffed peppers on each plate to look like a fan, open sides out. Put drops of sauce between each pepper.

OPTIONAL GARNISH: Cut desired shapes out of roasted red pepper with mini cookie cutters. Place decoratively around each plate.

Preparation Time: 30 minutes
Cook Time: 1 hour 30 minutes
Experience Level: Advanced

STUFFED MUSHROOMS

PARVE OR DAIRY   SERVES 8

30 large stuffing mushrooms, divided
2 tablespoons olive oil
1 medium red bell pepper, finely chopped
1 medium green bell pepper, finely chopped
4 scallions, thinly sliced
1½ teaspoons seasoned salt

1½ teaspoons garlic powder
½ teaspoon black pepper, or to taste
Scant ¼ cup white wine
¼ cup margarine, melted or ¾ cup shredded
   mozzarella cheese

Preheat oven to 400°F/200°C.

Prepare a lightly greased (15x10-inch) jelly-roll pan.

Remove stems from 24 mushrooms. Set caps aside. Finely chop stems and remaining 6 mushrooms. In a large skillet over medium-high flame, heat oil. Add chopped mushrooms, peppers and scallions. Sprinkle with seasoned salt, garlic powder and black pepper. Sauté for 10 minutes, stirring occasionally. Add white wine and continue cooking for 2 minutes. Remove from heat and let cool.

Place mushroom caps on prepared pan. Place about 1 to 2 tablespoons of filling in each mushroom cap. Drizzle tops with melted margarine. Bake uncovered for 12 minutes.

If preparing for a dairy meal, sprinkle stuffed mushrooms with shredded mozzarella cheese. Bake until cheese melts, about 15 minutes.

Preparation Time: 20 minutes
Cook Time: 12 to 15 minutes
Experience Level: Beginner

STUFFED WHITEFISH

PARVE   SERVES 10

1 (2 to 3-pound) whole whitefish, butterflied
½ teaspoon coarse salt
¼ teaspoon black pepper
Juice from 1 medium lemon
1 loaf salmon gefilte fish, defrosted
3 tablespoons fresh dill, chopped
6 medium scallions, chopped
1 (10-ounce) box frozen spinach, cooked according to package directions and drained

2 teaspoons olive oil
¾ teaspoon onion powder
1 teaspoon garlic powder
1 teaspoon paprika
3 plum tomatoes, sliced
⅓ cup brine-cured olives, kalamata or black, sliced
4 to 6 sprigs parsley

Preheat oven to 350°F/180°C.

Rinse fish and pat dry with paper towels. Season inside and out with salt, pepper and lemon juice.

In a medium bowl combine salmon gefilte fish, dill, scallions and spinach until well blended. Open fish and place salmon mixture evenly on bottom half of fish. Cover with top half, aligning edges neatly.

Place fish in a lightly greased glass baking dish large enough to accommodate fish. Sprinkle fish with olive oil. Season top of fish with the onion powder, garlic powder and paprika. Arrange sliced tomatoes in a row across length of fish. Sprinkle with sliced olives and parsley. Bake covered for 30 minutes. Uncover and bake an additional 30 minutes. Serve chilled or at room temperature.

Preparation Time: 45 minutes
Cook Time: 1 hour
Experience Level: Intermediate

SPICY GEFILTE FISH IN TOMATO SAUCE

PARVE   **SERVES 8**

A nice twist on traditional gefilte fish. Beware jalapeño peppers can be very spicy. The fish balls closer to the peppers will be spicier then those in the center. It is a good idea to keep this in mind when serving to family and friends.

1 loaf gefilte fish, defrosted	2 tablespoons onion powder
½ cup seasoned breadcrumbs	¼ cup dried parsley flakes
1 egg	1 teaspoon salt
1 (28-ounce) can crushed tomatoes	Black pepper to taste
2 tablespoons olive oil	2 jalapeño peppers, sliced in half crosswise
2 tablespoons paprika	

In a large bowl combine defrosted fish, breadcrumbs and egg. Refrigerate uncovered for 20 to 30 minutes.

Place an 8-quart stock pot ¾ full with water over high heat and bring to a boil.

Preheat oven to 350°F/180°C.

In a large baking dish mix tomatoes, oil, paprika, onion powder, parsley flakes, salt and pepper. Set aside.

Remove fish from refrigerator. Using wet hands, form fish mixture into 2-inch diameter balls and drop into boiling water. When fish balls begin to float, remove each fish ball with a slotted spoon. Place into sauce mixture in baking dish. Spoon a small amount of sauce over each fish ball. Place 1 piece of jalapeño pepper in each corner of baking dish. Cover tightly, place in preheated oven and bake for 1 hour and 15 minutes.

Serve chilled or at room temperature.

Preparation Time: 10 minutes
Cook Time: 1 hour 15 minutes
Chill Time: 20 to 30 minutes
Experience Level: Intermediate

*P*ASTALLIM

MEAT   SERVES 8

This is a traditional Moroccan dish. Although preparation takes a while, the results are well worth it. The light fried patties are a hit with both children and adults.

DOUGH
7 medium russet potatoes, peeled
3 tablespoons chicken soup flavoring

¼ cup fresh parsley or cilantro, chopped
Salt and white pepper to taste

FILLING
3 tablespoons canola or vegetable oil
1 pound ground beef
5 bay leaves

½ teaspoon white pepper
½ teaspoon cumin
2 tablespoons white vinegar

OUTER COATING
2 eggs beaten
½ cup flour

Canola oil

DOUGH: Place peeled potatoes in a large stock pot with water to cover over a high flame. Bring to a boil, lower heat and simmer for 30 to 40 minutes until potatoes are soft. Drain potatoes. While potatoes are still hot, mash with a potato masher. Add chicken soup flavoring, parsley, salt and white pepper to taste. Mix to combine. Taste and adjust seasonings as necessary.

FILLING: In a large skillet over medium-high flame, heat oil. Add ground beef, bay leaves, white pepper and cumin. Break up large chunks of meat while cooking. Cook until almost brown. Add white vinegar, and continue cooking until meat is browned. Remove bay leaves. Pass meat mixture through a meat grinder or food processor for a few seconds until coarsely ground.

Prepare a jelly-roll pan or a large clean dish to place shaped pastallim onto.

Form dough into a 3-inch diameter flat disk, approximately ⅛-inch thick. Place about 2 teaspoons of meat mixture in center of disk. Using both hands bring dough up around meat to form a ball. Flatten ball slightly to form a jelly doughnut shape. Place on prepared pan. Repeat with remainder of dough and filling.

OUTER COATING: Coat with beaten eggs, then dredge in flour.

In a large skillet, over medium-high flame, heat about 1-inch of oil. Fry pastallim for about 4 minutes on each side or until browned. Drain on paper towels. Serve hot.

Preparation Time: 45 minutes
Cook Time: 1 hour
Experience Level: Intermediate

VEAL ROLL WITH VEGETABLE SAUCE

MEAT   SERVES 16

VEAL ROLL

1 (17.3-ounce) package puff pastry dough, defrosted according to package directions
½ cup canola oil
2 medium ribs celery, sliced
2 medium carrots, sliced
1 medium onion, quartered

1½ cups flour
1½ teaspoons salt
1 teaspoon paprika
½ teaspoon black pepper
1 pound ground veal
1 egg, beaten

VEGETABLE SAUCE

2 tablespoons margarine
1 medium onion, chopped
1 medium rib celery, sliced
1 medium carrot, sliced
10 medium fresh white mushrooms, sliced

1¾ cups water
2 tablespoons cornstarch
¼ cup cold water
Salt and black pepper to taste

VEAL ROLL: Preheat oven to 350°F/180°C. Prepare 2 greased (15x10-inch) jelly-roll pans.

In a blender combine oil, celery, carrots and onion. Blend until a thick paste is formed. Transfer paste to a medium bowl. Add flour, salt, paprika and pepper. Stir to combine. Add veal and mix until thoroughly combined. Spread mixture evenly over each pastry sheet. Roll up jelly-roll style. Transfer to prepared pans.

Place beaten egg into a small bowl. Using a pastry brush, brush tops of rolled pastry with beaten egg. Place in oven and bake for 30 minutes or until top is golden brown.

VEGETABLE SAUCE: In a medium saucepan over medium heat, melt margarine. Add onion, celery, carrot and mushrooms. Cook until onion and celery are soft and transparent, about 10 minutes. Add water and bring to a soft boil.

In a small bowl combine cornstarch with cold water, slowly stir into saucepan. Cook, stirring frequently until sauce begins to thicken and turn slightly glossy, about 3 to 5 minutes. Season to taste with salt and pepper.

To serve, slice and spoon vegetable sauce over each slice.

Preparation Time: 1 hour
Cook Time: 30 minutes
Experience Level: Beginner

Wild Mushroom and Chicken Strudel

MEAT   YIELD 60 PIECES

STRUDEL AND FILLING
2 (10-ounce) boneless, skinless chicken
    breasts
Salt
Black pepper
2 tablespoons olive oil, divided
12 ounces fresh wild mushrooms, cleaned
    and chopped

2 tablespoons minced shallots
1 tablespoon margarine
1 tablespoon fresh basil, chopped
1 (16-ounce) box phyllo dough, defrosted
    according to package directions
6 to 8 tablespoons canola oil

SAUCE
4 roasted garlic cloves, peeled
4 tablespoons chicken stock
3 tablespoons white vinegar

½ cup canola oil
2 tablespoons dried basil

GARNISH, OPTIONAL
4 ounces arugula or watercress

STRUDEL and FILLING: Season chicken breasts on both sides with salt and pepper. In a large skillet over a medium high flame, heat 1 tablespoon olive oil. Add chicken and fry for 3 to 4 minutes on each side. Place on paper towels to absorb excess oil.

In the same skillet, over high flame, heat 1 tablespoon of olive oil. Add mushrooms and sauté 4 to 5 minutes. Add shallots and sauté for 2 minutes. Add margarine and basil, stir to combine. Transfer mixture to a large bowl to cool. Julienne chicken and add to mushrooms in large bowl. Stir to combine, adding salt and pepper to taste.

Prepare parchment lined (15x10-inch) jelly-roll pan.

While dough is still in plastic, cut off ¼ of log with a sharp serrated knife. Cover exposed end of larger log with plastic wrap. Refrigerate.

Prepare canola oil in a small bowl with a pastry brush.

Unroll the remaining ¼ of dough. Lay out one strip of dough crosswise in front of you. Brush with oil. Top with another sheet of dough. Place about 1½ teaspoons of filling on left end. Fold upper left corner down to lower edge, forming a triangle. Bring lower left corner up to upper edge. Left top to lower edge. Continue across phyllo dough. Be sure to seal edges and points well, maintaining triangle shape. The last fold will not be complete, tuck it under. Lightly brush with oil and place on prepared cookie sheet. Repeat with remaining dough and filling. See step by step photos for Fila with Cheese on page 271.

Preheat oven to 375°F/190°C.

Bake for 12 minutes or until golden and crisp.

Experiment with different napkin folds to create an ambiance for your table. Choose larger napkins to create a more elaborate fold. Add fresh or dried flowers at each napkin to further enhance your table setting.

SAUCE: Mash roasted garlic until smooth. In a small saucepan over medium high heat, pour stock and vinegar. Whisk garlic into stock. Bring to a boil, lower heat and slowly whisk in oil. Turn off heat. Add basil to sauce mixture.

Serve garlic sauce pooled on plate. Place arugula next to sauce and strudel on arugula.

Preparation Time: 30 minutes
Cook Time: 30 minutes
Experience Level: Advanced

*C*ABBAGE *S*TRUDEL

PARVE   SERVES 8

A classy appetizer with a delicate caraway flavor. The dough is crisp, the filling deliciously moist. May be prepared in advance and frozen up to 1 month. Do not defrost before baking.

1 tablespoon olive oil	1 tablespoon non-dairy creamer
1 large onion, coarsely chopped	1 large egg
1 large clove garlic, minced	5 sheets phyllo dough
1 small head green cabbage, shredded	¼ cup margarine, melted
1 tablespoon prepared stone ground mustard	¼ cup breadcrumbs
2 teaspoons caraway seeds	1 egg white, beaten
½ teaspoon salt	1 teaspoon water
¼ teaspoon freshly ground black pepper	1 tablespoon sesame seeds, optional

If phyllo dough is frozen defrost according to package directions.

In a large skillet over medium flame, heat oil. Add onion and garlic. Sauté until soft and golden, about 8 to 10 minutes. Gradually add cabbage, stirring frequently until cabbage is soft and wilted, about 10 minutes. Remove from heat. Stir in mustard, caraway seeds, salt and pepper. Add non-dairy creamer and egg, mix well to combine.

Preheat oven to 350°F/180°C. Prepare margarine in a small bowl with a pastry brush. Prepare breadcrumbs in a small bowl with a tablespoon. Prepare a greased (15x10-inch) jelly-roll pan.

Unroll phyllo dough. Remove 5 sheets and immediately cover remaining dough securely with wrapper. Refrigerate for another use.

Working quickly, with clean dry hands place the first sheet of phyllo dough in front of you short sides going across. Gently brush phyllo dough with melted margarine. Sprinkle with 1 tablespoon bread crumbs. Place additional sheet on top of first sheet. Brush with melted margarine. Sprinkle with 1 tablespoon bread crumbs. Repeat with remaining sheets of phyllo dough. Place the last sheet of phyllo dough on top. Brush with melted margarine.

Place cabbage mixture on top third of dough about 4-inches from top and sides. Fold long sides in, covering part of filling. Fold top side down, carefully fold down again until all dough is incorporated into roll. Brush end with melted margarine to secure closed. Place seam side down on prepared pan. May be covered in an airtight container and frozen at this point.

Mix egg white with water. Using a pastry brush, baste top of roll with egg white mixture and sprinkle with sesame seeds if desired.

Bake for 40 to 45 minutes or until golden brown. Let stand 45 minutes before slicing.

Preparation Time: 40 minutes
Cook Time: 40 to 45 minutes
Experience Level: Intermediate

Mushroom Pie with Mushroom Sauce

PARVE   SERVES 9

MUSHROOM SAUCE

1 tablespoon margarine
1 medium onion, chopped
1 cup fresh white mushrooms, sliced
1 cup boiling water

1 tablespoon cornstarch
¼ cup cold water
Salt and black pepper to taste

FILLING

2 tablespoons canola oil
1 medium eggplant, peeled and cubed
1 medium onion, chopped

1 (14-ounce) can sliced mushrooms with liquid
4 tablespoons mushroom soup mix

DOUGH

2½ cups flour, ½ cup more if necessary
14 tablespoons margarine, softened
⅔ cup orange juice

3½ teaspoons baking powder
1 egg white, beaten

MUSHROOM SAUCE: In a small saucepan over medium-high heat, melt margarine. Add onion and cook until transparent, about 8 to 10 minutes. Add mushrooms and boiling water. In a small bowl, combine cornstarch with cold water. Pour cornstarch mixture into saucepan. Add salt and pepper to taste. Cook, stirring until thickened, about 5 minutes, set aside. Reheat before serving.

FILLING: In a large skillet over medium-high flame, heat oil. Add eggplant and onions. Cook until onions are transparent, about 10 minutes. Add mushrooms with liquid and 4 tablespoons of mushroom soup mix to skillet. Heat through. Remove from heat and allow to cool for about 20 minutes.

Preheat oven to 350°F/180°C. Prepare a greased (9x13-inch) baking dish.

DOUGH: On a lightly floured surface, using hands, knead together flour, margarine, orange juice and baking powder. Knead to form a soft dough. Add additional flour if necessary. Divide dough in half. Using a rolling pin roll dough to form a large rectangle to fit on bottom and up the sides of prepared baking dish. Pour filling into crust. Roll out remaining dough and gently place on top of filling or make a lattice. Baste with beaten egg white.

Bake for 45 minutes until top is golden.

To serve, cut into squares and serve on appetizer plates topped with mushroom sauce.

Preparation Time: 35 minutes
Cook Time: 1 hour and 10 minutes
Experience Level: Intermediate

CHICKEN AND PASTRAMI IN PASTRY WITH SWEET SAUCE

MEAT   SERVES 16

CHICKEN AND PASTRAMI IN PASTRY

3 tablespoons canola oil
2 medium yellow onions, chopped
1 medium shallot, finely chopped
2 scallions, finely chopped
1 clove garlic, finely chopped
1½ cups chicken stock or water
1 cup basmati rice, rinsed
1 teaspoon salt
½ teaspoon black pepper

1 teaspoon garlic powder
1 teaspoon onion powder
1 (17.3-ounce) package puff pastry dough, defrosted according to package directions
2 to 3 pounds boneless, skinless chicken breasts, pounded thin
Onion powder
Garlic powder
½ pound sliced pastrami

SWEET SAUCE

1 cup Cantonese-style duck sauce
1 tablespoon honey

2 tablespoons soy sauce
1 teaspoon garlic powder

CHICKEN and PASTRAMI IN PASTRY: In a medium saucepan over medium-high flame, heat oil. Add onions, shallot, scallions and garlic. Sauté until slightly brown, about 10 minutes. Add stock, rice, salt, pepper, garlic and onion powder. Lower flame, cover and cook for 10 to 15 minutes until liquid is absorbed.

Preheat oven to 400°F/200°C. Prepare a parchment lined (15x10-inch) jelly-roll pan.

On a lightly floured work surface unfold pastry dough. You should have 2 rectangles. Place half of pounded chicken breasts on ⅔ of each rectangle. Sprinkle lightly with onion powder and garlic powder. Lay pastrami slices over chicken breasts. Place rice mixture evenly over pastrami. Carefully roll dough jelly-roll style beginning from first third going inwards.

Place both logs on prepared pan. Bake for 20 minutes or until puffed and golden brown.

SWEET SAUCE: In a small saucepan over low heat, combine duck sauce, honey, soy sauce and garlic powder. Bring to a boil, mix until thick.

Slice roll into 1-inch slices and serve with sauce spooned over top.

Preparation Time: 20 minutes
Cook Time: 35 minutes
Experience Level: Intermediate

EGG ROLLS

MEAT   SERVES 12

Homemade egg roll skins are simple to prepare and add to the freshness of this recipe. If you find yourself short on time, egg roll skins are available at most supermarkets. Serve with duck sauce or hot mustard for dipping.

FILLING

2 tablespoons canola oil
1 cup thinly sliced cabbage
2 medium ribs celery, thinly sliced
½ cup shredded cooked chicken

½ cup fresh bean sprouts
1 teaspoon salt
¼ teaspoon white pepper
Cornstarch for dusting

EGG ROLL SKINS

2 cups flour
½ teaspoon salt

½ cup ice water
1 egg, beaten

FOR COOKING

Canola oil

FILLING: In a large skillet over a high flame, heat oil. Add cabbage and cook 5 minutes, stirring occasionally. Add celery, chicken, bean sprouts, salt and white pepper. Cook 10 minutes, stirring occasionally. Taste and adjust seasonings if necessary. Drain off excess liquid. Cool for 30 minutes.

EGG ROLL SKINS: In a large mixing bowl, combine flour and salt. Add water and egg, mixing with a spoon until a soft ball forms. Transfer dough to a lightly floured surface. Knead dough by hand until a smooth dough is formed, about 2 minutes. Cover with a damp towel and refrigerate for 30 minutes.

Remove dough and divide into 6 equal pieces. On a lightly floured surface, working with one piece at a time, roll dough into a 7x14-inch, paper-thin rectangle. Cut in half to make two 7-inch squares. Cover dough that is not being used with a damp towel. Repeat with remaining dough.

Dust each square with cornstarch. Place 3 to 4 tablespoons of filling in the center of each square. Fold envelope style, wetting the corners lightly to seal.

FOR COOKING: In a deep skillet over medium-high flame, heat about 1-inch of oil for frying. Fry egg rolls for about 4 minutes each side or until golden.

Preparation Time: 30 minutes
Cook Time: 25 minutes
Chill Time: 1 hour
Experience Level: Intermediate

Pot Stickers

MEAT   SERVES 12

FILLING
10 ounces ground beef
2 medium onions, finely chopped
1 cup napa cabbage, finely chopped
1 tablespoon grated fresh gingerroot
1 tablespoon sesame oil

1 tablespoon soy sauce
Salt to taste
Freshly ground black pepper to taste
36 won ton wrappers, trimmed into circles

FOR COOKING
Canola oil for frying
2 cups chicken broth

Chinese chives for garnish or chive flowers,
   optional

FILLING: In a large bowl combine ground beef, onions, cabbage, gingerroot, sesame oil, soy sauce, salt and pepper to taste. Mix well.

Prepare a parchment lined jelly-roll pan or a clean dish. Prepare a small bowl with water.

Place a won ton wrapper on a clean work surface. Place about 2 teaspoons of meat mixture a little off center. Using fingertips, moisten dough to be joined with a little water. Fold wrapper over filling, edges meeting. Pinch edges to form 6 little pleats. Place on prepared pan until ready to cook. Repeat with remaining pot stickers. May be frozen in an airtight container at this point.

FOR COOKING: In a large skillet over high heat, add enough oil to cover bottom of skillet. Swirl to coat sides. When oil is hot, reduce heat to medium. Place pot stickers in skillet, smooth side down, side by side. Increase heat in order for oil to sizzle. Cook until bottoms are brown. Turn over pot stickers. Carefully add enough chicken broth to come half way up sides of pot stickers. Cover and cook until liquid is almost absorbed. Uncover and cook until bottoms of pot stickers are crisp, adding oil as necessary.

Remove from heat. Garnish with chives and flowers.

Preparation Time: 1 hour
Cook Time: 15 minutes
Experience Level: Advanced

Marinated Salami

MEAT   SERVES 8

This is a very versatile recipe, we have 3 serving suggestions. Prepare puff pastry rings and fill with mustard. Serve salami slices plated with marinade ladled on top, and pastry rings to accompany the slices. Serve as a cocktail, slice into cubes and spear with toothpicks. Or simply cut into cubes and serve over a bed of rice.

1 (2-pound) whole salami, plastic wrapper removed

2 cups apricot preserves
1 cup Dijon mustard

Grease a (9x13-inch) baking pan. Using a sharp knife, score salami well and place in greased pan.

In a medium bowl combine preserves and mustard for marinade. Pour over salami. Cover pan and refrigerate for 6 to 12 hours, turning occasionally.

Preheat oven to 350°F/180°C.

Bake salami in covered pan for 2 hours, basting and turning salami every 30 minutes.

Remove from oven and let stand for 10 to 15 minutes. Slice salami at an angle into ½-inch slices. Return slices to marinade in pan. Bake uncovered for an additional 40 minutes. Refer to serving suggestions above.

Preparation Time: 10 minutes
Cook Time: 2 hours 40 minutes
Chill Time: 6 to 12 hours
Experience Level: Beginner

Apricot Chicken Pot Stickers

MEAT   **SERVES 10**

A twist on a traditional Chinese recipe. The tangy filling makes a sauce unnecessary, but you may offer it to those who like to dip.

2 cups plus 1 tablespoon water, divided
2 small boneless, skinless, chicken breasts
2 cups finely chopped shredded cabbage
½ cup all-fruit apricot preserves
2 medium scallions, finely chopped
2 teaspoons soy sauce

½ teaspoon grated fresh gingerroot
⅛ teaspoon black pepper
30 (3-inch) won ton wrappers
Non-stick cooking spray
Sweet and sour duck sauce, optional for serving

In a medium saucepan over high heat, bring 2 cups of water to a boil. Add chicken, cover, reduce heat to low and simmer for 10 minutes, or until no longer pink. Remove chicken from water.

In a large skillet over medium-high heat, add remaining 1 tablespoon of water and cabbage. Cook for 1 to 2 minutes until water evaporates. Remove from heat. Let cool for 5 minutes.

Chop chicken finely and add to skillet. Add preserves, scallions, soy sauce, ginger and black pepper.

To assemble pot stickers, place a heaping tablespoon of chicken mixture in center of won ton wrapper. Brush edges with water and bring corners together. Press to seal. Repeat with remaining filling and won ton wrappers.

Spray basket of a steamer with non-stick cooking spray. Add water to steamer to come ½-inch below bottom basket. Arrange pot stickers in basket so they are not touching. Cover and steam for 5 minutes. Serve with sweet and sour duck sauce on the side.

Preparation Time: 45 minutes
Cook Time: 30 minutes
Experience Level: Intermediate

Chummus Sauce for Fish

PARVE   SERVES 8

Colorful and full of textures, this is a great accompaniment to our Whitefish with Chili Peppers on page 214. Can also be served as a dip.

3 (15-ounce) cans chickpeas, drained
3 large dried chili peppers
½ bunch cilantro, chopped
½ medium head garlic, chopped
½ cup olive oil

1 tablespoon chicken soup flavoring
½ tablespoon paprika
¾ teaspoon turmeric
1 teaspoon cumin
1 cup water

In a 4-quart saucepan over high heat, place chickpeas and water to cover. Bring to a boil, lower flame and cook for 30 to 40 minutes to soften chickpeas. If waxy skins float to top of saucepan, skim with a slotted spoon. Drain, rinse with cool water and return chickpeas to saucepan. Break up chickpeas with hands.

Wash chili peppers, pull off tops and shake out seeds. Discard tops and seeds. Julienne peppers and add to chickpeas. Add cilantro, garlic, olive oil, chicken soup flavoring, paprika, turmeric, cumin and water. Stir to combine all ingredients. Place saucepan over medium heat, stir occasionally. Cook 10 to 12 minutes until thick. Serve warm.

If reheating, mix to recombine oil with other ingredients and warm over medium heat.

Preparation Time: 20 minutes
Cook Time: 50 minutes
Experience Level: Intermediate

Olive Oil and Sun-Dried Tomato Spread

PARVE   SERVES 12

¾ cup sun-dried tomatoes marinated in oil, reserve oil
¾ cup kalamata olives, pitted
1 cup fresh flat leaf parsley leaves

4 cloves garlic
½ cup pine nuts
Freshly ground black pepper to taste

In the bowl of a food processor combine sun-dried tomatoes, olives, parsley, garlic and pine nuts. Pulse to blend. Slowly add reserved oil through the chute of the food processor. Pulse until mixture reaches a spreadable consistency. Season with pepper to taste. Serve at room temperature on toasted French bread slices.

Preparation Time: 5 minutes
Experience Level: Beginner

CUBAN SALSA

PARVE   SERVES 6

Salsa is the Spanish word for sauce which can be cooked or fresh mixtures. This version is mild, some versions can be spicier for those who like it hot.

1 (28-ounce) can whole tomatoes, crushed
   by hand
1 large green bell pepper, finely chopped
10 cloves garlic, crushed

¼ cup plus 2 tablespoons canola oil
1 teaspoon crushed red pepper flakes
2 teaspoons garlic powder
Salt and black pepper to taste

In a medium saucepan over high heat, place tomatoes, green pepper, garlic, oil, crushed red pepper flakes, garlic powder, salt and pepper to taste. Mix to combine, breaking up large pieces of tomato. Bring to a boil. Once boiling, lower heat and simmer, covered for 2½ hours. Let cool. Refrigerate for 3 hours. Serve chilled.

Preparation Time: 5 minutes
Cook Time: 2 hours 30 minutes
Chill Time: 3 hours
Experience Level: Beginner

COLD HONEYDEW AND MINT PURÉE IN CANTALOUPE

PARVE   SERVES 6

As its name indicates this dish is wonderfully cold and refreshing, picture perfect for a summer appetizer. Mint is a fragrant herb that is easily adaptable to most soils. It's a perennial and once planted it will enhance your garden for years to come. Most large supermarkets have fresh herbs year round, so you are not limited by season or your garden space.

½ large honeydew melon, cut into 1-inch
   pieces
1 cup loosely packed fresh mint leaves
Juice from 1½ medium limes, about
   3 tablespoons juice

2 tablespoons sugar
⅛ teaspoon salt
3 medium cantaloupes, halved and seeded
6 sprigs mint leaves, optional garnish

In the bowl of a blender or food processor place honeydew, mint leaves, lime juice, sugar and salt. Purée until smooth, transfer to a bowl. Cover and chill for 1 to 48 hours.

Place cantaloupe halves on salad plates. Ladle purée into center of cantaloupe. Garnish each with a sprig of mint.

Preparation Time: 15 minutes
Chill Time: 1 to 48 hours
Experience Level: Beginner

131

*T*APENADE

PARVE   SERVES 10

*H*ere are 2 variations on a theme. The first is spicy with a deep olive flavor, a bit exotic tasting. The second has a more robust olive flavor. Make them both and discover which is your favorite. Spread tapenade on toasted French bread, serve with fish or top your favorite pasta.

VARIATION I

1 (8½-ounce) jar kalamata olives, drained 2 teaspoons lemon juice
3 medium cloves garlic, thinly sliced   ¼ teaspoon black pepper
½ teaspoon grated lemon zest   ⅓ cup olive oil
2 anchovy fillets

Gently press olives with flat side of a knife to crush in order to loosen pits. Remove pits and reserve.

In the bowl of a food processor place pitted olives, garlic, lemon zest, anchovies, lemon juice and black pepper. Pulse to create a coarse purée.

In a small saucepan combine olive pits with olive oil. Heat and simmer over low heat for 3 to 4 minutes. Strain oil into food processor and discard pits. Pulse to combine with olive purée.

Serve immediately or store in refrigerator up to 5 days. Bring to room temperature and stir before serving.

Preparation Time: 10 minutes
Cook Time: 3 to 4 minutes
Experience Level: Beginner

VARIATION II

PARVE   SERVES 6

4 ounces (⅔ cup) niçoise or kalamata olives 1 tablespoon capers, drained
3 anchovy fillets, 1 teaspoon of oil reserved 1 tablespoon olive oil

With the flat side of a heavy knife, crush olives lightly to loosen pits. Discard pits.

In the bowl of a food processor purée olives, anchovy fillets, anchovy oil, capers and olive oil. Scrape down sides often.

Serve immediately or store in refrigerator for up to 5 days. Serve cold or at room temperature.

Preparation Time: 5 minutes
Experience Level: Beginner

CRISPY SAUTÉED ROSEMARY

PARVE   SERVES 12

Rosemary's silvery green, needle shaped leaves are highly aromatic. Their flavor hints of both lemon and pine. This recipe calls for cooking whole fresh sprigs. A delicious garnish for meat or poultry or an elegant appetizer when served in a chilled julep cup.

¼ cup olive oil
12 fresh rosemary sprigs

¼ teaspoon coarse salt

In a medium skillet over medium flame, heat oil. Place rosemary in hot oil a few sprigs at a time. Cook for about 1 minute, turning once. Rosemary should be crisp but not browned. Carefully remove rosemary from oil with tongs or a slotted spoon and place on paper towels to drain.

Sprinkle with salt.

Cook Time: 5 minutes
Experience Level: Beginner

SUN-DRIED TOMATO AND ROSEMARY BUTTER

DAIRY   SERVES 12

The best bagel topper, ever!

10 sun-dried tomato halves, marinated in
    oil, finely chopped
8 tablespoons butter at room temperature

4 ounces cream cheese
1 tablespoon fresh chopped rosemary

In a medium bowl combine sun-dried tomatoes, butter, cream cheese and rosemary. Transfer mixture to a sheet of parchment paper. Roll into a log about 1-inch in diameter. Refrigerate until ready to serve, at least 2 hours.

Preparation Time: 5 minutes
Chill Time: 2 hours
Experience Level: Beginner

SHALLOT AND PARSLEY BUTTER

DAIRY OR PARVE   **SERVES 8**

Start an elegant meal with a warm loaf of bread and this simple to prepare spread. The results look and taste anything but simple.

8 tablespoons butter or margarine, divided
1 large shallot, finely minced
1 tablespoon dry white wine

1 tablespoon coarse salt
1 tablespoon finely chopped fresh parsley

In a small skillet over medium heat, melt ½ tablespoon margarine. Add shallots and sauté for 1 to 2 minutes. Add wine and cook until wine has evaporated, about 30 seconds. Remove from heat. Stir in salt and cool completely.

Place remaining 7½ tablespoons of margarine in a bowl. Add shallot mixture and parsley, combine well. Transfer mixture to a sheet of parchment paper. Roll into a log about 1-inch in diameter. Refrigerate for at least 2 hours.

Slice into 2-inch pieces.

Preparation Time: 5 minutes
Cook Time: 3 minutes
Chill Time: 2 hours
Experience Level: Beginner

ICE SLUSH

PARVE   SERVES 8

Just before your guests are expected to arrive, place the sherbet and drink mixture into parfait glasses. The sherbet creates a colorful foam on the top of each glass. Add a long straw and place at each setting, garnish with edible flowers if desired.

1½ cups cranberry juice

1½ cups pineapple juice

5¼ cups 7-Up soda

2 cups raspberry sherbet

In a large pitcher combine cranberry juice, pineapple juice, and 7-Up. Mix with a large spoon. Chill for 3 hours if beverages were not previously chilled.

To serve place a scoop of sherbet in each glass, pour juice mixture over sherbet.

Preparation Time: 5 minutes
Chill Time: 3 hours if beverages were not previously chilled
Experience Level: Beginner

ARTICHOKE DIP

DAIRY   SERVES 8

When this dip was served at one of our tasting parties the response was unanimous. Everybody loved it, regardless of whether or not they like artichokes.

2 (9-ounce) boxes frozen artichoke hearts, defrosted

¾ cup mayonnaise

¾ cup grated Parmesan cheese

2 cloves garlic, crushed

1 teaspoon dried minced onion

Preheat oven to 350°F/180°C. Prepare a lightly greased (15x10-inch) jelly-roll pan.

Cut artichokes into ½ to ¾-inch pieces and place in a medium sized bowl. Add remainder of ingredients to artichokes. Mix to combine. Pour mixture into prepared pan. Bake for 20 to 30 minutes or until browned.

Serve warm, in a bowl along with crackers, toasted bread slices, or an assortment of fresh cut vegetables.

Preparation Time: 10 minutes
Cook Time: 25 minutes
Experience Level: Beginner

MEATS

GRILLED LONDON BROIL

MEAT   SERVES 8 TO 10

2 tablespoons canola oil
1 medium green bell pepper, coarsely chopped
2 medium carrots, thinly sliced
2 onions, coarsely chopped
1 (20-ounce) can pineapple chunks, drained, 5 tablespoons juice reserved
4 tablespoons white vinegar
4 tablespoons ketchup
4 tablespoons sugar

5 tablespoons cold water
1 tablespoon cornstarch
1 teaspoon salt
1 cup soy sauce
1 (4 to 6-pound) London broil roast, gristle removed
1 head garlic, finely chopped
2 teaspoons garlic powder
½ teaspoon black pepper

In a 4-quart saucepan over a medium-high flame, heat oil. Add green pepper, carrots, onions and pineapple chunks. Cook until tender, about 10 minutes. Add vinegar, ketchup, sugar and reserved pineapple juice. Bring to a boil.

In a small bowl combine water and cornstarch. Stir cornstarch mixture into saucepan. Add salt. Stir until thickened, about 2 minutes. Reduce heat and simmer for 5 minutes. Stir in soy sauce. Remove from heat. Place half of the sauce in a bowl, cover and refrigerate.

Sprinkle roast with garlic, garlic powder and black pepper. Place in a dish large enough to accommodate roast. Pour remaining sauce over roast. Cover and refrigerate for 6 to 12 hours.

Heat barbecue grill to high. Remove meat from marinade. Cook meat on grill for 5 minutes on each side. Remove from heat and place in pan large enough to hold roast. Place in freezer for 1 hour.

Preheat oven to 350°F/180°C.

Remove roast from freezer and slice as thin as possible with a non-serrated knife. Place meat in a baking dish. Pour reserved sauce over meat. Cover and bake in preheated oven for 25 minutes until medium rare.

Preparation Time: 1 hour
Cook Time: 55 minutes
Chill Time: 7 to 13 hours
Experience Level: Intermediate
Wine Suggestion: Hagefen Nappa Valley Caberret Sauvinon

Lazy Texas Brisket

MEAT   SERVES 8

With minimal preparation time, this is the ideal brisket to put up in the morning to be ready at dinner time. The rich, spicy barbecue sauce enhances its flavor. If desired, make the sauce as a barbecue marinade for a southern-style barbecue chicken.

BRISKET

1 large clove garlic, minced	½ teaspoon sage
1 (4 to 5-pound) brisket	½ teaspoon sugar
1 tablespoon chili powder	½ teaspoon dried oregano
1 teaspoon paprika	¼ teaspoon cayenne pepper
1 teaspoon salt	¼ teaspoon black pepper
½ teaspoon cumin	

BARBECUE SAUCE

2 tablespoons margarine	2 tablespoons brown sugar
1 medium onion, coarsely chopped	2 tablespoons Worcestershire sauce
½ cup water	1 tablespoon molasses
½ cup chili sauce	2 teaspoons salt
½ cup ketchup	2 teaspoons mustard powder
¼ cup apple cider vinegar	½ teaspoon black pepper
2 tablespoons lemon juice	½ teaspoon paprika

BRISKET: Preheat oven to 200°F/93°C.

Rub garlic into both sides of brisket. In a small bowl combine chili powder, paprika, salt, cumin, sage, sugar, oregano, cayenne pepper and black pepper. Rub all over brisket.

Prepare a piece of heavy duty aluminum foil large enough to wrap the whole brisket. Place brisket, fat side up on foil. Wrap tightly. Place aluminum foil wrapped brisket in a shallow roasting pan. Place in oven for 8 hours or until tender. Let cool.

BARBECUE SAUCE: In a large skillet over medium heat, melt margarine. Add onion and sauté for 5 to 10 minutes or until translucent. Add water, chili sauce, ketchup, apple cider vinegar, lemon juice, brown sugar, Worcestershire sauce, molasses, salt, mustard powder, black pepper and paprika. Stir to combine. Bring to a boil. Reduce heat and simmer uncovered for 30 minutes, stirring occasionally. Serve at room temperature.

Slice cooled brisket against grain. Serve hot or cold with barbecue sauce.

Preparation Time: 20 minutes
Cook Time: 8 hours 40 minutes
Experience Level: Beginner
Wine Suggestion: Joseph Zakon Winery Val Cab 5761

Horseradish Crusted Prime Rib

MEAT   SERVES 8 TO 10

When garlic is roasted in a crock, it becomes as soft as butter and can be used as a wonderful spread. When roasting the unpeeled garlic, add an additional head or two to use as a spread for accompanying bread.

30 cloves garlic, unpeeled	½ teaspoon coarse salt
⅓ cup olive oil	1 (4 to 6-pound) prime rib roast
⅓ cup creamy horseradish sauce	

Preheat oven to 350°F/180°C.

Place unpeeled garlic cloves in a small oven proof crock. Drizzle with olive oil. Cover and roast for 30 minutes. Let cool.

Remove garlic cloves from oil, reserve oil.

Squeeze softened garlic out of peels and into the bowl of a food processor. Add reserved oil, horseradish sauce and salt. Process about 3 minutes until smooth.

Place roast in a large roasting pan. Pour garlic mixture over roast and rub mixture all over meat to coat. Cover and refrigerate for 6 hours or overnight.

Preheat oven to 200°F/93°C.

Roast uncovered for 1 hour per pound. During last hour of cooking, raise temperature to 225°F/115°C. Do not open oven during roasting.

Let stand about 15 minutes before slicing.

Preparation Time: 15 minutes
Cook Time: 4 hours 30 minutes to 6 hours 30 minutes
Chill Time: 6 hours or overnight
Experience Level: Intermediate
Wine Suggestion: Baron Philippe De Rothchild Mouton Cadet Bordeaux 1997

$\mathcal{I}$TALIAN $\mathcal{B}$EEF

MEAT   SERVES 6

$\mathcal{D}$epending on tastes, the heat level of this recipe can be adjusted by adding more or less pepperoncini. The result here is moderately spicy. Be sure to have plenty of bread on hand to soak up the gravy.

1 (2 to 3-pound) fertiloff	2 teaspoons onion powder
½ cup Italian salad dressing	½ teaspoon garlic powder
¼ cup white vinegar	¼ teaspoon dried dill
3 tablespoons water	1 teaspoon black pepper or to taste
3 to 4 tablespoons sugar	2 medium green bell peppers, sliced
5 tablespoons beef flavoring	½ (12-ounce) jar pepperoncini
2 teaspoons dried parsley	2 cups pickling liquid from pepperoncini

Place fertiloff, Italian dressing, vinegar, water, sugar, beef flavoring, parsley, onion powder, garlic powder, dill, black pepper to taste, green peppers, pepperoncini, and pickling liquid in the crock of a crock pot. Cook on high setting for 6 to 8 hours.

Remove meat from crock pot and shred. Return to crock pot until heated through. Serve on Italian bread as sandwiches.

Preparation Time: 15 minutes
Cook Time: 6 to 8 hours
Experience Level: Beginner

$\mathcal{F}$RENCH $\mathcal{R}$OAST

MEAT   SERVES 8

$\mathcal{T}$his roast is even more delicious when cooked in advance, refrigerated then sliced and reheated.

2 tablespoons canola oil	¾ cup brown sugar
1 onion, sliced	1 cup ketchup
1 (4-pound) French roast or boneless chuck roast	Garlic powder
	Salt
½ cup white vinegar	Black pepper

In a large skillet with high sides, heat oil over medium-high flame. Add onion and sauté until translucent, about 10 minutes. Place roast in skillet and sear on all sides.

In a small bowl, combine vinegar, brown sugar and ketchup. Sprinkle seasonings onto roast and pour liquid mixture over roast. Lower flame to medium-low and cook covered for 1 hour and 30 minutes. Roast should be tender on the outside and pink in center.

Preparation Time: 15 minutes
Cook Time: 1 hour 50 minutes
Experience Level: Beginner
Wine Suggestion: Teal Lake Pinot Noir 2001

Homemade Corned Beef

MEAT   SERVES 10

While this recipe needs to be started several days in advance, it does not include a tremendous amount of preparation. Perfect for a holiday or Shabbos main course, the leftovers make for great sandwich fare.

BRINE
16 cups water
1½ pounds coarse salt
1 pound dark brown sugar
3 bay leaves
2 teaspoons mustard seeds
1 sprig fresh thyme
10 juniper berries

20 whole black peppercorns
1 egg in shell
Salt
1 (5-pound) brisket
Cold water to cover
5 cloves garlic

FOR BOILING
1 teaspoon sugar

2 tablespoons pickling spice

GLAZE
4 tablespoons margarine
2 tablespoons prepared yellow mustard
10 tablespoons ketchup

6 tablespoons apple cider vinegar
⅔ cup brown sugar

In a large stock pot over high heat place water, salt, brown sugar, bay leaves, mustard seeds, thyme, juniper berries and peppercorns. Bring to a hard boil for 5 minutes. Remove from heat and let cool. To test the saltiness of the brine place raw whole egg in shell in cooled brine. If egg does not float add more salt until egg floats.

Using a trussing needle or skewer, pierce brisket all over. Place brisket in pot of cold water, cover and let stand for 45 minutes.

Remove brisket from water and place in large crock or clean bucket. Pour cooked brine over brisket. Add garlic. Place a plate on top of brisket to submerge. Place a lid or plastic wrap over crock. Store in refrigerator or a cool dry place at a temperature below 60°F/13°C. Salting time depends on thickness of meat. Allow 3 to 10 days for salting time.

FOR BOILING: Rinse pickled brisket and place in a large stock pot. Add water to cover. Over high heat bring water to a boil. Add sugar and pickling spice. Lower heat and simmer covered for 2 hours or until easily pierced with a fork.

Remove brisket from water and transfer to a baking dish large enough to accommodate corned beef.

GLAZE: Preheat oven to 350°F/180°C.

In a medium saucepan over medium-high heat, melt margarine. Add mustard, ketchup, cider vinegar and brown sugar, stir to combine. Bring to a boil. Reduce heat and simmer for 5 minutes. Pour over corned beef. Cover and place in oven for 15 minutes. Uncover and bake an additional 15 minutes. Chill and slice. Serve cold or hot.

Preparation Time: 45 minutes
Cook Time: 2 hours 40 minutes
Chill Time: 3 to 10 days
Experience Level: Advanced

$\mathscr{C}$HUNKY $\mathscr{B}$EEF $\mathscr{C}$HILI

MEAT   SERVES 6

1 tablespoon canola oil
1½ pounds boneless chuck steak, cut into
    ¾-inch pieces
5 medium cloves garlic, chopped
1 large onion, chopped
3 tablespoons chili powder
2 teaspoons cumin
1 cup water

3 tablespoons tomato paste
2 tablespoons brown sugar
½ teaspoon salt
1 large red bell pepper, chopped
2 (15-ounce) cans red kidney beans, rinsed
    and drained
1 (14½-ounce) can diced tomatoes

CILANTRO TOMATO TOPPING, OPTIONAL

1 cup non-dairy sour cream
1 plum tomato, seeded and chopped
¼ cup fresh parsley or cilantro, chopped

1 tablespoon lime juice
1 teaspoon cumin
¼ teaspoon salt

In a 4 to 6-quart pressure cooker over medium-high flame, heat oil. In 3 batches add meat, garlic and onion. Stir occasionally and cook for 4 to 5 minutes, until meat is well browned on all sides. Using a slotted spoon transfer meat, onions and garlic to a large bowl.

Add chili powder and cumin to pan drippings. Cook for 30 seconds, stirring constantly. Add 1 cup water and bring to a boil. Deglaze by loosening browned bits from bottom of pan. Boil for 1 minute. Add in tomato paste, brown sugar, salt, red pepper, kidney beans, tomatoes and meat mixture.

Use pressure cooker according to manufacturers directions. Cover pressure cooker. Bring up to pressure and cook under pressure for 15 minutes. Release pressure quickly.

Cilantro Tomato Topping: In a small bowl combine sour cream, tomato, parsley, lime juice, cumin and salt. Set aside.

To serve, skim and discard fat from top of chili. Ladle into bowls. Place a dollop of topping on chili.

Preparation Time: 40 minutes
Cook Time: 30 minutes
Experience Level: Intermediate

Sloppy Joes

MEAT   SERVES 6

For a new twist, serve over garlic bread, rice, or noodles. Satisfying for the whole family.

1 pound ground beef
1 medium onion, chopped
1 to 2 medium cloves fresh garlic, crushed
1 (8-ounce) can tomato sauce
1 tablespoon chili sauce

1 tablespoon chili powder
1½ tablespoons sugar
½ to 1 teaspoon seasoned salt
½ to 1 teaspoon black pepper

In a large skillet over low to medium heat, sauté ground beef, onion and garlic. Break up any large chunks of meat and sauté until meat is browned. Add tomato sauce, chili sauce, chili powder, sugar, seasoned salt and black pepper. Mix to combine, cook for 20 minutes uncovered.

Preparation Time: 10 minutes
Cook Time: 30 minutes
Experience Level: Beginner

Braised Stuffed Veal Breast

MEAT   SERVES 6

Cooking the veal with the bone gives the veal a richer flavor. The idea is the same as using bones in a soup, causing the wine and sauce to thicken as it's cooking.

2 cups day old Italian bread cut into
   ½-inch squares
1 cup rice milk
½ cup fresh flat leaf Italian parsley, chopped
4 medium cloves garlic, slivered
½ pound sliced pastrami, chopped into
   ½-inch pieces
½ cup pine nuts, toasted
½ cup dark raisins soaked in warm water to
   rehydrate, drain

Coarse salt
Freshly ground black pepper
Olive oil
1 (4-pound) veal breast, request butcher to
   separate meat from bone, take bone to
   cook with meat
4 hard boiled eggs, shelled
1 cup red wine
1 (15-ounce) can tomato sauce
½ cup water

In a large bowl, soak bread in rice milk for 5 minutes. Using clean dry hands, squeeze out excess rice milk. Add parsley, garlic, pastrami, pine nuts and raisins. Season lightly with salt and pepper. Drizzle with olive oil to moisten, mix thoroughly to combine.

Line counter with one or two 18-inch pieces of plastic wrap. Place veal on plastic wrap. Make a deep slice along side of veal breast and fan open like a book. Lay another piece of plastic wrap on top. Using the smooth side of a mallet pound veal until veal is about ½-inch thick, being careful not to tear veal. Discard top sheet of plastic wrap. Rub surface of veal with olive oil and season with salt and pepper. Lift

veal and place 5 strands of kitchen twine across plastic wrap. Place veal across twine. Spread stuffing evenly over veal leaving a 1-inch boarder all around. Place the eggs lengthwise down center. Roll up veal jelly-roll style, using plastic wrap for support. Tie twine securely around veal.

Rinse veal bone. In a large roasting pan over medium heat place about 2 tablespoons olive oil. Carefully lift veal roll and place in roasting pan. Sear stuffed veal breast on all sides. Add wine, tomato sauce, water and veal bone.

Cover and simmer for 1 hour, turning and basting occasionally. Discard bones before serving.

Preparation Time: 30 minutes
Cook Time: 1 hour
Experience Level: Intermediate
Wine Suggestion: Gamla Sauvignon Blanc 2000

*V*EAL IN *W*INE

MEAT   SERVES 4

¼ cup flour   4 veal chops
¼ teaspoon salt   1 small onion, thinly sliced
¼ teaspoon garlic salt   ¼ cup medium fresh white mushrooms, sliced
¼ teaspoon black pepper   1 cup canned tomatoes, drained
2 tablespoons canola oil   ½ cup red wine

On a large piece of plastic wrap or in a shallow dish, combine flour, salt, garlic salt and pepper.

Coat both sides of veal chops with flour mixture.

In a large skillet over medium flame, heat oil. Brown veal on both sides. Add onion, mushrooms, tomatoes and red wine. Bring to a boil, lower flame and simmer covered, for 1 hour to 1 hour and 15 minutes.

Preparation Time: 15 minutes
Cook Time: 1 hour 15 minutes
Experience Level: Beginner
Wine Suggestion: Alfasi Cabernet Sauvignon

Veal and Apple Dinner Pie

MEAT   SERVES 6

For a beautiful presentation, sweet potatoes can be piped using a pastry bag. Take a look at some of the tips for cake decorating on page 306 to make this a stand out centerpiece of a dinner pie.

FILLING

2 tablespoons canola oil
2 pounds veal for stew
2 medium onions, chopped
1½ teaspoons dried sage
1 teaspoon salt

¼ teaspoon black pepper
1 (10½-ounce) can chicken broth
2 tart cooking apples
2 tablespoons flour

SWEET POTATO TOPPING

3 pounds sweet potatoes, baked and cooled
¼ cup light brown sugar
4 tablespoons plus 1 teaspoon margarine, divided

¼ cup orange juice
1 medium tart cooking apple

FILLING: In a large skillet over medium-high flame, heat oil. Add veal and sauté until browned on all sides, about 5 to 7 minutes. Remove from skillet. Add onion and sauté until golden, about 5 minutes. Add sage, salt and pepper. Return veal to skillet and mix to combine. Add chicken broth and bring mixture to a boil. Lower flame and simmer covered for about 1 hour or until veal is tender.

Peel, core and slice apples into 8 wedges. In a small bowl toss apple wedges with flour. Add apples to skillet with veal. Stir to combine. Simmer covered, an additional 15 to 20 minutes, until apple is tender and sauce has thickened. Remove from heat.

SWEET POTATO TOPPING: Peel baked sweet potatoes. Place peeled potatoes in the bowl of a food processor or blender and process just until smooth.

In a medium saucepan over medium heat, combine sweet potatoes, brown sugar, 2 tablespoons margarine and orange juice. Stir and cook for about 5 minutes.

Turn veal mixture into a 2-quart round 10-inch diameter shallow baking dish, mounding in center. Spoon sweet potato mixture on top of filling, around edges of baking dish leaving a 3-inch diameter opening in center. Or place sweet potato mixture in a pastry bag fitted with a number 5 tip. Create a pleasing design around edge, leaving a 3-inch diameter opening in center.

Melt 2 tablespoons margarine and spoon over sweet potatoes. Place pie under broiler 6-inches from heat for about 5 minutes or until lightly browned.

Peel, core and slice apple. In a small skillet over medium heat, melt margarine and sauté apple slices until soft. Arrange in spoke fashion on top of sweet potatoes.

Preparation Time: 1 hour
Cook Time: 1 hour 30 minutes
Experience Level: Intermediate
Wine Suggestion: Châteaueuf Herzog Selection Bordeaux

Tongue with Mushrooms and Artichoke Hearts

MEAT   SERVES 10

3 tablespoons canola or vegetable oil
1 tongue
2 tablespoons chicken soup flavoring, divided
2 teaspoons paprika, divided
2 teaspoons white pepper, divided
1 teaspoon turmeric, divided
1 teaspoon cumin, divided
Salt to taste

10 bay leaves
2 medium tomatoes, peeled
2 whole onions, peeled
½ medium head garlic
¼ bunch cilantro, chopped
Juice from ½ medium lemon
1 (13-ounce) can sliced mushrooms, drained
2 (14-ounce) cans artichoke hearts, drained
Cilantro or parsley for garnish, optional

In a 5-quart Dutch oven over medium-high flame, heat oil. Add tongue and brown on one side. While browning sprinkle with 1 tablespoon chicken soup flavoring, 1 teaspoon paprika, 1 teaspoon white pepper, ½ teaspoon turmeric, ½ teaspoon cumin and salt to taste.

Turn tongue over and sprinkle with remaining seasonings; 1 tablespoon chicken soup flavoring, 1 teaspoon paprika, 1 teaspoon white pepper, ½ teaspoon turmeric, ½ teaspoon cumin and salt to taste. When browned, add bay leaves and enough water to cover tongue. Add tomatoes and onions to Dutch oven. Bring to a boil. Reduce heat and simmer, covered for 1 hour.

While still hot, remove tongue from liquid and place on cutting board. Set liquid in Dutch oven aside. Make a slit in the skin, hold tongue down with a fork and peel all skin off by pulling away from meat. Use a sharp knife if necessary to peel off skin.

Wrap tongue in aluminum foil. Place in freezer for 1 hour. Remove tongue from freezer, slice thinly with a sharp knife.

Remove tomatoes, onions and bay leaves from cooking liquid, and place cooking liquid over medium heat. Add sliced tongue, garlic, cilantro, lemon juice, mushrooms and artichoke hearts. Cook over medium heat uncovered for 30 minutes until liquid has thickened. Adjust seasonings as necessary.

Serve garnished with fresh cilantro or parsley.

Preparation Time: 35 minutes
Cook Time: 1 hour 30 minutes
Chill Time: 1 hour
Experience Level: Intermediate
Wine Suggestions: Tishbi Estate 1999 Cabernet Sauvignon or
Merlot or Layla Vineyards Malbec

LAMB STEW WITH COUSCOUS

MEAT

SERVES 8

2 pounds lamb for stew, cut into 1-inch pieces
2 tablespoons olive oil, divided
2 cloves garlic, minced
1½ teaspoons ground cumin
1½ teaspoons ground coriander
1 large onion, cut into 8 wedges
1 (14½-ounce) can stewed tomatoes
1 cinnamon stick
1¼ teaspoons salt

¼ teaspoon cayenne pepper
1 cup water
2 medium sweet potatoes, peeled and cut into 1½-inch pieces
1 cup black raisins
1 (15-ounce) can chickpeas, drained
2 cups couscous
¼ cup fresh cilantro, divided

In a 5-quart Dutch oven over medium-high flame, heat 1 tablespoon of oil. Add half of lamb and brown on all sides. Set aside in a medium bowl. Repeat with remaining oil and lamb.

Add garlic, cumin and coriander to pan drippings in Dutch oven. Cook for 30 seconds. Add browned lamb. Stir in onion, stewed tomatoes, cinnamon stick, salt, cayenne pepper and water. Raise flame to high. Bring mixture to a boil. Cover, reduce heat to low and simmer 45 minutes, stirring occasionally.

Add sweet potatoes. Cover and cook for 30 minutes or until lamb and sweet potatoes are fork tender.

Add raisins and chickpeas, cover and cook for 5 minutes until heated through.

Prepare couscous according to package directions. Stir in 1 tablespoon chopped cilantro.

Add remaining cilantro to stew just before serving. Serve over couscous.

Preparation Time: 20 minutes
Cook Time: 1 hour 45 minutes
Experience Level: Intermediate
Wine Suggestion: Primitivo di Manduria 2001

HARVEST LEG OF LAMB

MEAT   **SERVES 6**

This exceptional recipe has the lamb roasted tender with a full, decadent flavor. Put your knife and fork down, you'll want to eat this one off the bone.

6 (1-pound) legs of lamb, fat trimmed, bone in	3 tablespoons fresh flat leaf parsley, chopped or 1½ tablespoons, dried
3 tablespoons lemon juice	1 tablespoon Italian seasoning, crushed
6 cloves garlic, minced	1 teaspoon black pepper
3 tablespoons olive oil, divided	

Place legs of lamb in a (9x13-inch) baking pan. With the tip of a sharp knife cut several ¼-inch long slits into each leg. Brush meat with lemon juice. In a small bowl, combine garlic with 1 tablespoon of the oil. Rub garlic and oil mixture all over lamb and specifically into cut slits. In same bowl combine parsley, 2 tablespoons oil, Italian seasoning and black pepper. Sprinkle mixture evenly over lamb and pat the parsley down.

Wrap each leg tightly with plastic wrap. Refrigerate overnight.

Preheat oven to 325°F/160°C.

Place legs fat side up on a rack in a shallow roasting pan. Roast for 2½ hours. Transfer meat to serving platter. Cover with aluminum foil and let sit 15 minutes before carving.

Preparation Time: 15 minutes
Chill Time: 6 to 24 hours
Cook Time: 2 hours 30 minutes
Experience Level: Intermediate
Wine Suggestion: Herzog Selection French Cabernet Sauvignon 1999

Cumin and Lime Grilled Skirt Steaks

MEAT   SERVES 6

The response from this recipe was so overwhelming, everyone who tasted it had to have the recipe and could not wait for the cookbook to be completed. The marinade is an unusual avocado green color, when the meat is cooked it returns to its normal color.

6 jalapeño peppers, stems removed, halved and seeded

4 cloves garlic, peeled

½ cup fresh lime juice from 3 to 4 fresh limes

1 teaspoon black pepper

3 tablespoons ground cumin

6 sprigs fresh cilantro

1½ cups olive oil

1 tablespoon salt

3 pounds skirt steak

In the work bowl of a blender place peppers, garlic, lime juice, black pepper and cumin. Blend until peppers are finely chopped. Add sprigs of cilantro, oil and salt. Purée until smooth. Cut steaks in half. Using a basting brush, generously brush both sides of steak with marinade and place in a large ziploc bag. Pour remaining marinade into bag and place in refrigerator for 12 to 24 hours.

Preheat barbecue grill or broiler to very hot. Cook steaks 3 to 4 minutes on each side, or until just seared for medium rare.

Preparation Time: 10 minutes
Cook Time: 8 minutes
Chill Time: 12 to 24 hours
Experience Level: Beginner
Wine Suggestion: Herzog Selection Syrah

MEAT OR CHICKEN KABOB MARINADE

MEAT

A simple marinade, perfect for preparing meat or chicken kabobs the day before a barbecue. Can also be used on steaks and for boneless, skinless chicken breasts.

2 medium cloves garlic, minced
¼ cup soy sauce
½ cup canola oil
½ cup dry red wine

2 tablespoons ketchup
½ teaspoon black pepper
¼ teaspoon ground ginger

In the work bowl of a food processor, process garlic for about 8 seconds. Add soy sauce, canola oil, red wine, ketchup, black pepper and ginger. Process until well blended.

Place desired meat or poultry in marinade. Refrigerate covered for 12 hours. Turn once after about 6 hours.

Preparation Time: 5 minutes
Chill Time: 12 hours
Experience Level: Beginner
Wine Suggestion: Yarden Merlot 1999 or 2000

CHINESE NOODLE CAKES WITH VEGETABLES AND BEEF

MEAT   SERVES 16

A gourmet Chinese dish that is fun to prepare. The noodle cakes are crispy on the outside and moist on the inside. Topped with stir-fry, they resemble a pizza and are served in wedges.

BEEF AND MARINADE
1 tablespoon cornstarch
1 tablespoon soy sauce
1 tablespoon rice wine or sherry
2 large cloves garlic, minced

1 tablespoon fresh minced ginger
12 ounces boneless beef cut into 2x½-inch pieces

NOODLE CAKES
2 tablespoons vegetable or peanut oil, additional if necessary

1 pound fresh or dried Chinese noodles or thin spaghetti, cooked according to package directions, drained and tossed with 2 tablespoons soy sauce

STIR-FRY

4 tablespoons vegetable or peanut oil, divided

4 cups sliced fresh vegetables, red bell peppers, carrots, snow peas and broccoli florets

2 tablespoons soy sauce

GARNISH

¼ cup toasted sesame seeds (to toast raw sesame seeds preheat oven to 400°F/200°C, toast for 10 minutes)

1 medium scallion, julienned

BEEF and MARINADE: In a medium bowl combine cornstarch, soy sauce, rice wine, garlic and ginger. Add beef and stir to coat. Marinate for 15 minutes.

NOODLE CAKES: In a flat bottomed (9-inch) skillet over high flame, heat oil. Spread half of the noodles onto bottom of skillet. Do not stir. Cook until crisp and golden on bottom, about 4 to 5 minutes. Add oil as necessary to keep noodles from sticking to skillet.

Slide noodles onto a plate, cover with another plate. Flip and return noodle cake to pan, adding oil if necessary to prevent sticking. Cook until crisp and golden, about 2 to 3 minutes. Transfer to serving plate and cover with foil to keep warm. Repeat with remaining noodles.

STIR-FRY: In a large wok or skillet over a high flame, heat 2 tablespoons of oil. Swirl to coat pan. Add vegetables and stir-fry until crisp and tender, about 2 minutes. Remove vegetables with a slotted spoon and set aside.

Add 2 tablespoons of oil to pan over high heat, swirl to coat. Add marinated beef and stir-fry until browned, about 2 minutes. Return vegetables to pan. Add soy sauce and stir-fry until vegetables are heated through.

TO SERVE: Ladle half the beef and vegetable mixture over each noodle cake. Sprinkle with sesame seeds and garnish with julienned scallions. Slice into wedges to serve.

Preparation Time: 30 minutes
Cook Time: 30 minutes
Experience Level: Advanced
Wine Suggestion: Yarden Merlot

Szechuan Beef and Snow Peas

MEAT   SERVES 4

3 tablespoons cornstarch, divided
3 tablespoons soy sauce, divided
1 tablespoon sherry
1 medium clove garlic, minced
½ pound pepper steak
½ teaspoon crushed red pepper

¾ cup water
2 tablespoons canola or vegetable oil, divided
6 ounces fresh snow peas
1 large onion, cut into chunks
1 medium tomato, cut into chunks
Salt to taste

In a medium bowl combine 1 tablespoon cornstarch, 1 tablespoon soy sauce, sherry and garlic. Add pepper steak and toss to coat. Let stand 15 minutes.

In a small bowl mix 2 tablespoons cornstarch, 2 tablespoons soy sauce, crushed red pepper and water. Set aside.

In a wok or large skillet over high flame, heat 1 tablespoon oil. Add pepper steak and cook 2 to 3 minutes or until no longer pink. Remove from wok. Heat remaining tablespoon oil. Add snow peas and onion, sprinkle lightly with salt. Stir-fry about 3 minutes. Add pepper steak, soy sauce mixture and tomato. Stir until thick and heated through, about 3 to 5 minutes.

Preparation Time: 5 minutes
Cook Time: 10 minutes
Experience Level: Beginner

Beef and Asparagus Stir-Fry

MEAT   SERVES 4

A Californian take on a Chinese dish, this stir-fry is full of fresh vegetables, using crisp fresh asparagus, colorful peppers, mushrooms and carrots.

½ cup water
2 tablespoons soy sauce
2 teaspoons cornstarch
2 teaspoons beef bouillon, crushed
¼ teaspoon black pepper
1 tablespoon vegetable oil
¾ pound pepper steak
1 pound fresh asparagus, cut into 2-inch pieces

1 small red or yellow bell pepper, coarsely chopped
2 medium onions, thinly sliced
2 carrots, julienned
6 ounces small to medium fresh mushrooms, sliced
3 medium scallions, sliced
3 cups hot cooked rice

In a small bowl combine water, soy sauce, cornstarch, beef bouillon and black pepper. Heat wok or large skillet over high heat. Add oil to pan and swirl to coat. Add pepper steak and cook, stirring often, 5 minutes or until beef is no longer pink. Place asparagus, pepper, onion and carrots in wok. Stir often until vegetables are tender, about 5 minutes. Add mushrooms and scallions. Cook for 2 minutes. Stir in soy sauce mixture. Cook until liquid begins to thicken.

Serve over bed of rice.

Preparation Time: 20 minutes
Cook Time: 15 minutes
Experience Level: Beginner

Beef Stroganoff

MEAT   SERVES 8

½ cup flour
½ teaspoon black pepper
2 pounds pepper steak, thinly sliced
1 tablespoon canola oil
1 medium onion, chopped
8 ounces fresh medium white mushrooms

2 cups plain soy milk or water
2 tablespoons soy sauce
¼ cup fresh chopped parsley
¼ medium green or red bell pepper, chopped
3 medium tomatoes, chopped
Dill to taste, optional

In a large bowl combine flour and black pepper. Add pepper steak and toss to coat. Set aside.

In a large skillet over medium-high flame, heat oil. Add onion and sauté until transparent. Add mushrooms and sauté an additional 3 minutes. Remove onions and mushrooms with a slotted spoon, place in a medium bowl.

Add meat to skillet in batches until meat is browned on all sides, about 3 minutes on each side. Place all meat, mushrooms and onions back in skillet. Add soy milk and bring to a boil. Cook for about 5 minutes, sauce will thicken. Add soy sauce, parsley and pepper. Cook until meat is tender, stirring occasionally, about 10 minutes. Add tomatoes and dill to taste, if desired. Cook an additional 5 minutes.

Preparation Time: 20 minutes
Cook Time: 30 minutes
Experience Level: Beginner
Wine Suggestion: Gamla Merlot

TRI-COLOR MEAT ROLL

MEAT   SERVES 12

1 tablespoon canola oil
2 medium red bell peppers, chopped
1 large onion, chopped
1½ pounds ground beef
2 tablespoons ketchup
½ teaspoon salt
⅛ teaspoon black pepper

¼ teaspoon garlic powder
¼ cup breadcrumbs
1 pound puff pastry sheets, defrosted
   according to package directions
1½ pounds ground chicken breast
1 egg, beaten
Poppy or sesame seeds, optional for topping

In a large skillet over medium flame, heat oil. Add red peppers and onion. Sauté until transparent, about 10 minutes. Set aside.

In a large bowl, combine ground beef with ketchup, salt, black pepper, garlic powder and breadcrumbs. Set aside.

Prepare a lightly greased (15x10-inch) jelly-roll pan.

Preheat oven to 350°F/180°C.

On a clean work surface unfold 1 sheet of puff pastry dough. Spread ½ of ground beef mixture evenly over pastry dough. Spread ½ of ground chicken over ground beef, being careful not to mix, just layer. Place ½ of pepper and onion mixture over chicken. Roll into a log, jelly-roll style. Place on prepared jelly-roll pan. Repeat with remaining dough, meat, chicken, pepper and onion mixture.

Using a pastry brush, brush tops with beaten egg and sprinkle with sesame or poppy seeds, if desired. Using a fork, prick holes on top of pastry in a pleasing pattern. Place in oven for 1 hour or until golden brown.

Preparation Time: 30 minutes
Cook Time: 1 hour 10 minutes
Experience Level: Intermediate

Broccoli Meat Pinwheels

MEAT   SERVES 8

MARINADE

½ cup orange juice

2 teaspoons soy sauce

1 teaspoon sugar

1 pound pepper steak

VEGETABLES

3 teaspoons canola oil, divided

¾ cup broccoli florets

3 carrots, thinly sliced

1 small red bell pepper, julienned

1 scallion, thinly sliced

2 teaspoons cornstarch

¾ cup cold water

PINWHEELS

1 (16-ounce) box puff pastry squares or
   sheets cut into 3-inch squares, defrosted

1 tablespoon fresh orange zest, optional
   garnish

MARINADE: In a medium bowl combine orange juice, soy sauce and sugar. Add pepper steak to marinade and toss to coat. Let stand 30 minutes.

VEGETABLES: In a large skillet over high flame, heat 2 teaspoons of oil. Add broccoli, carrots, red pepper and scallion. Stir and sauté 2 minutes. Remove vegetables from heat, set aside.

Drain meat from marinade, reserve marinade.

In same skillet over medium flame, heat 1 teaspoon of oil. Add pepper steak and cook until no longer pink, about 6 minutes. Add cooked vegetables. Stir in reserved marinade and bring to a boil.

In a small bowl combine cornstarch with cold water. Add to vegetables and meat in skillet. Cook about 3 minutes until sauce thickens.

PINWHEELS: Prepare a greased (15x10-inch) jelly-roll pan.

Preheat oven to 350°F/180°C.

Place a pastry square on a clean work surface. Using a sharp knife cut from each corner towards the center, do not cut through center. Make an x but keep center intact. Take the upper right hand corner and place in center. Press down. Turn square to the right to bring the turned in corner to the right side. Repeat bringing each corner to center as described. Repeat for remaining pastry squares. Place on prepared jelly-roll pan. Bake 20 to 30 minutes or until golden and puffed.

Place pinwheel in center of plate, with vegetable and meat mixture in center of pinwheel. Sprinkle with orange zest.

Preparation Time: 30 minutes

Chill Time: 30 minutes

Cook Time: 1 hour

Experience Level: Intermediate

POULTRY

Spinach and Herb Stuffed Chicken

MEAT   **SERVES 4 TO 6**

The stuffing under the skin makes for a beautiful presentation. For individual servings use Cornish hens instead of a whole chicken.

1 teaspoon dried basil
1 teaspoon dried oregano
1 teaspoon parsley flakes

2 medium cloves garlic, crushed
1 tablespoon olive oil
1 (5-pound) whole chicken

UNDER SKIN STUFFING
2 (10-ounce) packages frozen chopped
   spinach, thawed and well drained
1 large red bell pepper, chopped
¾ cup breadcrumbs

4 medium scallions, sliced
⅓ cup pine nuts
¼ cup margarine, melted
¼ teaspoon black pepper

CAVITY STUFFING
½ medium orange
1 medium onion, halved
2 sprigs fresh rosemary

2 sprigs fresh basil
2 sprigs fresh thyme

In a small bowl combine basil, oregano, parsley and garlic. Rub olive oil all over chicken. Rub spices all over chicken. Cover and refrigerate for 6 to 24 hours.

UNDER SKIN STUFFING: In a small bowl combine spinach, red pepper, bread crumbs, scallions, pine nuts, margarine and black pepper. Slip hand between skin and flesh of chicken breast. Distribute mixture evenly under skin.

Preheat oven to 325°F/160°C.

CAVITY STUFFING: Squeeze orange inside cavity and place inside. Add onion halves, rosemary, basil and thyme to cavity.

Place chicken breast side up in a shallow roasting pan. Roast uncovered for 1 hour and 45 minutes to 2 hours, basting occasionally with pan juices. When juices run clear remove chicken from oven and cover with aluminum foil for 10 minutes. Remove cooked herb sprigs from cavity before serving.

Preparation Time: 45 minutes
Cook Time: 1 hour 45 minutes to 2 hours
Chill Time: 6 to 24 hours
Experience Level: Intermediate
Wine Suggestion: Bartenura Soave 2001

SWEET ROASTED CHICKEN

MEAT   SERVES 4 TO 6

2 tablespoons honey
¼ cup lemon juice
¼ teaspoon cinnamon
¼ teaspoon ground ginger

¼ teaspoon cumin
¼ teaspoon allspice
2 cloves garlic, finely chopped
1 (3½-pound) whole chicken

Preheat oven to 375°F/190°C.

In a small bowl combine honey, lemon juice, cinnamon, ginger, cumin, allspice and garlic.

Coat chicken with spice mixture. Place in roasting pan breast side down. Roast for 20 minutes. Turn chicken breast side up. Cook an additional 40 minutes or until juices run clear. Baste occasionally with pan juices.

Preparation Time: 5 minutes
Cook Time: 1 hour 10 minutes
Experience Level: Beginner
Wine Suggestion: Gamala Chardonnay

SOUTH SIDE FRIED CHICKEN

MEAT   SERVES 8 TO 10

3 cups flour
2 cups potato chips, crushed
4 tablespoons seasoned salt
6 eggs, beaten
½ cup rice milk or non-dairy creamer

Mild red hot pepper sauce, to taste
2 (3½-pound) chickens, cut in eighths, skinned
Canola oil for deep frying

In a large ziploc bag combine flour, potato chips and seasoned salt.

In a medium bowl combine eggs, rice milk and hot pepper sauce.

Shake chicken in flour mixture. Dip in eggs then again dip into flour.

In a large skillet over medium-high heat, add enough oil to come half way up sides. To expedite cooking time use 2 large skillets. When oil is hot carefully place chicken pieces in skillet. Cover and let cook for 10 minutes. Turn chicken over, cover and cook 5 minutes. Uncover for an additional 5 minutes. Place on paper towels to absorb excess oil.

Preparation Time: 10 minutes
Cook Time: 20 minutes using 2 skillets, 40 using 1 skillet
Experience Level: Intermediate

Roast Chicken with Rosemary and Roasted Garlic

MEAT   SERVES 6

A beautiful and delicious main course. Slice the breast meat and arrange on serving platter with legs, thighs, potatoes and garlic head. Be sure to have bread on the table for spreading the garlic cloves on and for dipping in the gravy.

1 head garlic	Black pepper
2 tablespoons olive oil	1 tablespoon margarine, melted
2½ pounds baby red potatoes, scrubbed, unpeeled	2 tablespoons chopped fresh rosemary
	4 cloves garlic, chopped
2 tablespoons olive oil	1 (5 to 6-pound) whole chicken
Salt	3 sprigs fresh rosemary

Preheat oven to 400°F/200°C.

Cut top off head of garlic. Place garlic in a small crock or on a piece of heavy duty aluminum foil. Drizzle garlic with olive oil. Cover tightly and place in preheated oven.

Arrange potatoes in the bottom of a large roasting pan. Toss with olive oil and season with salt and pepper. Place roasting pan in oven with garlic. Roast both 45 minutes, stirring potatoes occasionally.

In a small bowl combine margarine with chopped rosemary and chopped garlic. Sprinkle chicken and cavity liberally with salt and pepper. Rub margarine mixture all over chicken. Remove whole garlic from crock and place in chicken cavity with fresh rosemary sprigs. Tie chicken legs together with cooking twine. Place chicken in roasting pan with potatoes. Shift potatoes if necessary to make room for chicken. Roast chicken uncovered for 1 hour and 30 minutes, basting occasionally.

Preparation Time: 15 minutes
Cook Time: 2 hours
Experience Level: Beginner
Wine Suggestion: Alfasi Sauvignon Blanc

Display your wine in a beautiful setting. An elegant wine rack will enhance the decor of your dining room or kitchen. Fine wines are best stored on their sides at cool to room temperature and kept away from direct light.

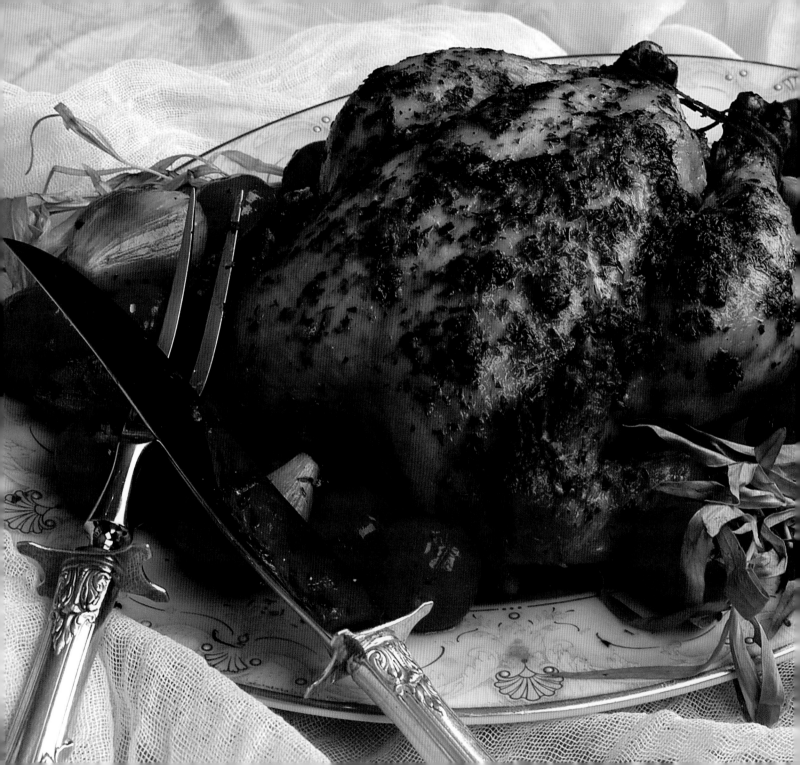

Whole Roasted Tarragon Chicken

MEAT   **SERVES 4**

The aroma of tarragon will fill your home when this chicken is cooking. If available place 1 or 2 sprigs of fresh tarragon in cavity of chicken before roasting.

1 (2½ to 3-pound) whole chicken	½ teaspoon black pepper
3 tablespoons olive oil	½ teaspoon coarse salt
2 cloves fresh garlic, minced	1 pound cherry tomatoes
2½ teaspoons dried tarragon, crushed	8 small shallots, peeled

Preheat oven to 375°F/190°C.

Tie chicken legs together at tail with kitchen twine. Place chicken breast side up on a rack in roasting pan.

In a medium sized bowl combine olive oil, garlic, tarragon, pepper and salt. Add cherry tomatoes and shallots. Toss to coat. Remove tomatoes and shallots from bowl and set aside. Using a pastry brush, baste chicken with remaining oil mixture.

Place chicken in oven uncovered for 1 hour 15 minutes to 1 hour 30 minutes or until juices run clear. Baste every 15 minutes from the first ½ hour onward. During last 25 minutes of roasting, arrange tomatoes and shallots under rack in roasting pan.

When juices run clear, remove chicken and vegetables from pan. Cover chicken with aluminum foil and allow to stand for 10 minutes before carving.

Serve vegetables over hot mashed potatoes or rice.

If desired, garnish chicken with fresh parsley and tarragon sprigs.

Preparation Time: 15 minutes
Cook Time: 1 hour 30 minutes
Experience Level: Beginner
Wine Suggestion: Alfasi Sauvignon Blac 1999

SECRET INGREDIENT CHICKEN

MEAT   SERVES 4 TO 6

What! One of the oddest combinations of ingredients you'll find. Your guests will want to know what the secret is because the chicken is so delicious, but we recommend you don't tell them. It wouldn't be a secret if you did.

Non-stick cooking spray
⅔ cup creamy peanut butter
2 cups ketchup
4 tablespoons prepared white horseradish
1 teaspoon salt

1 (3½-pound) chicken cut in eighths, skinned
2 tablespoons cinnamon sugar or 1½ tablespoons sugar combined with ½ tablespoon cinnamon, divided

Preheat oven to 350°F/180°C.

Generously spray a (9x13x2-inch) baking dish with non-stick cooking spray.

In a medium bowl combine peanut butter, ketchup, horseradish and salt.

Dip chicken pieces in sauce mixture. Place in prepared baking dish, presentation side down and pour remaining sauce over chicken. Sprinkle with 1 tablespoon cinnamon sugar.

Bake uncovered for 45 minutes. Turn chicken over, baste with sauce in baking dish. Sprinkle with remaining tablespoon of cinnamon sugar. Bake for an additional 45 minutes.

Preparation Time: 10 minutes
Cook Time: 1 hour 30 minutes
Experience Level: Beginner

THAI PEANUT CHICKEN

MEAT   SERVES 4

Peanut butter and curry combine to create an authentic Thai flavor that is both sweet and nutty.

½ cup crunchy peanut butter
⅓ cup honey
¼ cup soy sauce

2 tablespoons curry powder
2 cloves garlic, minced
1 (3-pound) chicken, cut in eighths

In the bowl of a food processor combine peanut butter, honey, soy sauce, curry powder and garlic. Process until smooth.

Pour mixture into large ziploc bag. Place chicken in bag with marinade. Refrigerate for 2 to 12 hours. Preheat oven to 350°F/180°C.

Place chicken in a roasting pan, pour marinade over chicken. Place in oven, uncovered for 1 hour, or until juices run clear.

For a cooking variation, place chicken with marinade in crockpot. Cook on low for 4 to 6 hours.

Preparation Time: 5 minutes
Cook Time: 1 hour
Chill Time: 2 to 12 hours
Experience Level: Beginner

*S*AKE *C*HICKEN

MEAT   SERVES 4 TO 6

Sake is a Japanese alcoholic beverage fermented from rice, often translated as rice wine. Once opened it will keep, tightly sealed in refrigerator for at least 6 weeks.

½ cup soy sauce
¼ cup orange juice
2 tablespoons canola oil
2 tablespoons white vinegar
¼ cup Sake

1 tablespoon honey
1 tablespoon orange marmalade
2 teaspoons grated fresh ginger
1 (4-pound) chicken, cut in eighths

In a medium bowl, combine soy sauce, orange juice, oil, vinegar, sake, honey, orange marmalade and ginger.

Place marinade in large ziploc bag with chicken. Marinate in refrigerator for about 12 hours.

Place chicken in a broiler pan. Broil chicken for about 10 minutes on each side, basting occasionally with marinade.

Place remaining marinade in a small sauce pan over medium heat. Bring to a boil for about 2 minutes. Serve with chicken.

Preparation Time: 10 minutes
Cook Time: 22 minutes
Chill Time: 12 hours
Experience Level: Beginner

HONG KONG ORANGE CHICKEN

MEAT   **SERVES 8 TO 10**

For an elegant garnish, slice oranges and broil until edges are slightly blackened.

1⅓ cups orange juice
½ cup honey
¼ cup plus 2 tablespoons soy sauce
¼ cup toasted sesame oil
2 tablespoons minced fresh ginger

½ teaspoon crushed red pepper flakes
4 teaspoons finely minced garlic
Salt and black pepper to taste
2 chickens, each, cut in eighths

In a medium mixing bowl combine orange juice, honey, soy sauce, sesame oil, ginger, red pepper flakes, garlic, salt and pepper to taste.

Place chicken in a large rectangular pan or a large ziploc bag. Pour marinade over chicken. Refrigerate for 4 hours or overnight.

Preheat oven to 375°F/190°C. In a large roasting pan, place chicken skin side up, pour 2 cups of marinade over chicken. Bake uncovered for 1 hour, until chicken appears glazed and juices run clear.

In a small saucepan over medium-low flame, bring remaining marinade to a boil. Drizzle over chicken before serving.

Preparation Time: 15 minutes
Cook Time: 1 hour
Chill Time: 4 to 12 hours
Experience Level: Beginner

CHICKEN WITH CHICKPEAS

MEAT   **SERVES 6**

This traditional Moroccan style chicken, which has a thick sauce, is usually served over couscous. For a variation try serving over a nutty flavored rice such as Basmati or Jasmin.

2 tablespoons canola or olive oil
1 medium onion, chopped
1 teaspoon turmeric
1 (4-pound) chicken, cut in eighths
3 cups water

1 cup dried chickpeas, soaked overnight or canned, drained
Juice from 2 medium lemons
4 cloves garlic, crushed
Dash of black pepper
Salt to taste

In a large non-stick skillet over medium flame, heat oil. Sauté onion until transparent. Stir in turmeric. Add chicken in a single layer. Brown for about 7 minutes on each side.

Exquisite sterling serving pieces from generations past were forged with very ornate designs. Some were so detailed, a master craftsman would work a year on just one mold. Use elaborate serving pieces to lend a lavish quality to your meal.

Add water, chickpeas, lemon juice, garlic, black pepper and salt to taste. Raise heat to high, bring to a boil, cover and lower flame to a simmer. Cook for 1 hour 15 minutes until chicken and chickpeas are soft and water thickens.

Preparation Time: 30 minutes
Cook Time: 1 hour 40 minutes
Experience Level: Beginner
Wine Suggestion: Ha Gefen Sauvignon Blanc

ROASTED CHICKEN THIGHS WITH VEGETABLES

MEAT   SERVES 4 TO 6

A complete meal in a pan. Chicken, potatoes and vegetables come together in perfect harmony for a simply delicious dinner.

1 pound small red potatoes, halved
2 medium carrots, cut into 3-inch pieces
1 jumbo onion, cut in eighths
12 cloves garlic, unpeeled
2 tablespoons olive oil
1 teaspoon salt, divided

¾ teaspoon dried rosemary, crushed
½ teaspoon black pepper, divided
8 chicken thighs, skinned
1 medium red bell pepper, cut into 6 wedges
1 medium green bell pepper, cut into 6 wedges

Preheat oven to 425°F/220°C.

In a large roasting pan toss potatoes, carrots, onion and garlic with olive oil, ½ teaspoon salt, ½ teaspoon rosemary and ¼ teaspoon black pepper. Cover and roast for 20 minutes.

Remove roasting pan from oven. Uncover and add chicken and peppers. Sprinkle with ½ teaspoon salt, ¼ teaspoon rosemary and ¼ teaspoon black pepper. Roast uncovered for about 50 minutes, stirring and basting about every 20 minutes. Roast until chicken thighs are no longer pink in center and juices run clear.

As a serving option cut through garlic skin and spread roasted garlic over chicken.

Preparation Time: 20 minutes
Cook Time: 70 minutes
Experience Level: Beginner

Plum Chicken

MEAT   SERVES 4 TO 6

This simple to prepare chicken is sweet and tangy. The sauce thickens and coats the chicken while cooking.

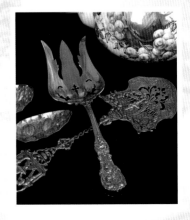

1 (4-pound) chicken, cut in eighths
¼ cup soy sauce
½ cup plum jam
¼ cup honey
¼ cup orange juice
1 clove garlic, crushed

Preheat oven to 350°F/180°C.

Place chicken, skin side down in a roasting pan.

In a small bowl combine soy sauce, jam, honey, orange juice and garlic. Pour over chicken.

Cover and bake for 25 minutes. Turn chicken pieces over, bake uncovered for an additional hour, basting every 15 to 20 minutes.

Preparation Time: 10 minutes
Cook Time: 1 hour 25 minutes
Experience Level: Beginner

Sautéed Chicken with Garlic and Balsamic Vinegar

MEAT   SERVES 4 TO 6

Balsamic vinegar is dark in color and has a pungent sweetness to it. In this chicken dish it is combined with wine and garlic to create a tangy sauce.

1 teaspoon dried thyme
½ teaspoon coarse salt
½ teaspoon freshly ground black pepper
2 teaspoons olive oil
3½ pounds chicken thighs and drumsticks, skinned
¼ cup balsamic vinegar
¼ cup dry red or blush wine
3 scallions, chopped
10 to 12 cloves garlic, thinly sliced
⅓ cup chicken stock or water

In a small bowl combine thyme, salt and pepper.

In a large skillet over medium flame, heat oil. Add chicken to skillet in a single layer. Sprinkle chicken with half of the seasoning mixture. Cover skillet and cook for about 12 minutes. Turn chicken over and sprinkle with half of remaining seasonings. Cover skillet and cook for an additional 12 minutes. Chicken should be well browned on all sides and cooked through. Remove chicken with tongs and keep warm.

Add vinegar and wine to skillet. Deglaze skillet by releasing any bits of chicken that may have stuck to bottom. Raise heat and bring mixture to a boil for 30 seconds. Add scallions, garlic, soup stock and remaining seasoning mixture. Boil for 2 minutes. Return chicken to pan and spoon scallions and garlic on top of chicken. Lower heat to a simmer to reheat chicken, about 3 minutes.

Preparation Time: 20 minutes
Cook Time: 30 minutes
Experience Level: Intermediate
Wine Suggestion: Yarden White Riesling

Honey Pecan Crusted Chicken

MEAT   SERVES 8 TO 10

For a crunchy fried look and taste use freshly crushed corn flakes. The flakes are bigger for a more satisfying crunch.

Non-stick cooking spray
1 cup honey
½ cup Dijon mustard
2 teaspoons paprika
½ teaspoon garlic powder

2½ cups corn flake crumbs or 7 cups corn flakes, coarsely crushed to 2½ cups
¾ cup finely chopped pecans
½ teaspoon salt
½ teaspoon pepper
2 chickens, cut in eighths

Preheat oven to 350°F/180°C.

Spray a baking dish large enough to accommodate both chickens, with cooking spray. Set aside.

In a small bowl combine honey, mustard, paprika and garlic powder. In a large shallow dish or on a piece of plastic wrap, combine corn flake crumbs and pecans.

Sprinkle salt and pepper evenly over chicken pieces. Dip chicken pieces into honey mixture coating well. Dredge in corn flake mixture and place in prepared baking dish. Lightly coat chicken with cooking spray.

Bake uncovered at 350°F/180°C for 1 hour 15 minutes or until chicken is tender and juices run clear.

Preparation Time: 20 minutes
Cook Time: 1 hour 15 minutes
Experience Level: Beginner
Wine Suggestion: Baron Herzog White Zinfendel

STARBURST CHICKEN

MEAT   SERVES 4

CHICKEN

2 tablespoons olive oil

1½ pounds boneless, skinless chicken breasts, sliced into ½-inch strips

2 cloves garlic, minced

¼ teaspoon ground ginger

1 (20-ounce) can crushed pineapple, drained, ⅓ cup juice reserved

2 medium carrots, sliced

1 medium green or red bell pepper, thinly sliced

2 scallions, thinly sliced

4 ounces spaghetti, cooked according to package directions, drained

SAUCE

⅓ cup reserved pineapple juice

¼ cup soy sauce

1 tablespoon cornstarch

1 tablespoon olive oil

CHICKEN: In a large skillet over medium-high flame, heat oil. Stir fry chicken and garlic, sprinkle ginger over chicken. Stir fry for about 2 minutes. Add drained pineapple, carrots, pepper and scallions. Reduce heat to medium. Cover and steam for 2 to 3 minutes. Stir in cooked spaghetti.

SAUCE: In a small saucepan away from heat combine pineapple juice, soy sauce, cornstarch and oil. Stir until cornstarch is dissolved. Place saucepan over medium heat, stirring constantly for 1 to 2 minutes until sauce thickens. Pour sauce over pasta with chicken. Toss and serve immediately.

Preparation Time: 10 minutes
Cook Time: 10 minutes
Experience Level: Beginner

ITALIAN CHICKEN

MEAT   SERVES 4

Stovetop cooking makes for chicken that is fork tender. With very little attention and minimal preparation this is an excellent choice for a weeknight meal. To fancy it up for a Yom Tov meal, double the recipe and place Italian Chicken into a Vol-Au-Vent on page 191.

3 tablespoons olive oil
1 clove garlic, chopped
1 medium red bell pepper, diced
1 medium onion, chopped
3 boneless, skinless, chicken breasts, cut
    into 1-inch cubes
½ cup dry white wine

1 (15-ounce) can tomato sauce
1 teaspoon Italian seasoning
½ teaspoon salt
½ teaspoon black pepper
¼ teaspoon chili powder
1 tablespoon sugar

In a large skillet over medium-high flame, heat oil. Add garlic, red pepper and onion. Cook for 4 minutes, stirring occasionally. Add chicken and wine, cook for an additional 5 minutes until chicken is cooked through. Add tomato sauce, Italian seasoning, salt, black pepper, chili powder and sugar. Stir to combine. Bring to a boil, lower heat and simmer uncovered for 40 minutes, stirring occasionally.

Preparation Time: 10 minutes
Cook Time: 50 minutes
Experience Level: Beginner
Wine Suggestion: Baron Herzog White Zinfendel

CHICKEN SESAME STIR-FRY

MEAT   SERVES 4 TO 6

4 boneless, skinless chicken breasts, cut
    into 1-inch pieces
2 tablespoons cornstarch
¼ cup water
½ cup soy sauce
½ cup chicken broth
1 large clove garlic, minced
1 tablespoon minced fresh ginger

2 teaspoons dark sesame oil
1 tablespoon sesame seeds
2 teaspoons canola oil
1½ pounds bok choy, stalks separated, cut
    crosswise into 1-inch pieces
1 red bell pepper, julienned
1 (14-ounce) can baby corn, ears halved
2 medium scallions, sliced

Place cornstarch and chicken pieces in a large ziploc bag. Seal bag and shake until chicken pieces are coated with cornstarch.

In a small bowl combine water, soy sauce, chicken broth, garlic, ginger and sesame oil. Set aside.

In a large skillet over medium heat, add sesame seeds. Stir constantly until lightly toasted. Place in a small bowl, set aside.

Heat canola oil in same skillet. Add chicken and stir-fry over medium-high heat until cooked through and lightly browned, about 4 minutes. Remove chicken with a slotted spoon, set aside.

Place bok choy and red pepper in skillet. Stir-fry 2 to 3 minutes, until tender. Stir in sauce and baby corn. Bring to a boil and cook for 1 to 2 minutes, until thickened. Return chicken to skillet to heat through. Transfer to a serving platter, sprinkle with toasted sesame seeds and sliced scallions.

Preparation Time: 15 minutes
Cook Time: 10 minutes
Experience Level: Intermediate

Hunter's Chicken

MEAT   SERVES 6

Orzo is a tiny, barley shaped pasta that can be used in place of rice. Cooked in the juices rendered from the chicken, the orzo absorbs all the wonderful flavors of this chicken dish.

4 cups water
1 cup raw orzo
1 tablespoons olive oil
10 ounces fresh white mushrooms, sliced
1 (28-ounce) can crushed tomatoes
1 red bell pepper, julienned
1 medium onion, thinly sliced

2 cloves garlic, minced
1 teaspoon dried basil
1 teaspoon oregano
1 teaspoon salt
6 boneless, skinless chicken thighs, cut in
   half crosswise
Fresh parsley, optional garnish

In a large non-stick skillet over medium-high heat, bring water to a boil. Add orzo, boil uncovered for 9 minutes, stirring occasionally. Drain well.

Dry skillet, place over medium flame and heat oil. Add mushrooms and sauté for 3 to 4 minutes. Remove mushrooms with a slotted spoon and place in a small bowl. Set aside.

Place tomatoes, pepper, onion, garlic, basil, oregano, salt and chicken into skillet. Mix to combine and bring to a boil. Lower heat, cover and simmer for 5 minutes, stirring once. Stir in orzo, cover and cook an additional 6 minutes, or until chicken is no longer pink in center. Add mushrooms and cook until heated through.

Garnish with chopped fresh parsley if desired.

Preparation Time: 30 minutes
Cook Time: 30 minutes
Experience Level: Beginner

PULLED CHICKEN SANDWICHES

MEAT   SERVES 4

1 (1½ to 2-pound) purchased rotisserie
  chicken
1 tablespoon olive oil
1 medium onion, sliced into rings
⅓ cup apple cider vinegar
½ cup tomato sauce

4 medium hot chili peppers, seeded and
  finely chopped
2 tablespoons fresh thyme, chopped
2 tablespoons molasses
2 tablespoons water
½ teaspoon salt

Remove all chicken from the carcass. Discard bones and skin. Using two forks, pull chicken into shreds, following the natural pattern of the muscle fibers.

In a large skillet over a medium flame, heat oil. Add onion and cook until tender, about 10 minutes, stirring occasionally to separate rings. Add vinegar and cook 1 minute. Stir in tomato sauce, hot peppers, thyme, molasses water and salt. Bring to a boil. Add the chicken, tossing to coat and heat through.

Serve on Basic Rolls on page 36 with pickle slices.

Preparation Time: 30 minutes
Cook Time: 20 minutes
Experience Level: Beginner

CHICKEN CHOP SUEY

MEAT   SERVES 4 TO 6

Chop Suey is a Chinese-American dish containing small pieces of chicken, mushrooms, bean sprouts, water chestnuts and bamboo shoots. Created in America in the mid-19th century, Chop Suey doesn't exist as a dish in China.

½ cup margarine
16 ounces fresh white mushrooms, sliced
1 medium green pepper, thinly sliced
6 whole scallions, thinly sliced
8 medium ribs celery, sliced diagonally
4 cups cooked chicken, diced
1 (16-ounce) can bean sprouts, drained
1 (8-ounce) can bamboo shoots, drained

1 (8-ounce) can sliced water chestnuts,
  drained
2 teaspoons salt
¼ teaspoon black pepper
3 cups chicken broth, divided
⅓ cup cornstarch
⅓ cup soy sauce

In a large skillet over medium-high heat, melt margarine. Add mushrooms, green pepper and scallions. Sauté for 4 minutes, remove with a slotted spoon. Add celery, set aside.

Place chicken, bean sprouts, bamboo shoots, water chestnuts, pepper and salt into a 6-quart stock pot. Add 2 cups chicken broth. Bring to a boil, lower heat and simmer 5 minutes, uncovered. Add sautéed vegetables and celery. Bring to a boil.

In a small bowl combine remaining 1 cup chicken broth with cornstarch. Stir into chicken mixture, add soy sauce. Simmer and stir until liquid becomes thick and clear, about 5 minutes.

Preparation Time: 10 minutes
Cook Time: 20 minutes
Experience Level: Beginner

*C*HICKEN WITH *O*LIVES AND *D*ATES

MEAT   SERVES 4

2½ tablespoons cumin
¼ teaspoon paprika
2½ teaspoons sugar
¼ teaspoon cinnamon
3 cloves garlic, minced

4 boneless, skinless chicken breasts,
   pounded thin
3 tablespoons olive oil
6 ounces pitted green olives, soaked in
   water for 20 minutes, drained
8 ounces pitted dates

In a small bowl combine cumin, paprika, sugar, cinnamon and garlic. Sprinkle over both sides of chicken. Cover and refrigerate for 2 to 6 hours.

In a large skillet over medium-low flame, heat oil. Place chicken in skillet, cook for 20 minutes. Turn chicken over and cover with olives and dates. Cook for an additional 20 minutes, or until no longer pink in center.

Preparation Time: 10 minutes
Cook Time: 40 minutes
Chill Time: 2 to 6 hours
Experience Level: Beginner

Green Thai Curried Chicken

MEAT   SERVES 6

Coconut milk is a traditional addition to Thai curries. Curry is a catch-all term that refers to hot, spicy, gravy based foods. If you prefer foods that are not spicy, omit the jalapeño peppers.

3 tablespoons canola oil
6 boneless, skinless chicken breast halves,
    cut into 1½-inch pieces
3 scallions, coarsely chopped
5 cloves garlic, chopped
2 thin slices fresh ginger
2 tablespoons fresh cilantro, chopped
2 jalapeño peppers, chopped, optional

Rind of 1 medium lemon
1 tablespoon curry powder
1 teaspoon cumin
Salt to taste
2 cups coconut milk, recipe to follow
1 (16-ounce) bag frozen green beans
1 tablespoon light soy sauce

In a large skillet over medium-high flame, heat oil. Add chicken and sauté on each side for about 6 minutes or until no longer pink. Remove from skillet with slotted spoon.

To skillet add scallions, garlic, ginger, cilantro, peppers, if desired, lemon rind, curry powder, cumin and salt to taste. Stir in coconut milk. Cook uncovered for 5 minutes. Return chicken to skillet. Add green beans and soy sauce. Cook for 10 minutes or until liquid thickens.

Preparation Time: 15 minutes
Cook Time: 35 minutes
Experience Level: Beginner

Coconut Milk

6 cups water   4 cups shredded coconut

In a medium saucepan over high heat, boil water. Add coconut. Immediately remove from heat. Let cool. When cooled strain liquid, discard coconut.

Preparation Time: 5 minutes
Cook Time: 2 minutes
Experience Level: Beginner

Vol-Au-Vent

MEAT   SERVES 8

A Vol-Au-Vent is a puff pastry shell that resembles a pot with a lid, originally created by a famous chef in France. An impressive centerpiece that works well filled with a double recipe of Italian Chicken on page 184 or a single recipe of Hunter's Chicken on page 185 without the orzo.

1 pound box puff pastry sheets   **1 egg beaten**

Preheat oven to 400°F/200°C.

Prepare a parchment lined (15x10-inch) jelly-roll pan.

Prepare a dome shaped ball of aluminum foil 6-inches across by 3-inches high.

On a lightly floured work surface roll out dough to form 2 (10-inch) squares.

Place one pastry square on prepared pan. Place foil ball in the center of square. Using a pastry brush and water, brush edges of pastry not covered with foil.

Place second pastry square on top of foil. Press firmly around edges of dough enclosing foil ball. Dough will stretch slightly because of domed shape of foil. Air will remain around foil ball.

Use a 9-inch cake pan or flan ring to mark a 9-inch diameter circle. Using a sharp knife cut out circle. Set trimmings aside, brush dough with water.

With the point of a knife, mark a 5-inch diameter circle in the center of the top of dough to mark lid. Cut strips from trimmings, place above and below lid marking for strength and for decoration. Brush vol-au-vent with egg wash. Using small cookie cutters or a knife, cut pretty leaves or other shapes from trimmings and place in a decorative fashion on pastry.

Decorate base edge of dough as one would the edge of a pie crust. Alternatively use the back of a knife to create a decorative edge by pushing in every ½-inch.

Pierce a hole in the center of the lid to allow steam to escape.

Bake in preheated oven for 30 minutes or until crisp and brown.

Let cool 10 minutes. Cut off lid. Squeeze ball of foil to make it smaller in order to fit through hole without disturbing opening. Remove foil. Gently place filling inside and serve.

Preparation Time: 30 minutes
Cook Time: 30 minutes
Experience Level: Advanced

Grilled Peanut Butter Chicken

MEAT   SERVES 4

Chicken grilled in this way is very versatile. It stands on its own, can be cut up and put in a salad, and is excellent picnic fare in a sandwich.

½ cup vegetable or canola oil
¼ cup soy sauce
⅓ cup creamy peanut butter
¼ cup dry red wine

4 cloves garlic, minced
1 teaspoon crushed red pepper flakes
4 boneless, skinless chicken breasts,
    pounded thin

In a medium bowl, whisk together oil, soy sauce, peanut butter, wine, garlic and red pepper flakes.

Pour into a ziploc bag. Add chicken and refrigerate for 8 hours or overnight.

Preheat barbecue grill. Discard marinade. Grill chicken for 7 minutes on each side, or until no longer pink in center.

Preparation Time: 10 minutes
Cook Time: 15 minutes
Chill Time: 8 hours or overnight
Experience Level: Beginner

Apricot Chicken Roll Ups

MEAT   SERVES 6

Boneless chicken breasts are wrapped around an apricot filling then breaded to create a pleasing jelly-roll design. This attractive presentation can take center stage at a dinner party or Sheva brachos.

Non-stick cooking spray
1 (6-ounce) package dried apricots, chopped
½ cup golden raisins
3 tablespoons honey
1½ teaspoons powdered ginger
⅔ cup breadcrumbs
2 tablespoons fresh parsley, chopped
1 tablespoon flour
1 teaspoon paprika
½ teaspoon sugar

½ teaspoon salt
½ teaspoon dried oregano
¼ teaspoon garlic powder
¼ teaspoon onion powder
¼ teaspoon black pepper
2 tablespoons shortening
2 eggs
6 medium, boneless skinless chicken breast
    halves

Preheat oven to 350°F/180°C. Have toothpicks available.

Prepare a 3-quart rectangular baking dish with cooking spray.

In a medium bowl combine apricots, raisins, honey and ginger, set aside.

In a shallow dish or on a sheet of plastic wrap combine breadcrumbs, parsley, flour, paprika, sugar, salt, oregano, garlic powder, onion powder and black pepper. Cut shortening into mixture until mixture resembles fine crumbs.

Place eggs in a small bowl, beat lightly with a fork.

Using a mallet, pound each chicken breast lightly between 2 pieces of plastic wrap. Pound into a rectangle about ⅜-inch thick. Remove plastic wrap. Spoon a scant ¼-cup of apricot mixture in the center of each chicken breast. Fold in bottom and sides. Roll up and secure with toothpicks.

Dip chicken in egg mixture then in breadcrumb mixture. Place in prepared dish, seam side down. Cover tightly and bake for 35 to 40 minutes or until no longer pink in center.

Discard toothpicks before serving.

Preparation Time: 45 minutes
Cook Time: 35 minutes
Experience Level: Intermediate

CLASSIC ROASTED TURKEY

MEAT   SERVES 12

A basic delicious turkey. Carving the turkey in advance and reheating in gravy ensures the turkey will be moist.

1 (12 to 17-pound) whole fresh turkey
1 large red delicious apple, washed, dried and cored
½ cup olive oil
Salt to taste
2 to 3 teaspoons black pepper

1½ tablespoons garlic powder
2 tablespoons paprika
1 teaspoon dried rosemary
2 large Spanish onions, sliced into rings
⅓ cup orange juice

Preheat oven to 350°F/180°C.

Place apple in cavity of turkey. Rub oil all over turkey. Sprinkle with salt, black pepper, garlic powder, paprika and rosemary.

Lay onion slices on bottom of a large roasting pan. Place turkey, breast side up on top of onions. Pour orange juice around turkey. Cover tightly with aluminum foil. Roast for about 3 to 5 hours or until meat thermometer placed in thickest part of breast, not touching bone, reads 180°F/82°C. Remove foil and baste turkey with pan juices. Cook uncovered for an additional 20 minutes to brown.

Let cool before carving.

Preheat oven to 350°F/180°C.

After turkey is carved, return to roasting pan and spoon gravy and onions on top of turkey. Reseal with aluminum foil. Reheat for approximately 25 minutes before serving.

Preparation Time: 1 hour
Cook Time: 3 hours 30 minutes to 5 hours 30 minutes
Experience Level: Beginner
Wine Suggestion: Yarden Sauvignon Blanc 1999

Roast Turkey with Vidalia Onions

MEAT   SERVES 8

Vidalia onions are extremely sweet and juicy. Mixed with apples, they form a jellied coating which pleasantly enhances the flavor of this roasted turkey.

1 head garlic
1 tablespoon olive oil
1 large Vidalia onion, finely chopped
½ cup finely chopped green apple
½ cup balsamic vinegar
½ cup sugar
1 (10 to 12-pound) whole turkey

Salt
3 tablespoons canola oil, divided
6 medium red onions, cut into wedges
10 to 12 cloves garlic, unpeeled
Chicken broth if necessary
¼ cup dry white wine or apple juice
3 tablespoons flour

Preheat oven to 350°F/180°C.

Slice off ¼-inch from top of garlic bulb. Place bulb, cut side up in a small crock or baking dish. Drizzle with olive oil. Cover and roast garlic for 1 hour or until cloves have softened. Let cool.

To make Vidalia onion coating, gently squeeze roasted garlic cloves and juices into a small saucepan over medium heat. Stir in onion, apple, balsamic vinegar and sugar. Bring to a boil, stirring occasionally. Reduce heat to simmer. Cook for about 30 minutes, stirring occasionally. Apple will soften, onions will turn transparent, and mixture will thicken.

Preheat oven to 325°F/160°C.

Remove neck, giblets and liver from turkey. Pat dry with paper towels. Sprinkle cavity with salt. Tie drumsticks securely to tail with cooking twine. Place turkey breast side up, on a rack in a shallow roasting pan. Brush with 1 tablespoon canola oil. Cover turkey loosely with aluminum foil. Roast for 1 hour.

In a large bowl toss onion wedges and unpeeled garlic cloves with 2 tablespoons of canola oil. Place mixture around turkey. Recover and roast for an additional 1 hour and 15 minutes.

Remove foil from turkey. Remove twine from drumsticks to ensure thighs cook evenly. Carefully spread the Vidalia onion coating over turkey. Roast for an additional 45 minutes or until juices run clear and drumsticks move easily.

Remove turkey from oven. Transfer turkey, garlic and onions to a platter. Cover and allow to stand for 15 to 20 minutes before carving.

Pour pan drippings into a large measuring cup. Skim fat from drippings. Add chicken broth, if necessary, to equal 1¾ cups of liquid. In a medium saucepan over medium heat combine wine and flour. Stir in pan drippings. Cook and stir until thick and bubbly, cook and stir one minute longer. Serve as gravy.

Preparation Time: 1 hour
Cook Time: 3 hours 30 minutes
Experience Level: Advanced

ROASTED TURKEY BREAST ON BONE

MEAT   SERVES 6

1 turkey breast, bone in, skin intact
Salt
Black pepper
Juice of 1 medium lime

¼ cup whole berry cranberry sauce
¼ cup barbecue sauce
1 cup dry white wine

Preheat oven to 375°F/190°C.

Trim excess fat off turkey breast. Season all over with salt and pepper. Place in roasting pan. Pour lime juice over turkey breast.

In a small bowl combine cranberry sauce with barbecue sauce. Coat turkey breast all over with mixture.

Pour white wine into bottom of pan. Roast uncovered basting occasionally. Cook for about 1 hour and 30 minutes, or until internal temperature reaches 180°F/82°C.

Preparation Time: 5 minutes
Cook Time: 1 hour 30 minutes
Experience Level: Beginner

ROAST DUCK

MEAT   SERVES 4

1 (3 to 4-pound) duck
Garlic powder
Paprika
1 medium onion, peeled

1 small orange, 4 slits cut almost to center, leaving center intact in order to remain 1 piece
1½ cups Cantonese-style duck sauce

Preheat oven to 500°F/250°C.

Remove excess fat from duck. Season cavity of duck with garlic powder and paprika. Place onion and orange in cavity. Season outside of duck with garlic powder and paprika and cover with duck sauce.

Place duck breast side down on a rack in roasting pan. Cover and roast in preheated oven for 20 to 25 minutes. Lower oven temperature to 350°F/180°C and continue cooking for 1 hour and 30 minutes or until juices run clear when fork is inserted in thickest part of thigh.

If crisp skin is desired, remove cover, prick skin with a fork, turn duck over and roast an additional 15 minutes.

Let stand 10 minutes before carving.

Preparation Time: 10 minutes
Cook Time: 2 hours 10 minutes
Experience Level: Beginner
Wine Suggestion: Yarden Merlot, savory, Gamla Sauvignon Blac, sweet

Rosemary Garlic Stuffed Turkey Roast

MEAT   SERVES 10

Cooking this type of roast in an oven bag guarantees moist results. The clean up could not be any easier. Turkey roasts are available in both white and dark meat. Ask the butcher for your preference.

10 medium cloves garlic, peeled
3 tablespoons dried, crushed rosemary
1 teaspoon paprika
1 tablespoon black pepper

1 teaspoon salt
2 tablespoons olive oil
1 (4 to 5-pound) turkey roast

Prepare a large oven bag according to package directions.

In the work bowl of a blender place garlic, rosemary, paprika, black pepper, salt and olive oil. Process until combined into a paste.

On a clean work surface unroll turkey roast. Spread ½ of garlic paste over inside and reroll. Tie with kitchen twine in several places. Spread remaining paste over outside of turkey roast. Place in oven bag. Refrigerate for 2 to 12 hours.

Preheat oven to 350°F/180°C.

Place oven bag in roasting pan. Roast for 2 hours.

Preparation Time: 15 minutes
Cook Time: 2 hours
Chill Time: 2 to 12 hours
Experience Level: Beginner
Wine Suggestion: Gamla Chardonnay 1999

STOVETOP DUCK

MEAT   SERVES 4 TO 6

This spectacular duck recipe requires a lot of kitchen time. The result is delicious and elegant. This recipe calls for making rendered duck fat, an ingredient that professional chefs prize. Use the leftover fat to add flavor to your basic sautéed foods.

If you want great results with less preparation time, a short cut recipe follows.

1 (5 to 6-pound) duck, reserve neck and giblets
1 bay leaf crushed
1 teaspoon salt
¼ teaspoon dried thyme

¼ teaspoon allspice
¼ teaspoon paprika
¼ teaspoon black pepper
¼ teaspoon dried sage

STOCK
1 medium onion, chopped
1 medium carrot, diced
1 rib celery, chopped
2 cups chicken broth
¼ teaspoon thyme
1 bay leaf
4 sprigs fresh parsley
1 plum tomato, chopped
2½ cups water

¼ cup dry white wine
¼ teaspoon salt
⅛ teaspoon black pepper
12 pearl onions, peeled (cut off root end, drop in boiling water for 1 minute, slip off peel)
¼ cup water
¾ pound assorted mushrooms, shiitake, oyster, brown, white

DE-BONE DUCK: Remove leg thigh portions from duck. Remove thigh bone by scraping edge of a sharp knife along bone to separate from meat. Cut bone at joint and leave leg bone behind. Repeat for other thigh bone. Remove wings and set aside. Remove breast meat from carcass by scraping a sharp knife along ribcage. Leaving each piece covered with skin, trim and reserve excess skin and fat. Using a sharp knife, carefully prick skin on duck pieces without piercing meat.

In a small bowl combine crushed bay leaf, salt, thyme, allspice, paprika, black pepper and sage. Season duck pieces with spice combination. Arrange on a platter, cover and refrigerate overnight.

Using kitchen shears, cut carcass into 2-inch pieces. Transfer to medium bowl with neck, giblets and wings.

Cut reserved fat and skin into thin strips. Place in a small skillet over low to medium heat. Cook until fat has melted into a clear golden liquid, about 30 to 50 minutes. Remove cracklings and reserve for another use. Transfer fat to a cup and refrigerate.

STOCK: In a large skillet over medium-high heat, melt 1 tablespoon of duck fat. Add carcass, giblets, neck and wings, cook in 2 batches for 5 to 10 minutes until well browned, turning occasionally. Using a slotted spoon, transfer pieces to a Dutch oven. Pour off fat from skillet and discard.

Add chicken broth to skillet and bring to a boil, stirring to scrape up brown bits from bottom of pan. Pour broth into Dutch oven. Add onion, carrot, celery, thyme, bay leaf, parsley, tomato and water. Raise heat, bring to a boil. Reduce heat, cover and simmer for 1 hour and 30 minutes.

Strain stock into a stockpot. Discard vegetables. Cool stock and refrigerate overnight.

Remove and discard fat from top of refrigerated stock. Bring to a boil over medium high heat. Add wine and continue boiling until liquid has been reduced by half, about 45 minutes. Add salt and pepper, set aside.

In a small saucepan over medium flame, heat 1 tablespoon of duck fat. Add onions and cook stirring occasionally 5 to 8 minutes or until browned. Add water and bring to a boil. Cover and simmer for 10 minutes. Discard liquid, set onions aside.

In a large skillet over medium-high flame, heat 1 tablespoon of duck fat. Add mushrooms and cook until softened, about 8 minutes. Set aside with onions.

In same skillet over medium-high flame, heat one tablespoon of duck fat. Add duck pieces, skin side down. Cook thigh portions 15 minutes until browned on both sides, cook breast portions 12 minutes, until well browned. Turn and cook for 3 additional minutes for medium rare. Transfer breasts to a plate. Cover skillet and reduce heat to low. Cook thigh portions for an additional 25 minutes, turning occasionally. Transfer thighs to plate with breasts.

Pour off fat and wipe skillet clean. Return duck to skillet with onions, mushrooms and reduced stock. Bring to a boil, cover and simmer 5 minutes, until heated through.

Remove duck and place on a cutting board. Slice breasts and thighs on the diagonal. Arrange duck, onions and mushrooms on a serving platter or on 4 dinner plates. Spoon stock over duck and serve.

Preparation Time: 1 hour 15 minutes
Cook Time: 2 hours 30 minutes
Chill Time: Overnight
Experience Level: Advanced
Wine Suggestion: Abarbanel Chateau de la Salle Beaujolais Villages 2002

STOVETOP DUCK SHORT CUT

MEAT
SERVES 4 TO 6

1 (5 to 6-pound) duck
1 bay leaf, crushed
1 teaspoon salt
1/4 teaspoon dried leaf thyme
1/4 teaspoon allspice
1/4 teaspoon paprika
1/4 teaspoon black pepper
1/4 teaspoon dried sage
3 tablespoons olive oil, divided

12 pearl onions, peeled (cut off root end, drop
   in boiling water for 1 minute, slip off peel)
1/4 cup water
10 ounces assorted mushrooms, shiitake,
   oyster, brown, white
1 (10.5-ounce) can condensed chicken broth
1/4 cup dry white wine
1/2 teaspoon dried leaf thyme

DE-BONE DUCK: Remove leg thigh portions from duck. Remove thigh bone by scraping edge of a sharp knife along bone to separate from meat. Cut bone at joint and leave leg bone behind. Remove wing and set aside. Remove breast meat from carcass by scraping a sharp knife along ribcage. Leaving each piece covered with skin, trim and reserve excess skin and fat. Using a sharp knife, carefully prick skin on duck pieces without piercing meat.

In a small bowl combine crushed bay leaf, salt, thyme, allspice, paprika, black pepper and sage. Season duck pieces with spice combination. Arrange on a platter, cover and refrigerate overnight.

In a small saucepan over medium flame, heat 1 tablespoon of olive oil. Add onions and cook for 5 to 8 minutes stirring occasionally, until browned. Add water and bring to a boil. Cover and simmer for 10 minutes. Remove onions with a slotted spoon, set aside. Discard liquid.

In a large skillet over medium-high flame, heat 1 tablespoon of olive oil. Add mushrooms and cook until softened, about 8 minutes. Remove with a slotted spoon and set aside with onions.

In same skillet over medium-high flame, heat remaining tablespoon of olive oil. Add duck pieces, skin side down. Cook thigh portions for 15 minutes, turning until browned on both sides. Cook breast portions 12 minutes or until well browned. Turn and cook for 3 additional minutes for medium-rare. Transfer duck breasts to a plate, cover skillet and reduce heat to low. Cook thigh portions for an additional 25 minutes, turning occasionally. Transfer thighs to plate with breasts. Pour off oil and wipe skillet clean.

In a small saucepan over medium-high heat, bring chicken broth, wine and thyme to a boil. Cover, lower flame and simmer for 5 minutes.

Return cooked duck pieces, onions, mushrooms and broth mixture to skillet. Bring to a boil over medium-high heat. Lower flame, cover and simmer for 5 minutes until heated through. Place duck onto cutting board. Cut breasts and thighs on the diagonal. Arrange duck, onions and mushrooms on a serving platter. Spoon broth over all.

Preparation Time: 30 to 40 minutes
Cook Time: 1 hour 20 minutes
Chill Time: Overnight
Experience Level: Advanced

*Delicate filigree
is handcrafted from long
thin strands of silver to
form intricate lacy designs.
Each piece is a unique
individual endowed with
a rare charm.*

FISH

An unusual set of kiddush cups depicts the story of Yosef Mokir Shabbos. Though poor, Yosef spent all his money to honor his Shabbos with fine and special foods. One week he spent the last of his money on an especially large fish and hurried home to prepare it for his Shabbos meal. Upon opening the fish he discovered a priceless jewel, a heavenly reward for his many sacrifices for the Shabbos.

SALMON TERIYAKI

PARVE · SERVES 4

Teriyaki is a term from Japanese cuisine referring to a food that has been marinated in a mixture of soy sauce, ginger and seasonings before being grilled, broiled or fried. The honey in this marinade gives the cooked salmon an appetizing glaze.

¼ cup tamari sauce or soy sauce	1 teaspoon fresh grated gingerroot
4 tablespoons sherry	1 teaspoon honey
¼ cup water	1 teaspoon toasted sesame oil, optional
1 clove garlic, crushed	4 (6-ounce) salmon steaks or fillets

In a small bowl combine tamari sauce, sherry, water, garlic, ginger, honey and toasted sesame oil if available. Pour into a ziploc bag and add salmon. Marinate in refrigerator for 1 to 2 hours.

Preheat broiler or barbecue grill.

Remove fish from marinade. Broil for about 5 minutes on each side or until fish flakes easily.

In a small saucepan over medium heat bring marinade to a boil. Lower flame and simmer for 5 minutes. Serve sauce as a dip for salmon.

Preparation Time: 10 minutes
Cook Time: 15 minutes
Chill Time: 1 to 2 hours
Experience Level: Beginner

SALMON WITH DIJON MUSTARD

PARVE · SERVES 6

½ cup oil	½ teaspoon black pepper
¼ cup honey	½ teaspoon salt
¼ cup Dijon mustard	6 (6 to 7-ounce) salmon fillets
4 cloves garlic, minced	3 tablespoons fresh chopped dill

In a small bowl combine oil, honey, mustard, garlic, pepper and salt to make a marinade.

Place salmon in baking dish large enough to accommodate fillets. Pour marinade over salmon. Refrigerate for 2 to 4 hours.

Preheat oven to 400°F/200°C.

Sprinkle dill on fish and bake for 8 minutes. Baste with marinade and bake for an additional 8 minutes or until fish flakes easily with fork.

Preparation Time: 5 minutes
Cook Time: 20 minutes
Chill Time: 2 to 4 hours

SALMON WITH OLIVE AND SUN-DRIED TOMATO CRUST

DAIRY OR PARVE   **SERVES 4**

Succulent salmon is topped by a moist, flavorful breadcrumb topping. This salmon can stand alone, add the sauce for a superb complement.

SALMON

¼ cup pitted and chopped, brine cured black olives

¼ cup pitted and chopped green olives

¼ cup chopped oil packed sun-dried tomatoes

3 medium cloves garlic, minced

3 tablespoons butter or margarine, melted

1½ teaspoons chopped fresh rosemary

1½ teaspoons chopped fresh thyme

5½ teaspoons Dijon mustard, divided

1 cup breadcrumbs

4 (5 to 6-ounce) salmon fillets

MUSTARD DILL SAUCE

⅓ cup white vinegar

½ cup Dijon mustard

2 teaspoons sugar

⅛ teaspoon ground cardamom

Salt and black pepper to taste

½ cup canola, or vegetable oil

⅓ cup finely chopped fresh dill

SALMON: Preheat oven to 400°F/200°C.

Lightly butter a (15x10-inch) jelly-roll pan with 1 tablespoon of butter.

In a medium bowl combine green and black olives, tomatoes, garlic, 2 tablespoons butter, rosemary and thyme. Stir in 1½ teaspoons of Dijon mustard and breadcrumbs. Mix to combine.

Arrange fillets on prepared jelly-roll pan. Spread each fillet with 1 teaspoon of mustard. Pack ¼ of breadcrumb mixture over each fillet. Place in preheated oven for 12 to 15 minutes or until fish flakes easily.

Serve with mustard dill sauce.

MUSTARD DILL SAUCE: In a medium bowl, whisk together vinegar, mustard, sugar, cardamom, salt and pepper to taste. Add oil in a steady stream, whisking constantly until sauce is emulsified. Chill for 1 hour. Sauce may be prepared 1 day in advance, kept covered and refrigerated. Whisk in dill 1 hour before serving.

Preparation Time: 25 minutes
Cook Time: 12 to 15 minutes
Chill: 1 hour, for Mustard Dill Sauce
Experience Level: Intermediate
Wine Suggestion: Golan Chardonnay

*C*UMIN *C*RUSTED *S*ALMON

PARVE **SERVES 6**

*M*iddle eastern spices blend to form a thick paste which coats this simple to prepare fish which can be served as an appetizer or a main course.

½ cup olive oil

¼ cup water

¼ teaspoon turmeric

1 tablespoon cumin

2 tablespoons parve chicken soup flavoring

¼ cup paprika

2 teaspoons dried crushed garlic

1 tablespoon ketchup

6 (6-ounce) salmon fillets

1 lemon

Chopped fresh cilantro, optional garnish

Preheat oven to 350°F/180°C.

In a small bowl combine oil, water, turmeric, cumin, chicken soup flavoring, paprika, crushed garlic and ketchup to form a thick paste.

Place fillets in a baking dish large enough to accommodate fish. Squeeze lemon over fish. Spread paste evenly over fillets. Cover and bake for 15 minutes. Remove cover and bake for an additional 10 minutes. Serve warm or at room temperature. Garnish with cilantro if desired.

Preparation Time: 10 minutes
Cook Time: 25 minutes
Experience Level: Beginner

*Q*UICK *M*ARINATED *S*ALMON WITH *A*RUGULA

PARVE **SERVES 4**

*A*rugula is an aromatic salad green with a peppery mustard flavor. It is sold in small bunches with roots attached. Look for bright green, fresh looking leaves.

¼ cup olive oil

2 tablespoons fresh lemon juice

2 tablespoons balsamic vinegar

2 tablespoons dry white wine

2 tablespoons fresh snipped chives

½ teaspoon course salt

Freshly ground black pepper

4 (6-ounce) salmon fillets

Salt

24 cherry tomatoes, halved

4 cups baby arugula, stems trimmed

Heat oven to 500°F/250°C.

Prepare an aluminum foil lined (15x10-inch) jelly-roll pan.

In a small bowl combine oil, lemon juice, vinegar, wine, chives, salt and pepper. Season salmon fillets with salt and pepper and arrange in a single layer on prepared pan. Spoon 1 tablespoon of marinade

over each fillet. Set remainder of marinade aside. Place salmon in preheated oven for about 7 minutes each side or until fish flakes easily.

Toss tomatoes with remaining marinade. Toss tomatoes with arugula.

To serve, arrange salmon on plate with a few leaves and tomatoes. Spoon pan juices over fillets. Serve immediately.

Preparation Time: 10 minutes
Cook Time: 10 to 14 minutes
Experience Level: Beginner
Wine Suggestion: Sauvignon Blanc 2000

*P*INE *N*UT *C*RUSTED *S*ALMON

DAIRY   SERVES 4

FISH

4 (6-ounce) salmon fillets

2 tablespoons Dijon mustard

½ cup breadcrumbs

½ cup chopped pine nuts

1 tablespoon butter

1 tablespoon olive oil

SAUCE

2 tablespoons lemon juice

¼ cup heavy cream

¼ cup cold butter, cut into ½-inch pieces

⅛ teaspoon salt

⅛ teaspoon pepper

FISH: Preheat oven to 350°F/180°C.

Using a pastry brush, brush salmon fillets with mustard.

In a small bowl, combine breadcrumbs and pine nuts. Pat mixture onto top of salmon.

In a large ovenproof skillet over medium flame, heat butter and oil until foaming. Add salmon, crust side down and cook for 3 to 5 minutes or until browned. Turn over and transfer to oven. Bake for 7 minutes.

SAUCE: In a small saucepan over medium-high heat, reduce lemon juice to 1 teaspoon. Add cream and boil until thickened, about 3 minutes. Whisk butter into sauce until smooth. Add salt and pepper.

Serve salmon accompanied by sauce.

Preparation Time: 10 minutes
Cook Time: 15 minutes
Experience Level: Beginner
Wine Suggestion: Delagrave Herzog Selection Bordeaux Dry White 2001

Smoked Salmon Quiches in Swiss Cheese Pastry

DAIRY   YIELD 18 MINI QUICHES

These little quiches make charming hors d'oeuvres for a party. Because of their tiny size, kids love them for lunches as well.

DOUGH

1 cup flour
½ teaspoon dried dill
¼ teaspoon salt

⅓ cup shortening
¼ cup shredded Swiss cheese
3 to 4 tablespoons cold water

FILLING

1 teaspoon butter or margarine
4 ounces fresh white mushrooms, chopped
1 small scallion, chopped
1 teaspoon lemon juice
3 egg yolks

½ cup milk
1 (3-ounce) package thinly sliced smoked
  salmon, cut into ½-inch pieces
Non-stick cooking spray
Fresh dill sprigs for garnish, optional

DOUGH: In a medium bowl combine flour, dried dill and salt. Using a pastry blender, cut in shortening until pea sized crumbs form. Add Swiss cheese and mix to combine. Sprinkle 1 tablespoon of water over part of mixture. Gently toss with a fork. Push dough to one side of bowl. Repeat, using 1 tablespoon of water at a time until all is moistened. Form dough into a ball. Wrap dough in plastic wrap until ready to use.

FILLING: In a large skillet over medium-high heat, melt butter. Add mushrooms, scallions and lemon juice. Cook until vegetables are tender, about 2 to 3 minutes. Remove from heat and drain liquid.

In a medium or large bowl, beat egg yolks slightly. Stir in milk. Add mushroom mixture and salmon. Cover and refrigerate for 30 minutes.

Preheat oven to 375°F/190°C.

Spray 18 (1¾-inch) mini muffin cups with non-stick cooking spray.

On a lightly floured surface, roll out dough to ⅛-inch thickness. Using a 3-inch round cookie cutter, cut dough into 18 circles. Fit circles into muffin cups, pinching dough as necessary to fit. Fill each crust with a scant tablespoon of filling. Bake for 30 minutes. Let stand for 5 minutes before removing from muffin cups. Serve warm, garnished with dill sprigs if desired.

Preparation Time: 45 minutes
Cook Time: 35 minutes
Chill Time: 30 minutes
Experience Level: Intermediate

FLOUNDER WITH A CRUNCH

DAIRY OR PARVE   **SERVES 4**

Crushed pretzels are a welcoming change from the basic breadcrumb topping. They add a nice crunch and a salty flavor, balancing the simplistic flavor of flounder.

1 pound flounder fillets
1 egg beaten
3 tablespoons Dijon mustard
1 tablespoon milk or non-dairy creamer
¼ teaspoon black pepper

¼ cup flour
1 cup coarsely crushed pretzels
2 tablespoons canola oil
1 lemon sliced, optional garnish

In a shallow bowl, using a fork, combine egg, mustard milk and pepper.

On a large piece of plastic wrap separately place flour and pretzels.

Coat fish with flour, dip fish into mustard mixture. Dredge fish in crushed pretzels to coat both sides well.

In a large skillet, over medium high flame, heat oil. Cook fish in batches for 3 to 4 minutes on each side or until golden and fish flakes easily with a fork.

Serve hot and garnish with lemon slices.

Preparation Time: 15 minutes
Cook Time: 15 minutes
Experience Level: Beginner

GREEK STYLE FISH IN MARINADE

PARVE   **SERVES 8 AS AN APPETIZER**

1 pound sole fillets, cut into 1½-inch strips
Salt
Black pepper
⅓ cup flour
6 teaspoons canola oil, divided
1 pound carrots, grated
1 medium onion, sliced into small strips
½ teaspoon salt

5 whole cloves
2 bay leaves, broken in two
5 peppercorns
3 teaspoons ketchup
1 cup boiled water
3 teaspoons white wine
⅓ cup fresh parsley, for garnish

Lightly salt and pepper fish slices. Dip in flour.

In a large skillet over a medium-high flame, heat 2 teaspoons of oil. Fry fish for about 4 minutes on each side or until fish flakes easily. Place on a platter that can accommodate marinade when ready. Refrigerate.

In same skillet over medium-high flame, heat 2 teaspoons of oil. Add carrots and onion and cook for about 10 minutes. Add salt, cloves, bay leaves, peppercorns, ketchup and water to skillet. Stir to combine. Add wine and cook for another 15 minutes over medium to low heat.

Pour over fish, cover and refrigerate until chilled about 1 hour.

Serve garnished with fresh parsley.

Preparation Time: 20 minutes
Cook Time: 40 minutes
Chill Time: 1 hour
Experience Level: Beginner

SOLE AMANDINE

DAIRY OR PARVE   **SERVES 4**

Sole has a delicately flavored flesh and a fine, firm texture. Sautéed almonds topping sole create a nutty, light and flavorful dish.

6 tablespoons butter or margarine, divided
1 cup sliced almonds
4 (4-ounce) sole fillets
Salt

Black pepper
¾ cup dry white wine
Juice from 1 medium lemon

In a large skillet over medium heat, melt 4 tablespoons of butter. Add sliced almonds and sauté until lightly browned. Remove almonds with a slotted spoon and set aside.

Lightly season fillets with salt and pepper. Add 2 more tablespoons butter to skillet, melt and add fillets. Cook uncovered over medium heat, turning fish halfway through cooking until barely firm. Place ¼ of almonds on top of each fillet. Add white wine to skillet with fish and bring to a simmer for 3 minutes.

To serve squeeze fresh lemon juice over each fillet.

Preparation Time: 15 minutes
Cook Time: 15 minutes
Experience Level: Beginner
Wine Suggestion: Châteauneuf Herzog Selection Bordeaux

Baked Moroccan Style Fish

PARVE   **SERVES 4**

Non-stick cooking spray
4 (6-ounce) sole, halibut or flounder fillets
3 tablespoons olive oil, divided
Salt
Black pepper
½ cup fresh breadcrumbs

1 small yellow onion, minced
⅓ cup chopped cilantro
1 teaspoon lemon zest
¼ teaspoon cumin
¼ teaspoon ground cardamom
⅛ teaspoon ground red pepper or hot paprika

Preheat oven to 425°F/220°C.

Prepare a (15x10-inch) jelly-roll pan with non stick cooking spray.

Place fish fillets on prepared pan and brush with 2 tablespoons olive oil. Season with salt and pepper. In a small bowl combine breadcrumbs, onion, cilantro, lemon zest, cumin, cardamom, red pepper and 1 tablespoon of olive oil. Divide breadcrumb mixture evenly over top of fillets. Bake for about 12 minutes or until fish flakes easily.

Preparation Time: 10 minutes
Cook Time: 12 minutes
Experience Level: Beginner
Wine Suggestions: Layla Dirty Lager or Abarbanel Riesling 1999 Estate Bottled
or Dalton Sauvignon Blanc Fume

WHITEFISH WITH TOMATOES AND CHILI PEPPERS

PARVE   **SERVES 6**

This fish has a spicy kick. You can adjust the intensity to suit your taste by adjusting the amount of chili peppers.

1 (1-pound) whitefish, butterflied, cut into
   1½-inch wide pieces resembling steaks
Coarse salt
½ cup plus 1 tablespoon canola oil, divided
3 tablespoons paprika

4 medium carrots, sliced
4 medium cloves garlic, chopped
16 ounces grape tomatoes, sliced
8 dried chili peppers, tops and seeds discarded
1 bunch fresh cilantro, divided

Rinse fish and pat dry. Salt fish liberally. In a small bowl combine ½ cup oil and paprika to form a paste. Spread paste over fish. Set aside.

In a large skillet over a medium flame, heat oil. Add carrots and garlic. Sauté until cooked through, about 7 minutes. Remove from heat.

Spread carrots and garlic over bottom of skillet in a single layer. On top of carrots and garlic, evenly place tomatoes, then chili peppers and half of cilantro. Gently arrange fish on top of chili peppers and cilantro. Sprinkle with remaining cilantro. Add enough water to skillet to come halfway up the sides of fish. Bring to a boil over medium heat. When it comes to a boil, lower heat and simmer uncovered for 6 to 7 minutes. Baste fish occasionally with pan juices. Lightly sprinkle salt onto liquid around fish. Baste by gently tilting pan from side to side. Cook an additional 6 to 7 minutes until fish flakes easily.

Remove from heat, cool. Serve at room temperature.

Preparation Time: 40 minutes
Cook Time: 12 to 14 minutes
Experience Level: Intermediate

HALIBUT CASSEROLE

DAIRY OR PARVE   SERVES 4

Halibut is available year round but is most abundant from March through September. Halibut meat is low-fat while firm and mild flavored.

½ cup butter or margarine, divided
1 large onion or 2 medium onions, sliced
    into 8 rings
1 medium green bell pepper, sliced into
    8 rings
1 medium rib celery, chopped

1 teaspoon dried basil leaves
1 teaspoon salt
½ teaspoon black pepper
1 (16-ounce) can stewed tomatoes
4 (4-ounce) halibut fillets
2 medium plum tomatoes, sliced

Grease a (12x8x2-inch) baking dish with 1 tablespoon of the butter.

In a large skillet over medium-high heat, melt butter. Add onion, green pepper, and celery. Sauté for about 5 minutes. Add basil, salt, pepper and stewed tomatoes. Stir to combine and bring to a boil. Lower heat and simmer uncovered for 15 minutes.

Preheat oven to 375°F/190°C.

Spoon 1 cup of sauce on bottom of prepared baking dish. Arrange fillets on top of sauce. Spoon green peppers, onion slices, stewed tomatoes and sliced tomatoes over each fillet. Pour remaining sauce over top. Cover and bake for 30 minutes. Uncover, baste with pan juices and cook for an additional 10 minutes.

Preparation Time: 15 minutes
Cook Time: 40 minutes
Experience Level: Intermediate
Wine Suggestion: Yarden White Riesling

HALIBUT WITH APRICOT SAUCE

PARVE   **SERVES 4**

Hot pepper sauce nicely balances the sweet flavor of dried apricots in the sauce for this halibut dish. Oregano adds a savory flavor. Add fresh oregano sprigs for garnish to add to the beautiful presentation.

8 dried apricot halves
½ cup boiling water
½ cup apricot nectar
⅓ cup apricot preserves
2 medium scallions, sliced
½ teaspoon dried oregano
⅛ teaspoon salt
1 tablespoon olive oil

1 to 2 teaspoons hot pepper sauce plus a few dashes, divided
Salt
Black pepper
4 halibut or salmon steaks, ¾-inch thick
Non-stick cooking spray
4 fresh oregano sprigs, optional garnish

In a small bowl cover apricots with boiling water. Set aside.

In a small saucepan over medium heat, combine apricot nectar, preserves, scallions, oregano and salt. Bring to barely boiling, stirring frequently. Reduce heat, simmer uncovered until sauce thickens slightly, about 8 minutes. Remove from heat. Keep warm. Reserve ¼ cup of sauce to baste on fish while cooking.

Drain apricots and add to sauce in saucepan with a few dashes of hot pepper sauce.

In a small bowl stir together olive oil and 1 to 2 teaspoons pepper sauce. Brush both sides of fish with oil mixture. Season fish lightly with salt and pepper.

Spray unheated grill rack or broiler pan with non-stick cooking spray. Preheat grill or broiler.

Grill fish over medium coals, uncovered for 3 to 5 minutes on each side or until fish flakes easily. Brush with reserved sauce during last 2 minutes of grilling time.

If broiling, broil 4 minutes per side about 5-inches from heat or until fish flakes easily. Brush with reserved sauce during last 2 minutes of broiling time.

Remove fish to serving platter. Spoon chunky apricot sauce on top. Garnish with fresh oregano sprigs.

Preparation Time: 20 minutes
Cook Time: 20 minutes
Experience Level: Beginner
Wine Suggestion: Gan Eden Late Harvest Gewürztraminer

PEPPER AND GINGER CRUSTED TUNA WITH RED WINE SAUCE

DAIRY OR PARVE   **SERVES 4**

Tuna resembles meat in both texture and color. This elegant recipe can be prepared with salmon in place of tuna if a lighter meal is desired.

TUNA
1 tablespoon olive oil
4 (8 to 10-ounce) tuna fillets, or steaks
2 tablespoons butter or margarine, melted, divided

2 teaspoons coarse salt
1½ teaspoons black pepper
1 tablespoon minced fresh ginger or
    ½ teaspoon ground ginger

RED WINE SAUCE
¼ cup unsalted butter or margarine, divided
3 shallots, minced
2 cloves garlic, minced
1 plum tomato, peeled, seeded and chopped
2 cups red wine (Pinot Noir)

1 tablespoon barbecue sauce
1 tablespoon balsamic vinegar
¼ teaspoon salt
Black pepper to taste
1 scallion thinly sliced, optional garnish

TUNA: Prepare a (9x11-inch) baking dish brushed with olive oil.

Using a pastry brush, brush both sides of tuna with 1 tablespoon of melted butter.

In a small bowl combine salt, pepper and ginger. Sprinkle seasoning mixture on both sides of fish, press seasonings into fish. Arrange fish in prepared baking dish and drizzle with remaining tablespoon of melted butter. Cover with plastic wrap and refrigerate for 20 minutes.

Preheat oven to 500°F/260°C.

Bake uncovered for 7 to 8 minutes on each side. Tuna should be slightly pink in center when fully cooked, do not overcook.

SAUCE: In a medium saucepan over medium heat, melt 2 tablespoons of butter. When butter begins to bubble add shallots and garlic. Cook for 1 minute. Stir in tomato and cook for 2 minutes. Add red wine and raise heat until wine begins to boil. Lower flame and simmer until liquid is reduced to about ½ cup. This will take approximately 10 to 15 minutes. Stir in barbecue sauce and vinegar. Whisk in remaining butter. Season with salt and pepper to taste.

Serve tuna over mashed potatoes and pour wine sauce over fish and tomatoes.

Garnish with green onions.

Preparation Time: 20 minutes
Cook Time: 30 minutes
Chill Time: 20 minutes
Experience Level: Beginner
Wine Suggestion: Teal Lake Pinot Noir

Tuna Olive Puff

PARVE   **SERVES 8**

Non-stick cooking spray
2 (6-ounce) cans tuna, drained
½ cup breadcrumbs or prepared cornflake
   crumbs
2 medium ribs celery, chopped
1 medium onion, chopped
¼ cup pitted black olives, finely chopped

Pinch of salt
Garlic powder to taste
⅓ cup mayonnaise
1 teaspoon lemon juice
½ teaspoon dried oregano
3 eggs, separated

Prepare an (8x8x2-inch) square baking dish with non-stick cooking spray.

In a medium bowl, flake tuna and combine with breadcrumbs, celery, onion, olives, salt and garlic powder.

In a small bowl, combine mayonnaise and lemon juice, add to tuna mixture. Season with oregano and add egg yolks to combine.

Preheat oven to 350°F/180°C.

In a medium bowl using a hand mixer, beat egg whites until stiff. Gently fold egg whites into tuna mixture.

Pour into prepared baking dish. Bake for 40 to 45 minutes, or until browned.

To serve cut into squares. May be eaten hot or cold.

Preparation Time: 20 minutes
Cook Time: 40 to 45 minutes
Experience Level: Beginner

Haddock Sauté

PARVE   SERVES 5

Haddock is a saltwater fish that is closely related to cod. This low-fat fish has a firm flesh that is lightly colored. In this recipe, its mild flavor is enhanced with sautéed vegetables and herbs.

5 (4-ounce) haddock fillets
Salt and black pepper to taste
2 tablespoons olive oil
2 medium onions, thinly sliced
4 cloves garlic, minced
1 small red bell pepper, chopped

1 pint grape tomatoes, sliced in rounds
2 tablespoons chopped fresh basil
1 tablespoon white wine vinegar
⅓ cup white wine
⅓ cup chopped fresh parsley

Season both sides of fillets with salt and pepper, set aside.

In a large skillet, over medium-high flame, heat oil. Add onions and sauté for about 5 minutes until soft. Add garlic and sauté for an additional 2 minutes, stirring frequently. Add red pepper, tomatoes, basil, vinegar and white wine. Cook until most of the liquid has evaporated. Add fillets and gently spoon vegetables on top of fish. Lower heat to medium, cover and simmer for about 10 minutes. Add parsley, cover and let cook an additional 5 minutes or until fish flakes easily.

Serve hot or at room temperature.

Preparation Time: 15 minutes
Cook Time: 20 minutes
Experience Level: Beginner

ASIAN SEARED RED SNAPPER

PARVE

SERVES 2

The flesh of red snapper is firm and contains very little fat. Traditional presentation calls for leaving the head and tail attached while serving.

1 (3-pound) whole red snapper, gills, scales and fins removed, head and tail left on
2 inches fresh ginger, peeled and sliced
3 cloves garlic, sliced

4 medium scallions, julienned
½ cup tamari sauce or good quality soy sauce
1 tablespoon Asian toasted sesame oil
2 tablespoons canola oil

Score fish, about half way through the flesh, with 3 diagonal slashes on each side.

Place fish in a pan large enough to accommodate fish. Stuff ginger and garlic in slits and inside belly of fish. Place ⅓ of the scallions inside fish and sprinkle ½ of remaining scallions on top. Pour tamari sauce and sesame oil over fish. Let marinate at room temperature for 15 minutes.

Preheat oven to 425°F/220°C.

Heat a heavy oven-proof skillet or a wok, large enough to accommodate the whole fish, over high heat. Reduce heat to medium high, add canola oil and carefully place fish in skillet. Cook on first side for about 5 minutes. Using a large spatula flip fish and cook second side for 5 minutes. Place fish in oven for an additional 5 to 10 minutes. Fish is done when flesh flakes easily.

To serve, garnish with remaining scallions.

Preparation Time: 15 minutes
Cook Time: 20 minutes
Experience Level: Beginner
Wine Suggestion: Gan Eden Cuvee "C'est Bouilli" (mevushal) Chardonnay

Pasta and Grains

Italian Spaghetti with Capers and Olives

PARVE   SERVES 6

This is an Italian original made with basic pantry staples. Cooked in just a few minutes, this gourmet Italian dish is easily a main course, accompanied by a simple salad and some bread.

8 ounces thin spaghetti
1½ tablespoons olive oil
3 to 4 cloves garlic, finely chopped

1 (14-ounce) can Italian plum tomatoes, crushed by hand
4 ounces pitted black olives, drained, sliced
4 tablespoons small capers

Prepare spaghetti according to package directions. Cook until al dente.

While spaghetti is boiling, in a medium saucepan, over medium flame, heat oil. Add garlic. Stir for about 1 minute. Add tomatoes, with juice from can, black olives and capers. Cook for 5 minutes.

When spaghetti is cooked transfer to a serving plate. Ladle sauce over spaghetti, toss to combine. Serve immediately.

Preparation Time: 5 minutes
Cook Time: 10 minutes
Experience Level: Beginner
Wine Suggestion: Bartenura Chianti 2000

Fettuccini Ala Pepolino

DAIRY   SERVES 6 TO 8

Fresh, juicy plum tomatoes are roasted then added to a traditional Italian tomato sauce. Top with freshly shaved Parmesan cheese for an authentic Italian classic.

8 medium plum tomatoes, halved lengthwise
3 tablespoons olive oil, divided
Salt
Black pepper
12 ounces fettuccini noodles

1 clove garlic, minced
1 (8-ounce) can tomato sauce
1 tablespoon fresh thyme, divided
¼ teaspoon crushed red pepper
¼ cup coarsely shaved Parmesan cheese

Preheat oven to 450°F/220°C.

Prepare a (15x10-inch) jelly-roll pan lined with aluminum foil.

Place tomato halves cut side up on prepared pan. Drizzle with 1 tablespoon of oil, sprinkle with salt and pepper. Roast for 25 minutes, until bottoms are dark brown. Halve each piece and set aside.

Prepare fettuccini according to package directions. Drain and set aside.

A mortar and pestle and a pepper mill are marvelous tools for preparing foods with fresh or dried herbs and spices. Freshly ground pepper and herbs yield a stronger and more robust flavor that will enhance any food to which they are added.

In a medium saucepan over medium-high flame, heat remaining 2 tablespoons of oil. Add garlic, cook for about 30 seconds. Add tomato sauce, ½ tablespoon thyme and crushed red pepper. Bring to a boil. Lower heat and simmer uncovered for 2 minutes. Add pasta, roasted tomatoes, remaining ½ tablespoon of thyme and ¼ teaspoon of black pepper. Cook until heated. Taste and adjust seasonings as necessary. Place on serving platter and sprinkle with Parmesan cheese.

Preparation Time: 20 minutes
Cook Time: 35 minutes
Experience Level: Beginner

FETTUCCINI WITH MUSHROOMS AND CREAM

DAIRY   SERVES 8

Shiitake mushrooms, also referred to as golden oak or forest mushrooms, add full bodied flavor to a creamy sauce which deliciously coats fettuccini noodles.

16 ounces fettuccini noodles
1 tablespoon olive oil
1 small shallot, finely chopped
8 ounces shiitake mushrooms, stems removed, caps thinly chopped
8 ounces white mushrooms, thinly sliced
½ teaspoon salt

¼ cup Marsala wine
1½ cups vegetable broth
⅓ cup heavy cream
1 cup fresh parsley or basil, chopped
¼ cup sun-dried tomatoes, marinated in olive oil, chopped

Prepare fettuccini noodles according to package directions. Drain and return to pot.

In a large non-stick skillet, over medium flame, heat oil. Add shallot and cook for 1 minute, stirring occasionally. Stir in mushrooms and salt. Cook until tender and golden, about 10 to 12 minutes.

Add wine to mushrooms and bring to a boil over medium-high heat. Cook for 3 minutes stirring constantly. Pour mushroom mixture into pot with fettuccini. Add parsley or and sun-dried tomatoes. Cook for 1 minute over medium heat until pasta is evenly coated. Serve immediately.

Preparation Time: 15 minutes
Cook Time: 25 minutes
Experience Level: Beginner
Wine Suggestion: Gan Eden Gewürztraminer

Spaghetti with Spring Garlic Pesto

DAIRY   **SERVES 8**

An Italian tradition, pestos are fresh sauces made with basil, garlic and pine nuts, crushed with a mortar and pestle. Our version blanches the basil leaves first then blends the cooked garlic with olive oil, pine nuts and Parmesan cheese.

15 cloves garlic or spring garlic
⅓ cup fresh basil leaves
1 pound spaghetti
1 tablespoon olive oil
½ to ¾ cup olive oil
⅓ cup pine nuts, toasted

4 teaspoons shredded Parmesan cheese
½ teaspoon salt
⅛ teaspoon black pepper
¼ cup grated Parmesan cheese
Basil leaves for garnish, optional

Fill a 4-quart saucepan ¾ full with water. Place over a medium-high heat and bring to a boil. Place garlic in boiling water for 8 minutes. Remove garlic with a slotted spoon and place in a small bowl with cold water, set aside.

Place basil in boiling water for about 5 seconds, remove with a slotted spoon and place on paper towels.

Add spaghetti and 1 tablespoon olive oil to garlic and basil flavored boiling water. Prepare spaghetti according to package directions. Drain pasta. Return to pot or place in a large bowl to toss with sauce.

Peel cooked garlic. In the bowl of blender place garlic, basil and ¾ cup olive oil. Blend until just combined. Add 2 tablespoons of the pine nuts, shredded Parmesan cheese, salt and pepper. Blend until nearly smooth. Toss with pasta.

Place on a serving platter and sprinkle with grated cheese and remaining pine nuts. Garnish with fresh basil leaves.

Preparation Time: 15 minutes
Cook Time: 20 minutes
Experience Level: Beginner

Bow Ties with Palamino Sauce

DAIRY   **SERVES 6 TO 8**

Bow tie pasta is coated with a creamy pink tomato sauce, sprinkle with fresh basil and Parmesan cheese for a final garnish.

16 ounces bow tie pasta
1 tablespoon butter
1 small onion, chopped
1 banana pepper or medium green bell
   pepper, chopped
2 cloves garlic, chopped
1 tablespoon flour

¾ cup whole milk
½ cup heavy cream
½ teaspoon salt
1¼ cups prepared marinara sauce
¼ cup grated Parmesan cheese
¼ cup fresh basil leaves, sliced

Prepare bow ties according to package directions. Drain and reserve in pot until sauce is ready.

In a large skillet over medium heat, melt butter. Add onion, pepper and garlic. Cook until tender, about 10 minutes, stirring occasionally. Stir in flour, cook 1 minute. Add milk, cream and salt. Bring to a boil over medium-high heat. Stir in marinara sauce and cook for an additional 10 minutes, stirring occasionally.

Toss bow ties with sauce. Transfer to a serving platter and toss with Parmesan cheese and sliced fresh basil leaves. Serve immediately.

Preparation Time: 10 minutes
Cook Time: 35 minutes
Experience Level: Beginner

Cheese and Noodles

DAIRY   **SERVES 8**

A twist on the traditional macaroni and cheese, mozzarella is added to a basic white sauce, mixed with pasta and baked with diced tomatoes. Experiment with different shapes of pasta to see which is your favorite.

16 ounces rigatoni pasta
7 tablespoons margarine
¼ cup flour
3½ cups milk
1¼ cups shredded mozzarella cheese, divided

1 teaspoon salt
1 cup diced tomatoes
1 to 2 teaspoons dried basil, optional
3 tablespoons butter
¼ cup breadcrumbs

Prepare rigatoni pasta according to package directions. Drain and place in a large ovenproof casserole dish. Preheat oven to 350°F/180°C.

In a medium saucepan over medium heat, melt margarine. Lower heat, stir in flour, cooking until brown. Whisk in milk and stir to thicken. Add 1 cup of cheese, and salt. Stir until smooth. Pour over pasta and mix to combine, place tomatoes on top. Sprinkle with basil if desired.

In a small saucepan over medium heat, melt butter. Remove from heat. Combine with breadcrumbs and remaining ¼ cup of cheese. Sprinkle on top of pasta and tomatoes. Bake for 30 minutes.

Preparation Time: 15 minutes
Cook Time: 45 minutes
Experience Level: Beginner

Dairy Noodle Pudding

DAIRY   SERVES 8 TO 10

A Shavuos favorite, this pudding is rich with cheeses. Dense and sweet, a small piece makes a nice side dish for dairy meals.

8 ounces medium egg noodles
Non-stick cooking spray
½ cup butter or margarine
5 eggs
1 cup sugar
16 ounces cottage cheese

8 ounces cream cheese, softened
2 cups sour cream
1 scant cup milk
2 teaspoons vanilla
Cinnamon

Prepare noodles according to package directions. Drain well and return to pot.

Preheat oven to 350°F/180°C.

Prepare a (13x9x2-inch) baking dish with non-stick cooking spray. Set aside.

Mix butter into noodles, let stand until butter melts.

To noodles add eggs, sugar, cottage cheese, cream cheese, sour cream, milk and vanilla. Mix to combine. Pour into prepared baking dish. Sprinkle top with cinnamon and bake until set, about 1 hour.

Preparation Time: 10 minutes
Cook Time: 1 hour 15 minutes
Experience Level: Beginner

GNOCCHI

DAIRY   SERVES 4

Gnocchi is a potato based pasta and is simply delicious paired with this butter and Parmesan sauce. Children enjoy helping with the preparation of gnocchi by rolling out the dough and cutting the individual pieces.

PASTA

3 medium potatoes, baked, pulp scooped
    out and mashed
1 egg

1½ cups flour, more if needed
5 teaspoons salt, divided

SAUCE

⅓ cup butter
1 medium clove garlic, crushed

¼ teaspoon dried sage
½ cup finely grated Parmesan cheese

PASTA: In a large bowl, mix mashed potatoes with egg. Add flour and 2 teaspoons of salt, mix with hands until dough is soft, smooth and a little sticky. Dough should not stick to hands, add flour as necessary to prevent sticking.

Divide dough into 8 equal pieces. Roll each piece into a 1-inch diameter log. Cut into ¾-inch long pieces (photo 1). For a decorative pasta, push each piece against the tines of a fork if desired (photo 2). Each piece should have the impression of your thumb on one side and the impression of the fork tines on the other.

Fill an 8-quart stock pot with water and place over high heat. Bring to a rapid boil and add 3 teaspoons of salt. Drop in about 30 gnocchi at a time. After about 2 minutes the gnocchi will rise to the surface. Cook for an additional 20 seconds. Remove with a slotted spoon and place in serving dish. Repeat with remaining gnocchi.

SAUCE: In a small sauce pan over low heat, melt butter with garlic and sage. When butter is melted, remove from heat and toss with gnocchi. Sprinkle with Parmesan cheese.

Preparation Time: 30 minutes
Cook Time: 13 minutes
Experience Level: Intermediate

Fresh Spinach Pasta with Spinach Sauce

DAIRY   **SERVES 4**

Once you have made fresh pasta you'll want to make it again and again. The results are a lighter pasta that sauces easily cling to. Spinach pasta uses cooked spinach in the dough, adding specks or completely turning the dough green, depending on how long it is kneaded.

SPINACH PASTA
1 cup flour
¼ teaspoon salt
1 egg, beaten

¼ cup finely chopped, cooked spinach, well drained
2 tablespoons water
½ teaspoon olive oil

SPINACH SAUCE
1 tablespoon butter
1 medium onion, thinly sliced
2 cups vegetable broth

¼ teaspoon black pepper
6 cups fresh baby spinach, stems discarded
¼ cup freshly shaved Parmesan cheese

SPINACH PASTA: In a large mixing bowl, combine flour and salt. Make a well in center.

In a small bowl, combine beaten egg, spinach, water and oil. Pour into center of well in flour. Slowly add flour from sides to center covering well. Mix with a fork to incorporate. Turn dough out onto floured work surface. Knead until dough is smooth and elastic, about 8 to 10 minutes.

Cover dough with a clean towel. Let rest for 10 minutes.

Divide dough in half.

On a lightly floured work surface using a rolling pin, roll dough into an 11-inch square. Cut into 1-inch wide strips. Repeat with remaining dough. May be air-dried until ready to cook.

SPINACH SAUCE: In a medium saucepan over medium heat, melt butter. Add onion and cook, stirring frequently until golden, about 7 minutes. Add broth and pepper to saucepan, bring to a boil. Stir in pasta and spinach. Cook covered for 2 minutes or until spinach and pasta are tender.

To serve, ladle into pasta bowls and top with Parmesan cheese.

Preparation Time: 45 minutes
Cook Time: 10 minutes
Experience Level: Intermediate
Wine Suggestion: Alfasi Flora

Fresh Ravioli with Spinach Ricotta Filling and Tomato Sauce

DAIRY

SERVES 6

RAVIOLI DOUGH
2 eggs
2 tablespoons water
2 teaspoons olive oil

1½ cups unbleached flour
¼ teaspoon salt

RAVIOLI FILLING
1 (10-ounce) package chopped frozen spinach
¾ teaspoon salt
1 cup whole milk ricotta cheese
¼ cup freshly grated Parmesan cheese

1 egg yolk
½ teaspoon freshly ground black pepper
Salt to taste

TOMATO SAUCE
3 tablespoons olive oil
2 medium onions, chopped
8 ounces fresh mushrooms, coarsely
  chopped, optional
1 large clove garlic, minced
1 large green bell pepper, chopped
2 teaspoons dried basil
1 teaspoon dried oregano
2 bay leaves

2 teaspoons salt
1 (1-pound 13-ounce) can tomato purée
1 (6-ounce) can tomato paste
2 tablespoons dry red wine
2 medium tomatoes, chopped
¼ teaspoon black pepper
½ cup fresh chopped parsley
½ cup freshly grated Parmesan cheese,
  optional

RAVIOLI DOUGH: In a large bowl, beat together eggs, water and oil. Add flour and salt. Using a circular motion, mix until well combined, scraping sides of bowl as necessary.

Turn dough out onto a lightly floured work surface. Sprinkle dough lightly with flour. Knead dough until no longer sticky and a smooth elastic dough is formed, about 5 minutes. Lightly rub all sides of dough with flour, place on floured work surface with a bowl upside down covering dough. Let rest for 15 minutes or up to 3 hours.

RAVIOLI FILLING: Cook spinach with salt, according to package directions. Drain well, squeeze to remove excess liquid. Gently dry with paper towels.

In a medium bowl, combine spinach, ricotta and Parmesan cheese. Beat in egg yolk, pepper and salt to taste. Cover and refrigerate until needed. After chilling, shape into ¾-inch balls.

TOMATO SAUCE: In a large sauce pan over medium flame, heat oil. Add onions, mushrooms if desired, garlic, green pepper, basil, oregano, bay leaves and salt. Sauté for about 10 minutes.

Add tomato purée, tomato paste, red wine, tomatoes and black pepper. Lower heat and simmer for about 45 minutes, stirring occasionally. Remove and discard bay leaves.

Toss in parsley. Taste and adjust seasonings as necessary. Stir in Parmesan cheese if desired.

RAVIOLI: If a pasta machine is available, continue following manufacturer's directions for ravioli.

By Hand: Divide dough into 2 equal portions. Flour and return one piece to under bowl. On a lightly floured work surface using a rolling pin, roll dough into a rectangle approximately 30-inches long, by 5½-inches wide and about ¹⁄₁₆-inch thick. You may use Popsicle sticks as a guide under rolling pin to help gage thickness (photo 1). Rolling, flipping and flouring as necessary. Neaten ends with a fluted pastry wheel or the tip of a sharp knife, flour and place scraps under bowl with other half of dough. Lightly score as many 1½-inch squares as possible.

Place a ball of filling in the center of each square (photo 2).

Roll out remaining dough the same size as the first piece. Lay over filling mounds, making sure that first strip is entirely covered (photo 3). Press down between filling mounds until the top layer of dough meets the bottom layer (photo 4).

With a floured pastry wheel or sharp knife, cut through dough sealing the 1½-inch squares (photo 5). Press down edges with fingers to insure a tight seal. Place on a floured cookie sheet until ready to cook. Let stand for 15 to 30 minutes to allow dough to relax, or place in freezer. Do not thaw ravioli before cooking.

Fill a large stock pot ¾ full with water, bring water to a boil over high heat. Add a pinch of salt. Place ravioli in boiling water for 8 to 10 minutes. Drain and serve topped with tomato sauce.

Preparation Time: 1 hour
Cook Time: 1 hour
Rising Time: 15 minutes to 3 hours
Experience Level: Advanced
Wine Suggestion: Alef Chianti Classico 2000, Abarbanel Selection

~

 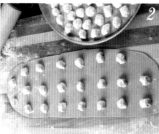 

Your meal has been cooked with love, enjoyed and appreciated. Recap the wonderful fare and friendship of your table with your hands deep in the warm suds of your washbasin. Take pride in the clean dishes knowing that they have many more wonderful events in their future.

Grilled Chicken Pasta Salad

MEAT   SERVES 6

2 boneless, skinless, chicken breast halves, pounded thin
½ cup steak sauce
12 ounces penne pasta
1 cup non-dairy creamer
1 cup mayonnaise
1 tablespoon vinegar or lemon juice
2 teaspoons dried, crushed parsley flakes

1 teaspoon onion powder
½ teaspoon garlic powder
½ teaspoon dill
1 teaspoon black pepper
1 medium Vidalia onion, or red onion, chopped
2 medium avocados, peeled, pitted and diced
1 cup halved cherry tomatoes

Place chicken and steak sauce in ziploc bag, turn bag to coat. Marinate for 1½ to 3 hours.

Prepare penne pasta according to package directions. Drain well, place on serving platter.

Preheat barbecue grill. Grill chicken for about 4 minutes on each side until no longer pink. Slice into ½-inch strips and add to pasta.

In a small bowl, whisk together non-dairy creamer, mayonnaise, vinegar, parsley, onion powder, garlic powder, dill and black pepper.

Add onion, avocado, and tomatoes to pasta and chicken. Pour dressing over all and toss to combine. Serve chilled.

Preparation Time: 15 minutes
Cook Time: 18 minutes
Chill Time: 1 hour 30 minutes to 3 hours
Experience Level: Beginner
Wine Suggestion: Ramon Cardova Rioja

Pine Nuts and Chicken Pasta

MEAT   SERVES 8 TO 10

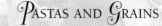

Pine nuts are extracted from the inside of pinecones and have a light, delicate flavor. Because of their high fat content, pine nuts turn rancid quickly and should be stored in an airtight container in the freezer.

16 ounces rotini pasta

2 tablespoons olive oil

2 pounds boneless, skinless chicken breasts, pounded and cut into strips

4 medium red, green and yellow peppers, thinly sliced

1 bunch scallions, minced

4 teaspoons fresh minced ginger

5 to 6 cloves garlic, minced

½ to ¾ cup pine nuts

½ cup soy sauce

½ cup lemon juice

Salt and black pepper to taste

Prepare pasta according to package directions, drain well, do not rinse. Place in a large bowl and keep warm.

In a large skillet or wok over high flame, heat oil. Sauté chicken with peppers and scallions for about 3 minutes.

Add ginger, garlic and pine nuts. Sauté an additional 3 minutes until pine nuts are golden. Add soy sauce and lemon juice, remove from heat.

Pour chicken and vegetables over pasta and toss well. Add salt and pepper to taste. Serve immediately.

Preparation Time: 20 minutes
Cook Time: 20 minutes
Experience Level: Beginner
Wine Suggestion: Dalton Sauvignon Blanc Fumé

BULGUR WITH LEEKS, CRANBERRIES AND ALMONDS

MEAT   SERVES 8 TO 10

Often an overlooked grain, bulgur wheat is a nutritious staple in the Middle East. This delicious side dish can accompany meat or turkey. The cranberries make it a perfect choice for your Thanksgiving day meal.

- 6 tablespoons margarine
- 5 medium leeks, white and pale green parts chopped
- 5 cups chicken broth, fresh or canned
- 3 cups bulgur wheat
- ⅔ cup dried cranberries
- ⅔ cup sliced almonds, toasted
- Salt and black pepper to taste

In a large saucepan over medium-high heat, melt margarine. Add chopped leeks and sauté until tender, about 12 minutes. Pour in chicken broth and bring to a boil. Stir in bulgur and return to a boil, lower heat and simmer uncovered for 5 minutes. Mix in cranberries, remove from heat, cover and let stand 15 minutes.

Fluff with a fork. Add salt and pepper to taste. Mix in sliced almonds.

Preparation Time: 10 minutes
Cook Time: 25 minutes
Experience Level: Beginner

TABOULI SALAD

PARVE   SERVES 6 TO 8

BULGUR WHEAT

1 cup bulgur wheat

1 cup boiling water

SALAD

1 cup finely chopped parsley

3 medium scallions, white and tender green parts, finely chopped

½ cup fresh chopped mint leaves, or 1 teaspoon dried mint

3 medium ripe tomatoes, seeded and finely chopped

DRESSING

Juice from 1½ medium fresh lemons

⅓ cup olive or canola oil

Salt

Black pepper

Garlic powder

BULGUR WHEAT: In a medium bowl place bulgur wheat and boiling water. Let stand until water is completely absorbed and bulgur is cooled.

SALAD: Add parsley, scallions, mint leaves and tomatoes to bulgur. Mix to combine.

DRESSING: In a small bowl combine lemon juice, oil, salt, pepper and garlic powder to taste. Pour over salad and toss. Taste and adjust seasonings if necessary. Chill for 30 minutes before serving.

Preparation Time: 10 minutes
Chill Time: 30 minutes
Experience Level: Beginner

BAKED RICE AND VEGETABLE MEDLEY

PARVE OR MEAT   SERVES 6

3 cups vegetable broth
⅛ teaspoon saffron threads
¼ cup olive oil
1 large red pepper, cut into strips
2 Japanese eggplants, cut into 1-inch cubes
1 small leek, white and tender green parts, thinly sliced
4 ounces French beans, trimmed and cut into 2-inch pieces
4 scallions, sliced

2 medium tomatoes, peeled, seeded and chopped
½ cup frozen artichoke hearts, thawed
2 cloves garlic, chopped
1 jalapeño pepper, seeded and finely chopped
½ teaspoon paprika
1½ cups short grain rice
Salt
Black pepper
2 boneless skinless chicken breasts, cooked, cut into ½-inch strips, optional

Preheat oven to 400°F/200°C.

In a medium saucepan heat vegetable broth with saffron. Keep warm over low heat.

In an oven-proof skillet over high flame, heat oil. Add pepper, eggplants, leek, green beans and scallions. Stir-fry for about 5 minutes, add tomatoes, artichoke hearts, garlic, jalapeño pepper and paprika. Stir to combine. Add rice and broth to vegetable mixture. Stir and bring to a boil. Cook for 5 minutes, stirring occasionally. Add salt and pepper to taste. Mix in chicken if desired, cover with rice and vegetables. Bake uncovered for about 20 minutes. Remove from oven when liquid is absorbed and rice is tender. Cover and let stand 5 minutes before serving.

Preparation Time: 20 minutes
Cook Time: 30 minutes
Experience Level: Intermediate

Wild Rice and Bean Salad

PARVE   SERVES 8

RICE
1 cup wild rice, rinsed well

2 cups water

DRESSING
¼ cup olive oil

3 medium cloves garlic, minced

2 medium shallots or very small yellow onions, finely chopped

¼ cup finely chopped flat leaf parsley or cilantro

2 teaspoons coarse salt

½ teaspoon freshly ground black pepper

Finely grated zest of 1 medium lemon

SALAD
1 (15-ounce) can cannellini beans, drained and rinsed

1 pint small cherry or grape tomatoes, quartered

RICE: In a medium sauce pan combine water and rice. Bring to a boil. Lower heat and simmer covered for about 45 minutes. Rice should be cooked yet slightly crunchy. Drain water if there is any remaining.

DRESSING: In a small bowl combine oil, garlic, shallots, parsley, salt, pepper and lemon zest.

Salad: Toss rice with dressing, beans and tomatoes. Chill for 1 hour before serving.

Preparation Time: 15 minutes
Cook Time: 45 minutes
Chill Time: 1 hour
Experience Level: Beginner

Song of India Rice

PARVE   SERVES 4 TO 6

1 tablespoon olive oil

1 medium onion, chopped

1 medium McIntosh apple, peeled, cored and thinly sliced

½ cup cashews

½ cup dark or golden raisins

1 teaspoon to 1 tablespoon curry powder, to taste

3 cups cooked brown rice

Salt and black pepper to taste

In a large skillet over medium-high flame, heat oil. Sauté onion for 2 minutes. Add apple slices, cashews, raisins and curry powder. Sauté until onions are transparent, and apples are tender, about 7 minutes. Mix in rice and add salt and pepper to taste.

Preparation Time: 15 minutes
Cook Time: 10 minutes
Experience Level: Beginner

Fragrant Persian Rice

PARVE   **SERVES 8**

Saffron is an expensive spice, but fortunately a little goes a long way. This aromatic spice adds a lovely yellow color to this delightful rice.

Zest of 1 small orange
½ cup boiling water
2½ cups basmati rice, divided
⅛ teaspoon saffron threads
2¼ teaspoons salt, divided
3 tablespoons margarine, divided

1 tablespoon sugar
¼ teaspoon cinnamon
½ cup pistachio nuts, shelled and unsalted
½ cup golden or black raisins
3½ cups water

Place zest in boiling water and blanch for about 2 minutes. Drain and pat dry.

Rinse rice. Place 1 cup of rice in a small bowl. Stir in saffron threads, set aside.

Place remaining rice in a medium bowl.

In a small skillet over medium heat, melt 1 tablespoon of margarine. Add zest and sauté for 15 seconds. Stir in sugar, cook for 30 seconds. Stir in cinnamon, pistachio nuts, raisins and ¼ teaspoon of salt. Sauté stirring continuously until nuts and raisins are coated. Combine with rice in medium bowl.

In a medium saucepan over medium heat, melt 2 tablespoons margarine. Add rice from medium bowl. Sprinkle with rice from small bowl. Pat down rice with a large spoon. Using the back of a wooden spoon, poke several holes in rice to the bottom of pan. Add water and 2 teaspoons of salt, bring to a boil. Cover and cook for 15 minutes.

Remove from heat. Let stand 10 minutes. Fluff with a fork.

Preparation Time: 15 minutes
Cook Time: 20 minutes
Experience Level: Intermediate

Pulao Rice

PARVE   **SERVES 6**

You will enjoy the combination of cashews, pumpkin seeds and raisins in this deep yellow rice. The color comes from the combination of turmeric and curry.

¼ cup margarine
1 cup basmati rice
3 cups water
1 tablespoon sunflower oil
½ teaspoon mustard seeds
1 teaspoon turmeric
1 cup frozen green beans

1 small green bell pepper, chopped
⅛ cup chopped cashews
¼ cup pumpkin seeds, optional
¼ cup dark raisins
½ teaspoon sea salt
1½ teaspoons curry powder

In medium saucepan over low flame, melt margarine. Add rice and stir constantly for 3 minutes. Add water, cover and cook until soft, about 15 minutes.

In a large skillet over medium flame, heat oil. Add mustard seeds. When seeds begin to pop add turmeric, green beans and pepper. Sauté for about 3 to 4 minutes. Add cashews, pumpkin seeds if desired and raisins. Combine with rice. Add salt and curry powder. Mix well.

Preparation Time: 20 minutes
Cook Time: 30 minutes
Experience Level: Beginner

Honeymoon Rice Salad

PARVE   **SERVES 16**

VINAIGRETTE
2 tablespoons Dijon mustard
½ cup red wine vinegar
2 tablespoons sugar
1 teaspoon salt

1 teaspoon freshly ground black pepper
Fresh minced parsley or snipped chives,
    to taste
1 cup olive oil

SALAD
8 cups freshly cooked white rice
1 red bell pepper, thinly julienned
1 green bell pepper, thinly julienned
1 medium red onion, diced
6 medium scallions, finely chopped
2 medium shallots, finely diced
1 (10-ounce) package frozen peas, thawed

½ cup pitted black olives, brine cured,
    finely chopped
1 cup dried currants or raisins
⅓ cup fresh parsley, chopped
½ cup fresh dill, chopped
Salt and freshly ground black pepper,
    to taste

VINAIGRETTE: In a medium bowl whisk together mustard, vinegar, sugar, salt, pepper and herbs to taste. Whisk mixture while slowly adding olive oil until mixture thickens. Adjust seasonings to taste. Cover until ready to use.

SALAD: Place warm rice in a large serving bowl, pour 1½ cups of vinaigrette over rice. Toss thoroughly. Cool to room temperature.

Add peppers, onion, scallions, shallots, peas, olives, currants, parsley, dill, salt and pepper to taste. Toss thoroughly, taste and adjust seasonings if necessary, adding additional vinaigrette as desired.

Serve immediately or refrigerate and bring to room temperature when ready to serve.

Preparation Time: 15 minutes
Experience Level: Beginner

Cantonese Fried Rice

MEAT OR PARVE   SERVES 10

4 cups water
2 chicken bouillon cubes
1 teaspoon margarine
2 cups white rice
2 tablespoons canola or vegetable oil

2 eggs, beaten
3 medium scallions, chopped
½ teaspoon black pepper
3 tablespoons soy sauce

In a medium saucepan over medium-high heat bring water, bouillon cubes, and margarine to a boil. Stir in rice, cover and cook for 15 minutes or until liquid is absorbed.

In a large skillet over medium-high flame, heat oil. Add eggs to skillet, scramble and mash into small pieces until cooked through, about 3 minutes.

Add eggs to rice. Mix in scallions, pepper and soy sauce. Add to skillet over medium heat. Combine well and heat through.

Preparation Time: 10 minutes
Cook Time: 20 minutes
Experience Level: Beginner

Richly colored glass jars are perfect for storing dry goods. The tint in the glass blocks damaging rays of light while the glass preserves without lending its own flavor to the stored items.

RICE WITH GREAT NORTHERN BEANS AND SAUCE

PARVE   **SERVES 8**

This is a delicious side dish that works well with shish kabob or steak. Add an Israeli salad for a perfect meal.

RICE

1 tablespoon canola oil
½ cup superfine egg noodles
3 cups water

½ teaspoon salt
2 cups white rice

BEANS WITH SAUCE

4 cups water
1 cup dry great northern beans, check for little rocks, discard
1 tablespoon canola oil

1 medium onion, finely chopped
1 (15-ounce) can tomato sauce
1 teaspoon coarse salt
½ teaspoon black pepper

RICE: In a medium saucepan over a medium flame, heat oil. Add egg noodles and continuously stir until lightly brown. Add water and salt, raise flame and bring to a boil. Mix in rice, cover and lower heat. Simmer for about 15 minutes or until water evaporates. A pot with a glass lid comes in handy for rice, do not open lid, just tilt pot to see if water has evaporated. Remove from heat.

BEANS WITH SAUCE: In medium saucepan over high heat, bring 4 cups of water to a boil. Add beans, lower flame and simmer, covered for 1 hour and 30 minutes. Water will remain.

In a small skillet over medium-high flame, heat oil. Add onions and sauté until transparent, about 10 minutes. Add onions to cooked beans and remaining water. Add tomato sauce, salt and pepper. Stir to combine. Cover and cook over medium-low heat for an additional 30 minutes.

Ladle beans and sauce over rice individually for each serving.

Preparation Time: 30 minutes
Cook Time: 2 hours 30 minutes
Experience Level: Intermediate

Vegetables and Sides

Marinated Asparagus

PARVE   SERVES 6 TO 8

This beautiful vegetable is one of the lily's cultivated forms. Although white and purple asparagus are similar to the common green asparagus, this marinade's flavor enhances the green variety best.

1 teaspoon salt	¼ teaspoon sugar
24 thin spears of asparagus	1 teaspoon coarse salt
3 tablespoons red wine vinegar	2 teaspoons pepper
6 tablespoons olive oil	2 teaspoons fresh chopped parsley
1 teaspoon Worcestershire sauce	1 tablespoon fresh chopped basil
½ teaspoon Dijon mustard	2 tablespoons finely chopped Vidalia onion, optional
½ teaspoon mustard powder	
½ teaspoon garlic powder	

Snap or cut off woody ends of asparagus. Fill a stock pot or large frying pan with water, add salt, bring to a boil over high heat. Add asparagus spears. Cover and cook for 5 minutes. Drain asparagus and rinse with cold water to stop the cooking process.

In a small bowl combine vinegar, oil, Worcestershire sauce, Dijon mustard, mustard powder, garlic powder, sugar, salt, pepper, parsley and basil. Toss with cooked asparagus. Refrigerate for 3 hours before serving.

Serve topped with finely chopped onion, if desired.

Preparation Time: 10 minutes
Cook Time: 5 minutes
Chill Time: 3 hours
Experience Level: Beginner

Garlic Green Beans

PARVE   SERVES 4

3 tablespoons margarine	8 cloves garlic, peeled
1 pound fresh green beans	½ teaspoon salt
8 pearl onions, or 1 small yellow onion, peeled	Black pepper

In a medium sauce pan over medium-low heat combine margarine, green beans, onions, garlic, salt and pepper to taste. Cover and stir occasionally until onions and garlic are golden, about 15 minutes.

Preparation Time: 10 minutes
Cook Time: 15 minutes
Experience Level: Beginner

ORIENTAL GREEN BEANS

PARVE   **SERVES 10**

Green beans are most appetizing when prepared tender crisp. A light sauce, such as this one, allows the fresh green bean flavor to come through. In addition adding a crunch with crushed walnuts is a fine finishing touch.

3 pounds fresh green beans
¼ cup canola oil
¼ cup soy sauce

¼ cup sesame oil
1 large clove garlic, minced
½ cup crushed walnuts

Steam green beans for 5 to 10 minutes to desired level of tenderness. Drain and place green beans in a large bowl.

Combine canola oil, soy sauce, sesame oil, minced garlic and walnuts in a small bowl. Pour over green beans and toss to coat. May be served hot or cold.

Preparation Time: 10 minutes
Cook Time: 5 to 10 minutes
Experience Level: Beginner

CARROT SOUFFLÉ

PARVE   **SERVES 9**

This soufflé may be baked in a 9x9-inch baking dish or a round soufflé dish, if available. The key to a successful soufflé is to serve it hot, straight out of the oven.

SOUFFLÉ

3 pounds carrots, peeled, cut into 1-inch
    chunks
¼ cup margarine
1 teaspoon baking soda

1 teaspoon baking powder
1 cup brown sugar
1 cup flour
1 egg

TOPPING

½ cup cornflake crumbs
5 tablespoons sugar

2 teaspoons cinnamon
2½ tablespoons margarine, melted

Fill a medium saucepan with water, add carrots and bring to a boil over high heat. Cook until carrots are fork tender, about 15 minutes.

TOPPING: In a small bowl, combine cornflake crumbs, sugar and cinnamon. Set aside.

Preheat oven to 350°F/180°C.

SOUFFLÉ: Drain carrots and mash with a potato masher. Add margarine and continue mashing until smooth. Add baking soda, baking powder, brown sugar, flour and egg. Mix until well blended. Pour into an ungreased (9x9-inch) baking dish. Sprinkle with topping and dot with melted margarine.

Bake in preheated oven for 30 minutes or until lightly browned.

Preparation Time: 15 minutes
Cook Time: 45 minutes
Experience Level: Beginner

Savory Roasted Baby Eggplants with Tomatoes and Onions

PARVE   SERVES 6

Baby eggplants, also called Italian eggplants have a more delicate skin and flesh and a lot less seeds than the common large variety. Here they are sliced in half and stuffed with a tomato filling that has been sautéed with fresh herbs and onions.

6 baby eggplants of equal size
Coarse salt
1 tablespoon canola oil
1 large Vidalia onion, sliced into ¼-inch slices
2 medium tomatoes, seeded and coarsely chopped
¼ cup fresh parsley, chopped

⅓ cup fresh basil, chopped
3 tablespoons lemon juice
1 teaspoon sugar, divided
½ teaspoon salt
½ teaspoon white pepper
⅓ cup water
3 tablespoons olive oil

Leaving tops in tact, slice unpeeled eggplants in half lengthwise. Score flesh with several x's, being careful not to pierce through to skin. Sprinkle liberally with salt and place cut side down in a colander. Place a dish or pot cover on top of eggplants to weigh them down. Place colander in sink or bowl to catch liquid that will drain out of eggplants. This removes bitterness from the vegetable. Let stand 20 to 30 minutes.

Preheat oven to 400°F/200°C.

Prepare a lightly greased roasting pan.

In a large skillet over medium flame, heat canola oil. Place onions in oil and sauté for about 10 minutes or until onions are soft. Add tomatoes, parsley, basil, lemon juice, ½ teaspoon sugar and salt.

In prepared roasting pan, place the eggplant halves skin side down. Season lightly with salt and white pepper to taste. Place vegetable mixture in a mound in the center of each eggplant half.

In a small bowl or cup stir together water, ½ teaspoon sugar and olive oil. Stir until sugar is dissolved. Add to roasting pan. Cover pan tightly with aluminum foil and place in center of oven. Cook covered for 45 minutes, basting occasionally with liquid. Uncover and cook for an additional 45 minutes. Eggplants will collapse and flatten slightly. Cooking liquid will begin to caramelize.

Serve at room temperature, drizzled with pan juices.

Preparation Time: 45 minutes
Cook Time: 1 hour 30 minutes
Experience Level: Intermediate

Ratatouille

PARVE   SERVES 4 TO 6

Originated in France, this popular dish can be served hot, cold or at room temperature. This makes an excellent choice for a Shabbos afternoon side dish, complementing even a simple roast chicken nicely.

1 large eggplant, cubed
1 medium onion, coarsely chopped
1 small red pepper, chopped
1 (4-ounce) can mushrooms, drained, ¼ cup of liquid reserved
⅓ cup olive oil
1 teaspoon salt

½ teaspoon pepper
½ teaspoon dried oregano
1½ teaspoons sugar
1 (6-ounce) can tomato paste
1 tablespoon white wine
1 tablespoon white vinegar

In a medium skillet combine eggplant, onion, pepper, mushrooms and oil. Simmer over medium heat for 10 minutes. Add salt, pepper, oregano, sugar, tomato paste, mushroom liquid, white wine and vinegar. Simmer for an additional 25 minutes.

Preparation Time: 15 minutes
Cook Time: 35 minutes
Experience Level: Intermediate

CHICKPEA STEW

PARVE   SERVES 4

1 tablespoon olive oil
1 small onion, thinly sliced
1 medium ripe tomato, cut into chunks
1 (15-ounce) can chickpeas, drained
3 tablespoons pimento stuffed green olives, drained

1 teaspoon paprika
Salt
Black pepper
¼ cup fresh spinach, coarsely chopped
1 tablespoon fresh parsley, chopped

In a medium skillet over medium flame, heat oil. Add onions and slowly brown for about 10 minutes. Add tomatoes and cook for 3 minutes. Add chickpeas and olives, cook for 2 minutes. Sprinkle with paprika, salt and pepper. Add spinach and parsley, stir to combine, cook until slightly wilted. Serve immediately.

Preparation Time: 10 minutes
Cook Time: 15 minutes
Experience Level: Beginner

SALAMI STUFFING

MEAT   SERVES 10

2 teaspoons canola oil
½ pound salami, chopped
12 ounces fresh white mushrooms, chopped
1 medium onion, chopped
3 ribs celery, chopped
½ cup dried parsley
1 teaspoon dried tarragon

1 teaspoon dried basil
1 teaspoon paprika
½ teaspoon nutmeg
6 to 8 cups day old or toasted white bread, cut into cubes
3 to 4 cups broth, water or non-dairy creamer

In a large skillet over medium-high flame, heat oil. Sauté salami, mushrooms, onion and celery for about 8 minutes. Add parsley, tarragon, basil, paprika and nutmeg. Stir to combine. Remove from heat.

Preheat oven to 350°F/180°C.

In a large mixing bowl, combine bread cubes with enough broth to moisten bread. Pour salami mixture over cubes and mix well. Place in a 2-quart casserole dish. Bake for 30 minutes.

Preparation Time: 20 minutes
Cook Time: 40 minutes
Experience Level: Beginner

Scrumptious Sage Stuffing

MEAT   SERVES 10

Using fresh sage and fresh breadcrumbs gives this cornbread stuffing an edge that sets it apart from a standard stuffing. It can be prepared a day in advance and kept covered in the refrigerator. When ready to cook bring to room temperature before baking.

CORNBREAD

Non-stick cooking spray
½ cup flour
⅜ cup yellow cornmeal
¾ teaspoon baking powder
¼ teaspoon baking soda
¼ teaspoon salt

½ cup non-dairy creamer or soy milk, mixed with ½ tablespoon vinegar
1 egg
⅛ cup margarine, melted and cooled
¼ teaspoon finely chopped fresh sage, optional

STUFFING

8 cups coarse fresh breadcrumbs, a mixture from several types of bread
Approximately 4 cups coarsely crumbled cornbread
¼ cup finely chopped fresh flat leaf parsley
3 tablespoons finely chopped fresh sage
1 teaspoon salt
½ teaspoon black pepper

1 cup margarine
2 medium onions, finely chopped
2 medium ribs celery, finely chopped
2 eggs lightly beaten
1 cup chicken or turkey broth
½ cup high fat content original soy milk
Non-stick cooking spray

CORNBREAD: Preheat oven to 425°F/220°C.

Prepare a greased (9x5x3-inch) loaf pan with non-stick cooking spray.

In a medium bowl combine flour, cornmeal, baking powder, baking soda and salt.

In a large bowl combine non-dairy creamer with vinegar, egg, melted margarine and sage.

Add dry ingredients to wet ingredients. Mix until just combined.

Spread into prepared loaf pan. Bake until golden, about 20 minutes.

Cool in pan on a wire rack then coarsely crumble.

STUFFING: Preheat oven to 325°F/160°C.

Prepare a well greased (9x13x2-inch) baking dish.

Spread breadcrumbs onto 2 (15x10-inch) jelly-roll pans. Place in oven for about 15 minutes. Let cool. Transfer to a large bowl. Stir in parsley, sage, salt and pepper.

In a large skillet over medium heat, melt margarine. Add onions and sauté for about 5 minutes. Add celery and cook for an additional 5 minutes. Remove from heat and add to breadcrumb mixture. Add eggs, broth and soy milk. Toss well.

Pour contents of large bowl into prepared baking dish. Bake covered in oven which is still 325°F/160°C for 30 minutes. Uncover and bake an additional 30 minutes until well browned.

Preparation Time: 25 minutes
Cook Time: 1 hour 25 minutes
Experience Level: Intermediate

Caramelized Onion and Beef Tartlets

MEAT   **YIELD 24 TARTLETS**

Bite sized tartlets can be served as party hors d'oeuvres, an appetizer or as a side dish. If desired they may be prepared, and refrigerated for up to 4 hours and baked just before serving.

2 teaspoons canola oil
1 large onion, finely chopped
1¼ pounds beef fry, finely chopped
1½ teaspoons mustard powder
Black pepper to taste

1 (17.3-ounce) package prepared short crust pastry dough
Non-stick cooking spray
2 eggs
½ cup non-dairy creamer

In a large skillet over medium-low flame heat oil. Add onion, cover and cook for about 30 minutes or until golden and caramelized in color. Do not rush this step, this slow cooking brings out the sweetness in the onions. Transfer onions to a medium bowl, set aside.

Add beef fry to skillet and cook until crisp. Add to onions. Stir in mustard powder and pepper to taste.

Prepare 2 mini muffin pans with non-stick cooking spray.

Preheat oven to 400°F/200°C.

On a lightly floured work surface, using a rolling pin roll out pastry to ¹⁄₁₆-inch thick. Using a 1½ or 2-inch round cookie cutter cut out circles. Place into prepared mini muffin pan, form to shape of interior of molds.

Fill each pastry lined mold with onion and beef-fry mixture.

In a small bowl, beat eggs with creamer. Pour a little into each tartlet. Bake for 15 to 20 minutes or until puffed and golden.

Preparation Time: 30 minutes
Cook Time: 1 hour
Experience Level: Intermediate

Sweet Stuffed Acorn Squash

PARVE   SERVES 2 TO 4

Acorn squash is an autumn vegetable that is mainly dark green with some shades of orange and is shaped like an acorn. This beautiful squash is a great side dish to turkey or a beautiful starter for any meal.

1 medium acorn squash	½ cup dark raisins
1 (8-ounce) can crushed pineapple, juice reserved	½ teaspoon cinnamon
	4 tablespoons apple juice concentrate, divided

Preheat oven to 350°F/180°C.

With a large sharp knife, slice squash in half with stem and point at the center bottom of each half. Remove seeds and clean squash. Cut stems and tip slightly in order for squash to stand straight and not tip over. Place in a (9x13x2-inch) baking dish.

In a small bowl, combine crushed pineapple, raisins and cinnamon. Place half of mixture in the center of each squash half. Pour 1 tablespoon of concentrated apple juice over the center of each squash. On the bottom of dish, pour reserved pineapple juice, remaining 2 tablespoons of apple juice concentrate and enough water so bottom of baking dish is covered with ¼-inch of liquid.

Cover tightly with aluminum foil and bake for 2 hours.

To serve place in appetizer plates or cut in half and plate as a side dish.

Preparation Time: 10 minutes
Cook Time: 2 hours
Experience Level: Beginner

Bite Size Spinach Egg Foo Yong with Sauce

PARVE   SERVES 4

A mini version of the classic Chinese-American dish this is designed to be served as an appetizer or side dish. You may want to experiment making Egg Foo Yong in different sizes to suit your tastes.

EGG FOO YONG

2 to 3 eggs, slightly beaten	½ medium green bell pepper, finely chopped
5 ounces frozen chopped spinach, cooked and drained well	1 small onion, finely chopped
1 medium rib celery, or ½ cup water chestnuts finely chopped	¼ teaspoon salt
	Black pepper
	Canola or vegetable oil for frying

BROWN SAUCE

2 tablespoons margarine

4 teaspoons cornstarch

2 teaspoons sugar

1 cup water

3 tablespoons soy sauce

EGG FOO YONG: In a medium bowl combine eggs, spinach, celery, pepper, onion, salt and pepper. In a large skillet over high flame, heat oil. Drop mixture by teaspoonfuls into skillet. Brown on both sides. Place on paper towels to drain excess oil. Continue until all of mixture has been fried.

BROWN SAUCE: In a small saucepan over medium heat combine margarine, cornstarch, sugar, water and soy sauce. Cook, stirring until thick and bubbly.

Serve hot Egg Foo Young topped with brown sauce.

Preparation Time: 25 minutes
Cook Time: 15 minutes
Experience Level: Intermediate

Herb Marinated Grilled Vegetables

PARVE   SERVES 8

A windowsill garden of potted herbs can greatly enhance your cooking experience. Snipping a few herbs can turn a simple vegetable dish into an aromatic delicacy.

3 large zucchini, thinly sliced, diagonally

3 large yellow squash, thinly sliced, diagonally

1 tablespoon olive oil

1½ teaspoons fresh rosemary

1½ teaspoons fresh thyme

1½ teaspoons chopped fresh chives

1½ teaspoons chopped fresh basil

2 cloves garlic, minced

Salt

In a large ziploc bag combine zucchini, squash, oil, rosemary, thyme, chives, basil and garlic. Refrigerate for 2 hours.

Preheat barbecue grill or broiler. Place marinated vegetables on vegetable grilling rack or on broiler pan. Season to taste with salt. Broil or grill until browned, turn over and brown on other side.

Preparation Time: 15 minutes
Cook Time: 20 minutes
Chill Time: 2 hours
Experience Level: Beginner

Zucchini Creole

PARVE   **SERVES 6 TO 8**

Fresh zucchini is available year round with a peak period during late summer. Here it is paired with tomatoes to make a delicious vegetable side dish.

3 tablespoons margarine
3 tablespoons flour
1 (14½-ounce) can stewed tomatoes
1 tablespoon brown sugar
1 teaspoon salt

1 small onion, chopped
6 medium zucchini, sliced
Non-stick cooking spray
¼ cup breadcrumbs

In a small saucepan over medium heat, melt margarine. Add flour and stir until smooth. Add stewed tomatoes, brown sugar, salt and chopped onion. Mix to combine, cook for about 5 minutes, stirring occasionally.

Preheat oven to 350°F/180°C.

Spray a 2-quart casserole dish with non-stick cooking spray.

Arrange half of sliced zucchini on bottom of prepared casserole dish. Pour half of the sauce over zucchini. Arrange remaining zucchini on top of sauce. Pour remaining sauce over zucchini. Sprinkle with breadcrumbs.

Place in preheated oven and bake for 40 minutes.

Preparation Time: 20 minutes
Cook Time: 40 minutes
Experience Level: Intermediate

Striped Zucchini Stuffed with Chickpeas and Rice

PARVE   **SERVES 8**

Stuffed zucchini can be used as a vegetarian main course or as a side dish. The combination of flavors are traditional Syrian seasonings which work well for awakening the taste buds.

6 tablespoons canola oil, divided
2 medium onions, chopped
8 zucchini, each about 7-inches long
2 teaspoon coarse salt, divided
1 (15-ounce) can chickpeas, drained and
   rinsed

1 cup white basmati rice, rinsed
½ teaspoon allspice
¼ teaspoon cinnamon
½ teaspoon black pepper
2½ cups water, divided

In a medium skillet over medium-high flame, heat 3 tablespoons of oil. Sauté onions until soft and wilted, about 10 minutes. Set aside onions with oil to cool.

Wash zucchini well. Using a peeler, peel strips the length of the zucchini, alternating between peel and non peel. Continue all around until the vegetable is evenly striped.

Measure about 3-inches from both ends and cut. Using a zucchini scooper or ½-inch melon baller, carefully scoop out pulp keeping a thin wall about ⅛-inch thick. Discard pulp.

Sprinkle insides of zucchini lightly with 1½ teaspoons of coarse salt.

In a medium bowl combine chickpeas, rice, 2 tablespoons oil, onions with oil used to fry the onions, salt, allspice, cinnamon and black pepper. Mix very well to ensure an even flavor. Add ½ cup water, mix well.

In bottom of a medium saucepan, place 1 tablespoon of oil, coat evenly. Stuff zucchini with filling, leaving about ¼ inch at opening, which will allow rice to expand during cooking. With the tines of a fork gently pierce zucchini 3 or 4 times, preferably closer to the ends where the skin is still on. Place zucchini close together around the edges of pot then in center of pot. Place a second level beginning with outer row. They should be packed in tightly. Place extra filling in center or anywhere there are gaps. Sprinkle with ½ teaspoon salt and pour 2 cups water to cover.

Place pot cover from a smaller pot directly over zucchini to keep the stuffing from expanding and falling out, alternatively you may use a glass dish. Cover pot with proper lid in addition to smaller lid. Place on a medium-low flame for about 20 minutes, or until Zucchini is soft and can be pierced easily with a fork.

Preparation Time: 45 minutes to 1 hour
Cook Time: 20 to 30 minutes
Experience Level: Intermediate

Roasted Zucchini with Red Peppers and Scallions

PARVE   **SERVES 6**

3 medium zucchini , sliced diagonally
2 large red bell peppers cut into 1-inch squares
3 medium scallions, white and tender green parts sliced

4 tablespoons olive oil
2 teaspoons coarse salt
1½ teaspoons balsamic vinegar

Preheat oven to 500°F/250°C.

In a well greased, baking pan, combine zucchini, peppers and scallions. Using a pastry brush, generously brush vegetables with olive oil. Place vegetables in oven and roast for 8 to 10 minutes until beginning to brown.

Transfer to a serving platter. Sprinkle with salt and drizzle with balsamic vinegar.

Preparation Time: 15 minutes
Cook Time: 8 to 10 minutes
Experience Level: Beginner

Vegetable Stuffed Zucchini

PARVE   **SERVES 10**

8 medium zucchini, ends trimmed
Salt
1 tablespoon olive oil
5 medium shallots, chopped
1 small onion, finely chopped
3 cloves garlic, minced

1 large red pepper, finely chopped
6 ounces fresh white mushrooms, chopped
12 ounces fresh or frozen spinach, chopped
¼ teaspoon salt
¼ teaspoon black pepper
Non-stick cooking spray

Cut each zucchini crosswise into 1½-inch lengths. Using a zucchini scooper or ½-inch melon baller, carefully scoop out ½ to ¾ of the zucchini pulp from each slice, keeping one end intact. Lightly sprinkle insides with salt. Reserve pulp.

In a large skillet over medium-high flame, heat oil. Add shallots and onion. Sauté for about 5 minutes. Add garlic. Finely chop reserved zucchini pulp, add to skillet. Stir in red pepper. Sauté for 5 minutes. Add mushrooms and spinach, lower heat to medium and sauté stirring occasionally for an additional 20 minutes or until liquid has evaporated. Season with salt and pepper.

Preheat oven to 350°F/180°C.

Grease a (9x13x2-inch) baking dish with non-stick cooking spray.

Fill each scooped out zucchini with vegetable mixture until heaping and place in prepared baking dish. Cover and bake for 30 to 40 minutes until zucchini is soft when pierced with a fork. Remove from oven and uncover immediately to stop cooking process. Serve warm.

Preparation Time: 45 minutes
Cook Time: 1 hour 10 minutes
Experience Level: Intermediate

Sweet Cheese Casserole

DAIRY   SERVES 8

BATTER

¼ cup butter or margarine

⅓ cup sugar

6 eggs

1½ cups sour cream

½ cup orange juice

1 cup flour

2 teaspoons baking powder

FILLING

8 ounces cream cheese, cut into ½ inch pieces

2 cups small curd cottage cheese

1 egg yolk

1 tablespoon sugar

1 teaspoon vanilla

Sour cream, optional garnish

Preheat oven to 350°F/180°C.

Prepare a (9x13x2-inch) glass baking dish with non-stick cooking spray.

BATTER: In the bowl of a mixer fitted with the whisk attachment, cream together margarine, sugar and eggs. Add sour cream, orange juice, flour and baking powder. Mix until smooth.

FILLING: In another bowl, cream together cream cheese, cottage cheese and egg yolk. Add sugar and vanilla, mix until combined.

Pour half of batter into prepared baking dish. Pour all of filling over first layer of batter. Pour remaining batter over filling.

Bake uncovered for 50 to 60 minutes or until knife inserted in center comes out clean.

Top with sour cream if desired.

Preparation Time: 15 minutes
Cook Time: 50 to 60 minutes
Experience Level: Beginner

Fila with Cheese

DAIRY   **YIELD 80 PIECES**

Here is an all-time Syrian favorite. Crisp phyllo dough topped with sesame seeds and filled with cheese. Batches can be prepared and frozen, to be baked as needed. A great Friday afternoon or Erev Yom Tov treat.

1 pound block mozzarella cheese, freshly grated	¾ cup butter, melted
2 eggs	½ cup sesame seeds
	1 (16-ounce) package phyllo dough

Prepare parchment lined (10x15-inch) jelly-roll pans. 3 if preparing to bake immediately 1 if preparing to bake at a later time.

Prepare melted butter in a small bowl with a pastry brush.

Prepare sesame seeds in a small bowl.

Line work surface with plastic wrap to prevent dough from drying out and for easy clean up.

In a large bowl using a fork, mix grated cheese with egg until well combined.

While dough is still in plastic, cut off ¼ of log with a sharp serrated knife. Cover exposed end of larger log with plastic wrap. Refrigerate.

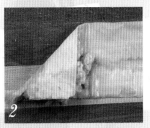
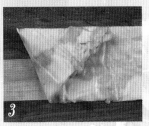

Unroll the remaining ¼ of dough. Lay out one strip of dough crosswise in front of you. Lay damp towel over dough not presently being used. Fold lower edge up to center, fold upper edge down to center. Brush across center with melted butter. Place about 1½ teaspoons of cheese mixture on left end. (Photo 1.) Fold upper left corner down to lower edge forming a triangle. (Photo 2.) Bring lower left corner up to upper edge. (Photo 3.) Left top to lower edge. Continue across phyllo dough. Be sure to maintain triangle shape. The last fold will not be complete, put a drop of butter and tuck under excess dough. Lightly brush triangle with melted butter. (Photo 4.) Place in bowl of sesame seeds, buttered side down. Brush on other side and turn over in sesame seeds. (Photo 5.) Place on prepared jelly-roll pan in a single layer. Repeat with remaining dough and filling only taking out ¼ of dough at a time.

Preheat oven to 375°F/190°C.

Bake for 15 to 20 minutes or until light golden brown. Delicious served warm.

If freezing, cover first layer on jelly-roll pan with plastic wrap and continue, covering each layer. Can be frozen up to 1 month. Do not defrost before baking.

Preparation Time: 1 hour
Cook Time: 20 minutes in 3 batches total 1 hour
Experience Level: Advanced

Moussaka

DAIRY   SERVES 10

Moussaka is Greek in origin and popular throughout most of the Near East. Every community has their own variation, ours replaces the traditional ground lamb with a sauce of sautéed mushrooms.

Non-stick cooking spray   Salt
3 medium or 2 large eggplants

MUSHROOM SAUCE
3 tablespoons butter   ½ teaspoon salt
2 pounds fresh white mushrooms, sliced   Black pepper
2 large onions, chopped   ⅛ teaspoon cinnamon
2 cloves garlic, minced   ⅛ teaspoon nutmeg
1 (6-ounce) can tomato paste   ¼ cup dry red wine
¼ cup fresh chopped parsley   ½ cup breadcrumbs
½ teaspoon dried oregano   ½ cup shredded mozzarella cheese
½ teaspoon dried basil   4 eggs, beaten

WHITE SAUCE
½ cup butter   2½ cups warm milk
½ cup flour   4 egg yolks

TOPPING
⅓ cup breadcrumbs   ¼ cup grated Parmesan cheese

Prepare a greased broiler pan with non-stick cooking spray. Slice eggplants into ½-inch thick slices. Lightly salt and place on prepared pan. Broil for 7 minutes on first side and 5 minutes on second side, cooking in batches until all eggplant has been broiled.

MUSHROOM SAUCE: In a large sauté pan over medium-high heat, melt butter. Add mushrooms and onions, sauté for about 8 minutes. Add garlic, sauté for an additional 2 minutes. Stir in tomato paste, parsley, oregano, basil, salt, pepper to taste, cinnamon, nutmeg and red wine. Simmer, stirring occasionally until liquid is absorbed. Remove from heat. Add breadcrumbs, mozzarella cheese and beaten eggs.

WHITE SAUCE: In a medium saucepan over low heat melt butter. Whisk flour into butter to make a roux. Add milk, whisking until thick. Beat in egg yolks, whisking constantly to prevent from curdling. Remove from heat.

Preheat oven to 350°F/180°C.

Butter a large lasagna pan. Cover bottom of pan with half of the eggplant slices, then half the mushroom sauce. Add remaining eggplant and cover with remaining mushroom sauce. Top with white sauce. Sprinkle breadcrumbs and Parmesan cheese over everything.

Bake covered for 40 minutes, uncover and bake an additional 15 to 20 minutes until browned and bubbly.

Preparation Time: 1 hour 30 minutes
Cook Time: 1 hour
Experience Level: Intermediate

Spanek U Giben

DAIRY **SERVES 6**

1 tablespoon canola oil
1 medium onion, chopped
2 (10-ounce) boxes frozen chopped spinach
¼ cup water

2 eggs
2¼ cups shredded mozzarella cheese
Non-stick cooking spray

In a medium saucepan over medium-high flame, heat oil. Add onion and sauté until soft and beginning to brown, about 10 minutes. Add frozen spinach and water to saucepan. Cover, lower heat to medium and simmer for about 10 minutes, breaking up frozen spinach occasionally. Drain well, pressing out excess water through strainer.

Preheat oven to 350°F/180°C.

Prepare a round 1-quart casserole dish with a generous amount of non-stick cooking spray.

In a bowl combine cooked spinach, sautéed onions, eggs and mozzarella cheese. Pour into prepared casserole dish. Bake for 45 minutes or until set and beginning to turn golden brown.

Preparation Time: 10 minutes
Cook Time: 1 hour 5 minutes
Experience Level: Beginner

Potato Torte with Cheese

DAIRY **SERVES 8**

Paprika
2¼ cups shredded cheese of choice
¼ cup plus 1 teaspoon butter or margarine,
  cut into ½-inch pieces, divided

2 teaspoons salt
¼ teaspoon pepper
9 medium potatoes, thinly sliced
1½ teaspoons Parmesan cheese

Preheat oven to 400°F/200°C.

Grease a (9x13-inch) or 2-quart casserole dish with 1 teaspoon butter. Sprinkle lightly with paprika.

In a medium bowl, combine cheese, butter, salt and pepper. Arrange potatoes in a thin layer on bottom of casserole dish. Sprinkle with a thin layer of cheese mixture. Repeat for several layers keeping layers thin. Arrange cheese on top layer, sprinkle with Parmesan cheese.

Cover and bake for 1 hour. Uncover and cook an additional 30 minutes, until potatoes are soft and golden.

Let rest 15 minutes before serving.

Preparation Time: 20 minutes
Cook Time: 1 hour 30 minutes
Experience Level: Beginner

Potato Cheese Casserole

DAIRY   SERVES 6

6 medium russet potatoes, peeled and cut
    into ¾-inch cubes
1 tablespoon butter
1 cup cottage cheese
1 small onion, finely minced
1 teaspoon coarse salt
⅛ teaspoon white pepper

⅛ teaspoon garlic powder
⅛ teaspoon dried basil
⅛ teaspoon dried thyme
⅛ teaspoon paprika
¾ cup heavy cream or milk
2 tablespoons fresh chopped parsley
¼ cup grated orange Cheddar cheese

Boil potatoes in a large saucepan over medium-high heat until fork tender. Drain.

Preheat oven to 400°F/200°C.

Grease a 2-quart casserole with butter. Place potatoes in casserole.

In a medium bowl combine cottage cheese, onion, salt, white pepper, garlic powder, basil, thyme, paprika, heavy cream and parsley. Pour over potatoes and mix gently.

Sprinkle cheese evenly over top. Bake for 15 to 20 minutes, or until browned.

Preparation Time: 15 minutes
Cook Time: 40 minutes
Experience Level: Beginner

CAKES

Strawberry Shortcake

PARVE   SERVES 16

CAKE

2 cups flour
1 teaspoon baking powder
1 teaspoon baking soda
½ teaspoon salt
¾ cup margarine, softened
1 cup sugar

1 cup non-dairy sour cream
¼ cup orange juice
1½ teaspoons grated orange peel, optional
1 teaspoon vanilla
2 eggs, at room temperature

STRAWBERRIES

24 ounces fresh strawberries, divided
2 tablespoons sugar

⅓ cup strawberry preserves

WHIPPED CRÈME FRAÎCHE

2 cups non-dairy whipping cream, cold
½ cup non-dairy sour cream
½ cup confectioners' sugar

1 teaspoon grated orange peel, optional
½ teaspoon vanilla

CAKE: Preheat oven to 350°F/180°C.

Line, grease and flour 2 (9-inch) round cake pans.

In a medium bowl, sift flour, baking powder, baking soda and salt.

In the bowl of a mixer fitted with a flat beater, beat margarine and sugar until blended. Beat in sour cream, orange juice, orange peel and vanilla. Add eggs 1 at a time. Add dry ingredients to combine. Batter will be thick. Pour batter into prepared cake pans, smooth top.

Bake for 20 to 25 minutes until golden. Cool in pans for 30 minutes, invert onto wire racks. Cakes may be frozen at this point.

STRAWBERRIES: Hull and slice 12-ounces of strawberries. In a medium bowl toss sliced strawberries with sugar. Let stand for 2 hours to allow juices to be drawn out.

WHIPPED CRÈME FRAÎCHE: In the bowl of a mixer fitted with a whisk, on high speed, whip together whipping cream, sour cream, sugar, grated orange peel and vanilla. Whip until a spreadable consistency is formed.

ASSEMBLY: Drain strawberries. Discard liquid.

Place 1 cake layer on cake stand, bottom side up. Arrange fresh strawberries evenly on top of cake. Spread 1¾ cups crème fraîche on top of strawberries. Arrange sugared berries on top of cream. Top with second cake, bottom side down. Frost whole cake with remaining crème fraîche, reserving ½ cup for garnish.

Place remaining crème fraîche in a pastry bag with a star tip. Make large rosettes around edge of cake. Place remaining strawberries, either sliced or whole decoratively around top of cake.

Warm strawberry preserves slightly and brush over strawberries and inside rosettes.

Preparation Time: 45 minutes
Cook Time: 20 to 25 minutes
Chill Time: 2 hours
Experience Level: Intermediate

BLACKBERRY JAM CAKE WITH BROWN SUGAR FROSTING

PARVE   SERVES 16

A spice cake with a delicious brown sugar frosting. Garnish with fresh berries and mint leaves for a simple yet beautiful presentation.

CAKE

1⅓ cups flour
1 teaspoon cinnamon
½ teaspoon baking soda
½ teaspoon ground nutmeg
½ teaspoon ground cloves
½ cup margarine, softened
½ cup sugar

½ cup brown sugar
2 eggs
½ cup non-dairy creamer mixed with
   1 tablespoon vinegar
½ cup blackberry jam
½ cup chopped pecans

FROSTING

½ cup margarine
1 cup brown sugar

¼ cup non-dairy creamer
3½ cups confectioners' sugar

CAKE: Preheat oven to 350°F/180°C. Grease and lightly flour 2 (8-inch) round pie pans.

In a small bowl combine flour, cinnamon, baking soda, nutmeg and cloves.

In the bowl of a mixer fitted with a flat beater cream margarine, sugar and brown sugar until light and fluffy, about 2 minutes. With mixer on medium speed, add eggs, one at a time. Scrape down sides of bowl with a rubber spatula, as necessary. With mixer on medium speed, alternate adding dry ingredients and non-dairy creamer until just combined. Turn mixer to low and stir in jam and pecans until just incorporated.

Pour batter into prepared pans and bake for 30 to 35 minutes or until toothpick inserted in center comes out clean.

Let cakes cool in pans on wire racks for 10 minutes. Invert cakes onto cooling racks and let cool completely before frosting.

THE FROSTING: In a medium saucepan on a medium low flame, melt the margarine. Stir in brown sugar. Continue stirring and cook until bubbling about 5 to 6 minutes. Remove from heat. Transfer to bowl of a mixer fitted with a whisk. Add non-dairy creamer and beat on high until smooth about 1 minute. Add confectioners' sugar and beat on medium speed until frosting is easily spread. If frosting is thick add extra non-dairy creamer, as necessary. Use immediately, while frosting is still warm.

Frost following directions for Cake Construction on page 306.

Preparation Time: 45 minutes
Cook Time: 30 to 35 minutes
Experience Level: Intermediate

Cakes

Sour Cherry Cake

PARVE   **SERVES 9**

2 eggs
1 cup sugar
½ cup margarine, melted
½ teaspoon vanilla

2 tablespoons cocoa
¾ cup flour
½ teaspoon baking powder
1 (15-ounce) can sour cherries, well drained

Preheat oven to 350°F/180°C.

Grease a (8x8-inch) square baking pan.

In the bowl of a mixer fitted with a whisk, beat together eggs and sugar until light yellow and fluffy. Add margarine and vanilla, stir to combine. Mix in cocoa, flour and baking powder. Pour batter into prepared pan. Press cherries into top of batter.

Bake for 45 minutes or until set. Best served on day of baking, cake will get soggy if covered.

Preparation Time: 10 minutes
Cook Time: 45 minutes
Experience Level: Beginner

Surprise Cake

PARVE   **SERVES 8**

The addition of dates creates a moist, delicious cake you'll want to prepare for any occasion.

1 cup chopped dates
1½ cups boiling water
2 teaspoons baking soda, divided
¾ cup shortening
1 cup sugar
2 eggs

1¾ cups flour
½ teaspoon salt
6 ounces semi-sweet chocolate chips
¼ cup sugar
1 cup chopped nuts, i.e. almonds, walnuts

Preheat oven to 350°F/180°C.

Prepare a greased (9-inch) round springform pan.

In a small bowl combine dates, boiling water and 1½ teaspoons baking soda. Let stand 2 minutes, drain well.

In the bowl of a mixer fitted with a flat beater, on medium speed cream together shortening and sugar. Add eggs, flour, remaining ½ teaspoon baking soda, salt and drained dates. Mix to combine.

Pour batter into prepared pan. Evenly sprinkle top of cake with chocolate chips, sugar and nuts. Bake for 35 to 40 minutes.

Preparation Time: 15 minutes
Cook Time: 35 to 40 minutes
Experience Level: Beginner

LEMON GLAZED POUND CAKE

PARVE   **SERVES 12**

The candy-like glaze keeps the moisture in this delicious pound cake. Perfect with a cup of coffee or tea. You will find yourself preparing this cake to have around for drop-in guests. It freezes beautifully.

CAKE

3 cups flour
2 teaspoons baking powder
½ teaspoon salt
1 cup margarine
2 cups sugar

4 eggs
½ cup non-dairy creamer or soy milk
½ cup orange juice
2 tablespoons lemon rind

GLAZE

⅓ cup fresh lemon juice

¾ cup sugar

CAKE: Preheat oven to 350°F/180°C.

Grease a Bundt pan and set aside.

In a medium bowl combine flour, baking powder and salt. Set aside.

In the bowl of a mixer fitted with a flat beater, on medium speed, cream together margarine and sugar. Add eggs, one at a time mix until well combined. Add non-dairy creamer and orange juice alternating with dry ingredients until all is incorporated. Add lemon rind and mix until smooth. Pour into prepared Bundt pan.

Bake in preheated oven for 50 to 60 minutes until cake tester comes out clean. Invert hot cake onto cake plate.

GLAZE: In a small bowl mix together lemon juice and sugar. Brush hot cake all over with lemon glaze. Allow to cool before serving.

Preparation Time: 15 minutes
Cook Time: 50 to 60 minutes
Experience Level: Beginner

Coconut Pecan Whipped Cream Cake

PARVE   SERVES 16

While preparing this recipe for one of our tasting parties the person baking it felt something just was not right. The author of the recipe, a known baker and cook, could not be reached. The person baking it was assured it must be right. When the cake was brought to the party everybody loved it. It wasn't as pretty as we would have preferred, but it was delicious. Then, as the party was ending the author of the recipe called. "Oh, No! I forgot the flour!" she cried. We'd like to assure you this recipe has the flour, but even without, it's still delicious.

CAKE
2 cups flour
1½ cups sugar
2 teaspoons baking powder
½ teaspoon salt

1½ cups non-dairy whipping cream
3 whole eggs, or ¾ cup egg beaters
1½ teaspoons vanilla

FROSTING
7 cups confectioners' sugar
1 cup margarine
2 teaspoons vanilla
4 tablespoons non-dairy creamer

4 cups sweetened shredded coconut
2 cups chopped pecans plus 2 tablespoons
   for garnish

CAKE: Preheat oven to 350°F/180°C.

Grease and flour 2 (9-inch) round cake pans.

In a medium sized bowl combine flour, sugar, baking powder and salt. Set aside.

In the bowl of a mixer fitted with a whisk, on high speed, beat whipping cream until stiff. Transfer to a large bowl. Set aside.

Wash and dry mixer bowl. In mixer bowl fitted with a whisk, on high speed, beat eggs with vanilla until thick and lemon colored, about 3 to 5 minutes. Gently fold into whipping cream. Fold dry ingredients into whipping cream and egg mixture.

Pour into prepared cake pans. Bake for 30 to 35 minutes until a toothpick inserted in center comes out clean.

Let cakes cool in pans on wire racks for 10 minutes. Invert cakes onto cooling racks. Cool completely.

Cut each layer in half with a large serrated knife to make total of 4 layers. See directions for Torting a Cake on page 306.

FROSTING: In the bowl of a mixer fitted with a flat beater, on medium speed, cream sugar, margarine, vanilla and non-dairy creamer. Add coconut and pecans until combined. Fill and frost 4 layered cake. Sprinkle 2 tablespoons pecans on top of cake.

VARIATION: Eliminate pecans in frosting. Use 2 tablespoons of shredded coconut for garnish.

Preparation Time: 45 minutes
Cook Time: 30 to 35 minutes
Experience Level: Intermediate

Hazelnut Torte

PARVE · SERVES 16

BUTTERCREAM
4 egg yolks, slightly beaten
⅔ cup sugar
3 tablespoons water

1 tablespoon instant coffee
1 teaspoon vanilla
1 cup margarine

MOCHA GANACHE
8 ounces semi-sweet chocolate, coarsely chopped
1 cup non-dairy whipping cream

3 tablespoons margarine
2 teaspoons coffee granules

TORTE
2 cups ground hazelnuts
2 tablespoons flour

6 egg whites, at room temperature
1 cup sugar

GARNISH
¼ cup ground hazelnuts

16 chocolate dipped hazelnuts

BUTTERCREAM: In a medium bowl place beaten egg yolks and set aside.

In a medium saucepan over medium-high heat, combine sugar and water. Stir constantly and bring to a boil. Remove from heat. Slowly stir half of sugar and water mixture into egg yolks. Pour egg yolk mixture into saucepan and bring to a gentle boil. Reduce heat. Cook and stir for about 2 minutes. Remove from heat. Stir in coffee and vanilla. Cool to room temperature.

In the bowl of a mixer fitted with a flat beater, on high speed, beat margarine until fluffy. Add cooled sugar mixture, beat until combined. Chill until mixture is of spreading consistency.

MOCHA GANACHE: In a medium saucepan over low heat, combine chocolate, whipping cream, margarine and coffee granules. Cook, stirring until chocolate is melted. Don't rush this step.

Remove from heat. Place saucepan in a bowl of ice water. Using a rubber spatula, stir constantly for 6 to 8 minutes or until mixture thickens to a spreading consistency.

TORTE: Grease and line 3 (8x1½-inch) round baking pans with waxed paper.

In a medium bowl, combine hazelnuts and flour. Set aside.

Preheat oven to 300°F/150°C.

In the bowl of a mixer fitted with a whisk, beat egg whites on medium-high speed until soft peaks form. Gradually add sugar, 1 tablespoon at a time, beating on high speed until very stiff peaks form and sugar is almost dissolved, about 8 minutes.

Fold hazelnut mixture into egg white mixture. Spread evenly into prepared baking pans. Bake in preheated oven for 40 to 45 minutes or until just set and very lightly browned. Cool on wire racks for 10 minutes. Carefully loosen sides of cakes from pans. Invert onto cooling racks. Peel off waxed paper. Cool completely on racks.

ASSEMBLY: Place 1 cake on a cake stand. Spread half of the mocha ganache on top to within ¼-inch of edge. Chill in freezer for 5 minutes. Spread ½ cup buttercream on top of mocha ganache. Top with second cake. Spread remaining mocha ganache on top of second cake. Top with third cake. Chill in freezer for 5 minutes. Spread remaining buttercream on sides and top of torte.

GARNISH: Press ground hazelnuts gently into buttercream on sides of torte. Place hazelnuts along perimeter of cake within 1-inch all around.

Preparation Time: 1 hour
Cook Time: 55 minutes
Experience Level: Advanced

*F*OOLPROOF *C*HOCOLATE *C*AKE

PARVE   **SERVES 16**

2 eggs
½ cup plus 2 tablespoons cocoa
1 cup canola oil
3 cups flour
¾ cup non-dairy creamer or water
¼ cup apple cider vinegar

2 cups sugar
2 teaspoons baking soda
1 teaspoon salt
1 teaspoon vanilla
1 cup hot water

Preheat oven to 350°F/180°C.

Grease a (9x13-inch) baking dish, set aside.

In the bowl of a mixer fitted with a flat beater, on medium speed, mix eggs, cocoa, oil, flour, non-dairy creamer, apple cider vinegar, sugar, baking soda, salt, vanilla and water. Mix until well combined.

Pour into prepared baking dish. Bake for 40 minutes or until toothpick inserted in center comes out clean.

Preparation Time: 10 minutes
Cook Time: 40 minutes
Experience Level: Beginner

*K*OKOSH

This recipe was submitted to the original Arie Crown cookbook which was printed in 1981. The rich chocolate filling and the moist dough form a treat that stands the test of time.

DOUGH
4½ teaspoons dry yeast

¼ cup water

3½ cups flour

½ cup sugar

2 eggs

½ cup margarine, softened

½ cup non-dairy creamer or orange juice

FILLING
1 cup margarine, softened

5 tablespoons cocoa

2 cups sugar

½ teaspoon lemon juice

1½ teaspoons vanilla

DOUGH: In the bowl of a mixer fitted with a dough hook, dissolve yeast with water. Let stand 5 minutes. Add flour, sugar, eggs, margarine, and non-dairy creamer. Mix to form a soft dough. Cover and allow to rise for 1 hour or until doubled in bulk.

Preheat oven to 375°F/190°C.

Grease a tube pan. Wrap bottom of outside of pan with aluminum foil, to prevent leaking.

FILLING: In bowl of mixer fitted with a flat beater, on low speed, combine margarine, cocoa, sugar, lemon juice and vanilla. Mix to a gritty spreading consistency.

Using a rolling pin, roll out dough into a large ⅛-inch thick rectangle. Spread ¾ of filling evenly over entire rectangle. Roll up jelly-roll style. Place in prepared tube pan, seam side down joining edges to form a ring. Smooth dough at seam, ensuring dough is distributed evenly in pan. Spread remaining filling evenly over top of ring.

Place in preheated oven, on a jelly-roll pan to catch drips. Bake for 1 hour. Let cool for 10 minutes before turning out of pan. Cool completely before slicing.

Preparation Time: 30 minutes
Cook Time: 1 hour
Experience Level: Intermediate

Mocha Cake
with Waferroll Cookies

PARVE   SERVES 16

Packaged waferroll cookies give this cake an impressive appearance that will make it look as if you spent hours in the kitchen. Prepare it whenever you need a beautiful and delicious cake as a centerpiece.

MOCHA CAKE

1 cup canola oil

2½ cups sugar

3 teaspoons vanilla

4 eggs

2 cups boiling water

2 teaspoons instant coffee

1 cup cocoa

3 cups flour

1½ teaspoons salt

2 teaspoons baking soda

½ teaspoon baking powder

FROSTING

½ cup shortening, no substitutions

1 egg white

1 teaspoon vanilla

6 tablespoons warm, not hot water

2 teaspoons instant coffee

3 tablespoons cocoa

4 cups, 1-pound confectioners' sugar

ASSEMBLY

2 (3½-ounce) boxes waferroll cookies

1 (3½-ounce) truffle filled Swiss dark or bittersweet chocolate bar

MOCHA CAKE: Preheat oven to 350°F/180°C.

Grease 3 (8-inch) round cake pans, set aside,

In the bowl of a mixer fitted with a flat beater, combine oil, sugar, vanilla and eggs. Mix coffee with water and add to bowl alternating with cocoa. Add flour, salt, baking soda and baking powder. Combine until smooth. Pour into prepared pans and place in preheated oven for 30 minutes or until toothpick inserted in center comes out clean. Let cool. Reserve 1 cake for another use.

FROSTING: In a large mixing bowl fitted with a flat beater, combine shortening, egg white, vanilla, water, coffee and cocoa. Add sugar 1 cup at a time mixing until smooth and creamy.

ASSEMBLY: Place 1 cake on cake stand. Evenly spread ¼ of frosting on top. Place second cake on top of first. Frost top and sides of cake. Does not need to be perfect, as it will be covered. Place waferroll cookies around cake, completely surrounding it with a fence of cookies.

Using a vegetable peeler peel chocolate curls, or shavings from bar of chocolate. Place chocolate curls and shavings decoratively on top of cake.

Refrigerate until ready to serve.

Preparation Time: 35 minutes
Cook Time: 30 minutes
Experience Level: Intermediate

Cinnamon Crumb Coffee Cake

PARVE   SERVES 6 TO 8

TOPPING

4 tablespoons margarine, softened

1 cup brown sugar

2 teaspoons cinnamon

¼ cup flour

CAKE

¼ cup margarine

¾ cup sugar

1 egg

½ cup non-dairy creamer

½ teaspoon vanilla

1½ cups flour

2 teaspoons baking powder

½ teaspoon salt

½ cup raisins or crushed walnuts

TOPPING: In a medium bowl mix together margarine, sugar, cinnamon and flour until combined. Set aside.

CAKE: Preheat oven to 375°F/190°C.

In the bowl of a mixer fitted with a flat beater, cream margarine and sugar. Add egg, non-dairy creamer and vanilla. Sift together flour baking powder and salt. Add dry ingredients to mixing bowl. Beat until a smooth batter is formed. Add raisins or nuts. Mix to combine.

Grease an (8x8x2-inch) baking dish. Pour batter into baking dish, sprinkle topping evenly over batter. Bake for 30 minutes.

Preparation Time: 15 minutes
Cook Time: 30 minutes
Experience Level: Beginner

For a simple yet decadent treat, melt twelve ounces of semi-sweet chocolate with one tablespoon of shortening in the top of a double broiler, stirring until smooth. Use as a dip for luscious fresh strawberries, candied rinds or dried fruit. Lay to harden on parchment paper and savor the sensation of indulgence you will experience with every bite.

289

Sour Cream Pound Cake

PARVE   SERVES 10

Extremely sweet and moist, this scrumptious cake is an ideal companion to a good cup of coffee.

TOPPING
1 cup chopped pecans   ¾ cup sugar
1 tablespoon cinnamon

CAKE
1 cup margarine   2 eggs
2 cups sugar   2 cups flour
1 cup non-dairy sour cream   1 tablespoon baking powder
1 tablespoon vanilla   ¼ teaspoon salt

Preheat oven to 350°F/180°C. Set oven rack in the center of the oven.

Prepare a greased and floured tube pan, set aside.

TOPPING: In a small bowl combine pecans, cinnamon and sugar. Set aside.

CAKE: In the bowl of a mixer fitted with a flat beater, on medium speed, cream margarine and sugar. Add sour cream, vanilla and eggs and mix to combine.

In a medium bowl, sift together flour, baking powder and salt. Fold dry ingredients into creamed mixture until combined. Pour half of batter into prepared tube pan. Sprinkle half of the nut mixture onto the batter in the tube pan. Pour the remaining batter over the nuts. Sprinkle with remaining nut mixture.

Bake in center of preheated oven for 1 hour or until a toothpick inserted in center comes out clean.

Preparation Time: 20 minutes
Cook Time: 1 hour
Experience Level: Beginner

MARBLE BUNDT CAKE

PARVE   SERVES 12

3 cups flour
2 teaspoons baking powder
½ teaspoon salt
1 cup margarine
2 cups sugar

3 eggs
1 cup orange juice
1½ teaspoons vanilla
¾ cup chocolate syrup
¼ teaspoon baking soda

Preheat oven to 350°F/180°C.

In a medium bowl sift together flour, baking powder and salt. Set aside.

In the bowl of a mixer fitted with a flat beater, on medium speed, cream together butter and sugar. Add eggs. In a small bowl or glass combine orange juice and vanilla. Add orange juice and vanilla alternately with dry ingredients until all is incorporated.

Grease a (10-inch) Bundt or tube pan. Pour a scant ⅔ of batter into Bundt pan.

Blend chocolate syrup and baking soda into remaining batter. Pour over batter in pan. Run a knife through batter a few times to give batter a marbleized effect.

Bake for 50 to 55 minutes or until toothpick inserted in center of cake comes out clean.

Preparation Time: 15 minutes
Cook Time: 55 minutes
Experience Level: Beginner

GOLDEN BUNDT CAKE

PARVE   SERVES 12

CAKE
1 cup margarine, softened
2 cups sugar
4 eggs
2 teaspoons vanilla
1 teaspoon baking powder

1 teaspoon baking soda
1 teaspoon salt
1 cup orange juice
3 cups flour

GLAZE
¾ cup sugar
⅓ cup margarine

2 teaspoons vanilla
4 tablespoons water

CAKE: Preheat oven to 325°F/160°C. Grease and flour a (10-inch) Bundt pan.

In the bowl of a mixer fitted with a flat beater on medium speed, cream margarine and sugar. Add eggs, one at a time. Add vanilla, baking powder, baking soda and salt. Mix to combine. Alternate adding orange juice and flour. Beat on medium speed for 3 minutes. Pour batter into prepared pan.

Bake in preheated oven for 1 hour or until toothpick inserted in center comes out clean. Prick holes in cake with a toothpick while warm.

GLAZE: In a small saucepan over medium heat, combine sugar, margarine, vanilla and water. Cook until completely melted and combined. Do not boil.

Pour glaze over hot cake. Let cake cool completely before removing from pan.

Preparation Time: 20 minutes
Cook Time: 1 hour 10 minutes
Experience Level: Beginner

*A*PPLE *S*PICE *C*AKE

PARVE   SERVES 9

This simple, old fashion, cake is mixed by hand and prepared the same as when it was created in 1958. Simply delicious.

2 medium Granny Smith apples, peeled, cored and cubed	1 teaspoon cinnamon
1 cup sugar	½ teaspoon allspice
½ teaspoon salt	1 egg, lightly beaten
1½ cups flour	½ cup margarine, melted
1 teaspoon baking soda	½ cup nuts, optional
½ teaspoon nutmeg	½ cup raisins, optional

Preheat oven to 350°F/180°C.

Grease an (8x8-inch) baking dish.

In a large bowl combine apples and sugar. Let stand 10 minutes.

In small bowl sift together salt, flour, baking soda, nutmeg, cinnamon and allspice.

Pour egg and margarine over apples. Mix to combine. Mixing by hand, add dry ingredients and nuts and raisins if using, to apple mixture. Mix until just incorporated. Push mixture into prepared baking dish.

Bake for 50 to 55 minutes. Cool for 10 to 15 minutes. Invert onto wire rack to finish cooling, if left in baking dish it will get too moist.

Preparation Time: 15 minutes
Cook Time: 50 to 55 minutes
Experience Level: Beginner

Swedish Tea Ring

PARVE YIELD 3 CAKES, EACH SERVE 15

Perfect for a breakfast treat or after a fast day. This recipe makes 3 cakes, use one right away and freeze the other two for future use. If you prefer you may omit the nuts, or raisins, the cake will still be scrumptious.

CAKE

1½ cups non-dairy creamer	1½ teaspoons salt
1 cup margarine	7 cups flour, divided
½ cup sugar	3 eggs
4½ teaspoons dry yeast	½ teaspoon vanilla

TOPPING

6 tablespoons margarine, melted, divided	1½ cups chopped pecans, divided
1 cup sugar	1½ cups raisins, divided
1 tablespoon cinnamon	

GLAZE

2 cups confectioners' sugar	¼ cup non-dairy creamer

CAKE: In a medium saucepan over medium flame heat non-dairy creamer and margarine until about 120°F/50°C on a candy thermometer. Set aside.

In the bowl of a mixer fitted with a dough hook, on medium speed, combine sugar, yeast, salt and 2 cups of flour. Gradually add creamer mixture, beating for 2 minutes. Add eggs, vanilla and 2½ cups of flour. Beat for 2 more minutes. Gradually add remaining 2½ cups flour to make a soft slightly sticky dough.

Turn dough out onto a lightly floured work surface. Knead for 5 minutes until smooth and elastic. Or use dough hook for 5 minutes at medium-high speed. Cover and let rest for 10 minutes.

Shape dough into a ball. Place in a greased bowl, turning to coat. Cover and let rest in a warm place for 1 hour and 30 minutes or until doubled in bulk.

Punch down dough. Turn out onto a lightly floured work surface and divide into thirds.

Working with one third of dough at a time, using a rolling pin, roll dough into a 21x7-inch rectangle.

TOPPING: Brush 2 tablespoons margarine onto top of rectangle leaving a 1-inch margin all around without margarine. In a small bowl combine sugar and cinnamon, mixing well. Sprinkle ⅓ of cinnamon and sugar evenly over dough. Evenly sprinkle ½ cup raisins and ½ cup pecans over sugar. Beginning at the long end roll up dough jelly-roll style. Pinch edges to seal. Place roll on a greased (15x10-inch) jelly-roll pan, seam side down. Shape into a ring and pinch ends together.

Using a sharp knife, make cuts around ring at 1-inch intervals, cutting ⅔ of the way through. Separate dough at cuts, laying each piece on its side, slightly overlapping slices. Cover and let rise in a warm place for 30 minutes or until doubled in bulk.

Repeat with remaining ⅔ of dough.

Place oven rack on upper level. Preheat oven to 375°F/190°C.

Bake 1 ring at a time for 20 minutes or until golden brown. Carefully transfer to wire rack to cool.

GLAZE: In a medium bowl, combine confectioners' sugar and non-dairy creamer. Drizzle over warm rings. Serve warm or at room temperature.

Freezes well, do not glaze until defrosted. Can be made with only nuts or only raisins or omitting both.

Preparation Time: 50 minutes
Rising Time: 2 hours
Cook Time: 20 minutes in 3 batches
Experience Level: Advanced

BANANA CUPCAKES WITH FROSTING

PARVE   SERVES 12

The addition of banana to the frosting forms a loose frosting that will not harden. Keep the frosting in the refrigerator. Before serving swirl frosting over tops of cupcakes with the back of a spoon.

CUPCAKES

2 medium ripe bananas, mashed	1 teaspoon vanilla
1 teaspoon baking soda	1 teaspoon baking powder
1 teaspoon hot water	1 teaspoon salt
½ cup margarine	1½ cups flour
¾ cup sugar	1 cup chocolate chips, optional
1 egg, beaten	

FROSTING

1 banana, mashed	½ teaspoon lemon juice
¼ cup margarine, softened	4 cups confectioners' sugar

Preheat oven to 400°F/200°C.

Line a standard size muffin pan for 12, with paper liners.

In a small bowl combine mashed bananas with baking soda and hot water, set aside.

In the bowl of a mixer fitted with a flat beater, on medium speed, cream together margarine and sugar. Add egg and vanilla mix to combine. Add baking powder, salt and flour mixing until incorporated. Mix in banana mixture and add chocolate chips if using.

Pour batter into prepared liners, filling ¾ full. Bake for 15 minutes. Cool before frosting.

FROSTING: In the bowl of a mixer on medium-high speed, combine banana, margarine, lemon juice, and confectioners' sugar until smooth. Frost cupcakes.

Preparation Time: 15 minutes
Cook Time: 15 minutes
Experience Level: Beginner

PARVE CHEESECAKE

PARVE   **SERVES 16**

You won't believe that this isn't dairy. Beating the egg whites balances the dense tofu cream cheese, forming a light fluffy cake that will wow your guests. A garnish of fresh strawberries is a pretty complement to this cheesecake.

CRUST

8 ounces cinnamon graham crackers, crushed   6 tablespoons margarine, melted

CHEESECAKE

2 (8-ounce) tubs non-dairy cream cheese   4 eggs, separated

1 (12-ounce) tub non-dairy sour cream   1 tablespoon fresh grated lemon rind

1 teaspoon vanilla   ½ teaspoon lemon juice

1 cup sugar, divided   1 tablespoon flour

CRUST: Grease a (9-inch) springform pan.

In a medium bowl, combine graham crackers and margarine. Evenly coat the bottom of pan with the crust mixture. Refrigerate while preparing filling.

Preheat oven to 350°F/180°C. Place oven rack at highest position.

In the bowl of a mixer fitted with a flat beater, on high speed, beat cream cheese until smooth. Add sour cream, vanilla, ¾ cup sugar, egg yolks, lemon rind, lemon juice and flour. Mix until well combined.

Place egg whites in a clean and dry bowl of a mixer fitted with a whisk. Whip whites until soft peaks begin to form. Gradually add remaining ¼ cup sugar, beating until stiff peaks form. Gently fold egg white mixture into cream cheese mixture until combined. Pour into crust.

Place springform pan into a large baking pan, large enough to accommodate water going half way up the side of springform pan. Place pan in oven. Pour enough water into pan to come ½-inch up side of springform pan. Bake on upper rack in water bath for 40 to 50 minutes or until set. Turn heat off and keep cheesecake in oven with door ajar, for 30 minutes.

Preparation Time: 25 minutes
Cook Time: 40 to 50 minutes plus 30 minutes without heat
Experience Level: Intermediate

LORRAINE'S CHEESECAKE

DAIRY   SERVES 16

Light and fluffy, this cheesecake was a favorite with all of our testers. The batter needs minimal mixing so stop as soon as the ingredients are combined. Overbeating cheesecake batter causes cracks when baking.

⅓ (16-ounce) package chocolate graham crackers, mashed into crumbs
1 pound small curd cottage cheese, California style if available
2 (8-ounce) packages cream cheese
1½ cups sugar

4 eggs
⅓ cup cornstarch
2 tablespoons lemon juice
1 teaspoon vanilla
½ cup margarine, melted
2 cups sour cream

Preheat oven to 325°F/160°C. Grease a (9-inch) springform pan.

Evenly sprinkle graham cracker crumbs on sides and bottom of springform pan. Set aside.

In the bowl of a mixer fitted with a whisk combine cottage cheese and cream cheese. Beat on high speed until well blended with no visible curds remaining. Add sugar and eggs. Reduce to low speed and add cornstarch, lemon juice, vanilla, margarine and sour cream beating until smooth. Pour into prepared pan.

Bake for 1 hour and 10 minutes. Turn off heat and keep cheesecake in oven for an additional 2 hours. A gentle baking and cooling process is still present.

Preparation Time: 15 to 20 minutes
Cook Time: 1 hour 10 minutes plus 2 hours without heat
Experience Level: Beginner

WHITE CHOCOLATE CHEESECAKE

DAIRY   SERVES 10

CRUST
1½ cups crushed shortbread cookies
4½ tablespoons finely chopped toasted almonds

½ cup butter, melted

CHEESECAKE
2 (8-ounce) packages cream cheese, softened
1 (6-ounce) white chocolate baking bar, melted and cooled
⅔ cup sugar

3 eggs
⅔ cup sour cream
1 teaspoon vanilla

RASPBERRY SAUCE
1 (10-ounce) jar seedless raspberry preserves

1 cup fresh or frozen raspberries

CRUST: Prepare a greased (8-inch) springform pan.

In a small bowl, combine crushed cookies, almonds and melted butter. Press mixture evenly into bottom of prepared pan, set aside.

CHEESECAKE: Preheat oven to 350°F/180°C. In the bowl of a mixer fitted with a flat beater, beat cream cheese and melted baking bar on high speed until combined. Add sugar and beat until smooth. Add eggs, sour cream and vanilla. Beat on low speed until just combined. Do not overbeat. Pour into prepared crust.

Bake for 45 minutes or until center is nearly set. Do not over bake. This cake will puff from baking then settle as it cools. Cool for 45 minutes to 1 hour on a wire rack. Cover and refrigerate for at least 4 hours.

RASPBERRY SAUCE: In a small saucepan over low heat, melt preserves. Add raspberries and heat gently until sauce simmers. Remove from heat. Cool.

To serve, remove sides from springform pan. Slice cheesecake into wedges and drizzle raspberry sauce over each slice.

Preparation Time: 20 minutes
Cook Time: 50 minutes
Chill Time: 4 hours
Experience Level: Beginner

BUTTERSCOTCH CHEESECAKE

DAIRY   SERVES 16

A traditional New York cheesecake crowned with a creamy white chocolate mocha topping. Rich and indulgent. If using a non-stick springform pan reduce heat to 300°F/150°C.

CRUST
1 cup graham cracker crumbs   3 tablespoons sugar
3 tablespoons butter, melted

FILLING
5 (8-ounce) packages cream cheese, softened   3 tablespoons flour
1 cup sugar   1 cup sour cream
1 tablespoon vanilla   4 eggs

TOPPING
1½ (3½-ounce) choco blanc chocolate bars,   ½ teaspoon instant coffee
    broken into ½-inch pieces   1 teaspoon light corn syrup
3 tablespoons hot water   Chocolate curls, optional

CRUST: Preheat oven to 325°F/160°C.

Wrap the outside of a (9-inch) springform pan in aluminum foil. Grease pan.

In a medium bowl, combine graham cracker crumbs, melted butter and sugar. Press mixture evenly into prepared pan. Bake for 10 minutes.

FILLING: In the bowl of a mixer fitted with a flat beater, beat cream cheese, sugar, vanilla and flour. Add sour cream and mix well. Add eggs, one at a time, mix until just combined.

Pour filling into crust. Place springform in a large roasting pan and place in oven. Pour boiling water into roasting pan to come half way up side of springform pan. Bake for 1 hour and 10 minutes. Raise heat to 350°F/180°C and bake for an additional 20 minutes.

Carefully remove springform pan from water. Loosen cheesecake from sides of pan. Cool to room temperature. Refrigerate for 2 to 4 hours.

TOPPING: In a medium saucepan over low heat, combine and melt chocolate bars, hot water, instant coffee and corn syrup. Stir until smooth. Pour over cooled cheesecake. Garnish with chocolate curls if desired.

Preparation Time: 25 minutes
Cook Time: 1 hour 40 minutes
Chill Time: 2 to 4 hours
Experience Level: Beginner

CHOCOLATE CHEESECAKE

DAIRY   SERVES 10

Dark, rich and creamy, you will want to eat the whole thing yourself.

CRUST
1½ cups graham cracker crumbs   ⅓ cup butter, melted
⅓ cup sugar

CHEESECAKE
2 (8-ounce) packages cream cheese, softened   1 teaspoon vanilla
1¼ cups sugar   2 eggs
⅓ cup cocoa

TOPPING
1 cup sour cream   1 teaspoon vanilla
2 tablespoons sugar

CRUST: In a medium bowl combine graham cracker crumbs, sugar, and butter. Grease a (9-inch) springform pan. Evenly coat the bottom of pan with crust mixture. Set aside.

Preheat oven to 375°F/190°C.

CHOCOLATE CHEESECAKE: In the bowl of a mixer fitted with a flat beater, cream together cream cheese, sugar, cocoa and vanilla. Add eggs and mix to combine. Pour into prepared crust and bake for 25 minutes. Let cool 15 minutes.

TOPPING: Raise oven temperature to 425°F/220°C.

In a small bowl mix together sour cream, sugar and vanilla. Place on top of cheesecake and bake for 10 minutes.

Preparation Time: 20 Minutes
Cook Time: 35 minutes
Experience Level: Beginner

CRUMB CAKE WITH CREAM FILLING

DAIRY   SERVES 8

The custard filling for this cake needs refrigeration. If you are short on space in the refrigerator, store cake covered on the counter. Assemble 2 hours before serving, when pulling your main course food out to heat.

CAKE
½ cup margarine at room temperature
½ cup sugar
2 eggs

1 teaspoon vanilla
2¼ cups self-rising flour

CREAM FILLING
8 ounces sour cream
1 cup sugar
1 teaspoon vanilla

½ cup milk
1 package instant vanilla pudding
8 ounces heavy cream

CAKE: Preheat oven to 350°F/180°C.

Prepare a greased deep dish pie pan or (10-inch) straight sided pie pan and another available pan for baking cake for crumbs.

In the bowl of a mixer fitted with a flat beater, on medium speed, cream together margarine and sugar. Add eggs and vanilla. Mix to combine. Add flour and mix until a sticky dough is formed. Spread ⅔ of batter into prepared deep dish pie pan. Pour remaining batter into other prepared pan. Bake both pans at the same time in preheated oven for 20 minutes. Cool completely.

CREAM FILLING: In a medium bowl, using a wooden spoon mix together sour cream, sugar, vanilla, milk and instant pudding. Stir in heavy cream. Pour onto cake in deep dish pie pan.

Crumble cake in other pan to consistency of coarse crumbs. Sprinkle cream filling with cake crumbs. Refrigerate at least 2 hours before serving.

Preparation Time: 15 minutes
Cook Time: 20 minutes
Cool Time: 3 hours
Experience Level: Beginner

Chocolate Wrapped Fudge Cake

DAIRY   SERVES 16 TO 20

Decorating this cake is as simple as wrapping a present and making a bow. The topping is a dough that rolls out like clay and is easy to work with.

WHITE CHOCOLATE DOUGH
12 ounces white chocolate, chopped or white chocolate chips

7 tablespoons light corn syrup

DARK CHOCOLATE DOUGH
1 cup semi-sweet chocolate chips

¼ cup light corn syrup

CHOCOLATE CAKE
⅓ cup plus 1 tablespoon cocoa
2 tablespoons margarine, softened
½ cup boiling water
1 teaspoon vanilla

6 eggs, separated
¾ cup sugar, divided
2 tablespoons flour

WHITE CHOCOLATE FROSTING
8 ounces white chocolate, chopped or white chocolate chips
¼ cup whipping cream
½ cup margarine, softened

2 egg yolks, pasteurized if available, if not place in double boiler and slightly warm yolks
1 tablespoon chocolate liqueur

WHITE CHOCOLATE DOUGH: In the top of a double boiler over medium heat, melt white chocolate and syrup. Stir with a heat-proof rubber spatula until smooth, about 5 minutes. Transfer to a bowl. Place a piece of plastic wrap directly on the surface of the chocolate mixture. Refrigerate at least 4 hours until dough is firm. Bring to room temperature before using.

DARK CHOCOLATE DOUGH: In the top of a double boiler, melt chocolate chips and syrup. Stir with a heat proof rubber spatula until smooth, about 5 minutes. Transfer to a bowl. Place a piece of plastic wrap directly on the surface of the chocolate mixture. Let stand in a cool place for 4 to 8 hours or until a soft, shiny, pliable dough is formed. Do not refrigerate.

CHOCOLATE CAKE: Preheat oven to 350°F/180°C. Line a (15x10-inch) jelly-roll pan with parchment paper extending parchment over short ends of pan. Grease and flour.

In a small bowl stir together cocoa, margarine, boiling water and vanilla.

In the bowl of a mixer fitted with a whisk, on high speed, beat egg yolks with ½ cup sugar until thick and lemon colored, about 4 minutes. Add chocolate mixture and flour. Mix on low speed until combined.

In a clean bowl with clean beaters, beat egg whites until soft peaks form. Slowly add remaining ¼ cup sugar, beating until stiff peaks form. Stir a bit of whites into chocolate mixture to lighten. Fold in remaining whites until no white appears in mixture. Pour into prepared pan and spread batter so top is level.

Bake for 20 to 24 minutes or until toothpick inserted in center comes out clean. Cool in pan on wire rack.

WHITE CHOCOLATE FROSTING: In a double boiler melt white chocolate with cream, stirring until smooth.

In the bowl of a mixer fitted with a flat beater, on medium speed, cream margarine until light. Add

yolks one at a time, mixing until light and fluffy. Add chocolate mixture and liqueur on low speed until combined. If frosting is thin refrigerate for 30 minutes to thicken.

ASSEMBLY: Prepare a piece of cardboard 5x10-inches long. Cut a piece of parchment paper a little bigger than cardboard, fold over edges and tape underneath. Remove cake from pan by placing a large cutting board on top of cake. Flip and place on counter. Remove paper carefully. Trim edges of cake and cut into 3 sections 5-inches wide. Place 1 section of cake on parchment covered cardboard. Spread with half of frosting. Top with another section of cake. Spread with remaining frosting. Top with third layer of cake. Refrigerate until firm.

WRAPPING THE CAKE: Divide white chocolate dough in half. With a rolling pin, roll one half between 2 sheets of wax paper until about ¼-inch thick. If dough is too thick place in microwave oven for 2 seconds and roll. Place dough over half of cake, trimming edges to be even with bottom of cake. Fold in corners like wrapping paper. Repeat with remaining half of dough to cover second half of cake.

Roll out dark chocolate between 2 sheets of waxed paper until about ¼-inch thick. Again, if dough is too thick place in microwave oven for 2 seconds and roll. If dough is still too thick, repeat process. If dough is too sticky to pull off paper, let stand until dough becomes firm. Cut dough into strips about 1-inch wide. Wrap one strip around the width of cake, covering seam of the white chocolate dough. Wrap another strip around the length of the cake. Top the dark chocolate with thinner strips of white chocolate dough if desired. Make bows by forming loops of dark chocolate dough and white chocolate dough. Press gently into center of cake. Refrigerate until ready to serve. To serve, cut in thin slices.

Preparation Time: 1 hour 15 minutes
Cook Time: 25 minutes
Chill Time: 8 hours
Experience Level: Advanced

*C*AKE *C*ONSTRUCTION

TORTING THE CAKE:

Torting a cake is the process in which you can bake 1 cake and divide it in half or thirds to make a layer cake.

To prepare the cake for filling, remove dome from top of cake to form an even surface. Torte cake by marking cake with a knife, evenly spaced on cake (photo 1). Use a serrated bread knife or a cake leveler and slice cake across by slicing around the outside of the cake in a circular motion continuing until the knife cuts through the cake completely. A rotating turntable comes in handy to torte the cake.

Carefully lift up a small enough section of cake so that the edge of the cake board will be in between the bottom of the top layer and the top of the next layer (photo 2). Slide cake board underneath the top layer while guiding it on the cake board gently with the other hand. Repeat with next layer.

Each layer of cake will be on its own cake board. The bottom layer of cake will now serve as the top layer of your cake due to its smooth uncut and even surface which was on the bottom of the pan. Place a cake board on top of this layer and flip it over to expose the flat bottom.

Prepare decorating bag by placing the coupler in the bag according to manufacturers directions. Fold top of bag over. Using a spatula or large spoon, scoop frosting into bag. Flip the top of the bag back up. Grasp the bag close to the frosting and twist the bag between the thumb and forefinger. Place the other finger around the center of the bag. The thumb and forefinger will serve to hold the bag closed and the other finger around the center of the bag will control the squeezing of the bag. The more pressure you exert on the bag will control how quickly the frosting comes out of the bag. This requires a little practice but once you get control of the decorating bag, the more professional your cake will look.

FILLING THE CAKE:

To keep layers moist and preserve the cake it is helpful to use cake syrup on each layer. Flavors and liqueur can be added to enhance the taste. Prepare cake syrup in advance, cooled in time for cake construction.

2 cups sugar **4 cups water**

In a medium saucepan combine sugar and water. Place over medium heat until syrup comes to a boil. Remove from heat. Cover and set aside to cool. Keep refrigerated for up to 10 weeks in a covered container.

Brush the first layer with cake syrup using a pastry brush.

Place a ring of frosting around the perimeter of the cake (photo 3). One hand should squeeze out the frosting while the other hand slowly turns the turntable. If you turn the turntable too quickly, while not exerting enough pressure on the bag, the ring of frosting will thin out and break before completing the circle. If you turn the turntable too slowly while exerting too much pressure on the decorating bag, the line will be uneven and bumpy. This isn't difficult but will require a little practice.

Place a large spoonful of frosting, pudding or jam inside the ring of frosting, make sure the ring is not broken or the filling will leak out of the cake. The ring serves as a dam for the filling.

Place the next cake layer on top of the first, using one swift motion, hold the cake board in one hand and slide cake onto bottom layer while at the same time pulling the cake board away (photo 4). Do not push the cake, merely guide it with your hand. Do not allow cake board to touch the layer below it while pulling away or you may wipe away the frosting. Repeat with each layer.

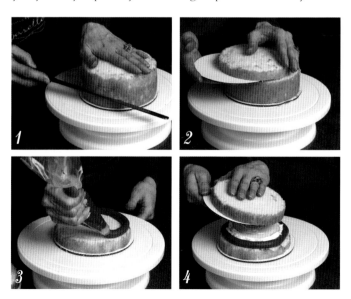

For top layer brush with cake syrup but do not frost at this time. Place cake in refrigerator for about 1½ hours to allow the frosting to chill and become firm.

When cake has chilled sufficiently, place a large amount of frosting on top (photo 5). Using an offset spatula with a rocking motion, carefully spread frosting over the top surface of cake while letting frosting go over sides (photo 6). Do not lift spatula from the cake itself or you will mix crumbs into frosting which is unsightly. Rather, lift spatula from cake by sliding it back into frosting and sliding it off cake. Continue spreading frosting on the sides in the same manner until the cake is completely covered.

To smooth out frosting, fill a pan with steaming water. Heat offset spatula in water, wipe off spatula to dry slightly. Allow flat blade of angled spatula to slide against cake with very slight amount of pressure, while at the same time turning the turntable with the other hand (photo 7). Keep dipping the knife into the water, then drying it, to keep the blade warm until the cake is completely smooth.

DECORATING THE CAKE:

FOR VINES: Attach tip #4 to coupler on decorating bag. Squeeze bag while slowly moving around to make vines.

FOR FLOWERS: Attach tip #102 to coupler on decorating bag. Position bag so opening is face down onto the cake with the wide end of tip at top. Hold bag in position while applying pressure to bag. Icing will build up to a small arch. At this point stop pressure (photo 8), press down tip and remove tip from cake. Repeat this with bag facing slightly to the left of the first petal. Repeat this again to the right of the first petal.

FOR LEAVES: Attach tip #352 to coupler on decorating bag. Squeeze out leaves by holding the bag steady as the frosting builds up, Stop pressure and quickly jerk bag away leaving a point.

BEAD BORDER: Finish cake with a bead boarder, using tip #10. Squeeze bag without moving away until a ball of frosting builds up. Stop pressure and pull bag away by tilting the bag down and away. Repeat the next ball on the tail of the first all around cake (photo 9).

TO SERVE: Keep cake refrigerated until about 1 hour before serving. Dip cake knife in water between each cut to produce even and clean slices.

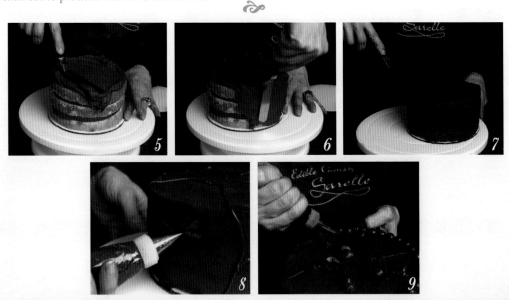

DESSERTS
AND PIES

Chocolate Indulgence

DAIRY OR PARVE   **SERVES 6**

Unmolding these chocolate indulgences can be tricky if the ramekins are not adequately greased and sugared. Place dessert plate onto hot ramekin and carefully flip. Place chocolate square on top and bring to the table in time for your guests to enjoy the melted chocolate.

CAKE

1⅓ cups milk chocolate chips or semi-sweet chocolate chips

6 tablespoons butter or margarine, cut into ½-inch pieces

½ cup flour

½ cup plus 2 tablespoons sugar

1 teaspoon salt

4 eggs

1 tablespoon butter or margarine, to grease ramekins with

2 teaspoons sugar, to sugar ramekins with

TOPPING

6 (1-ounce) milk or semi-sweet chocolate squares

6 strawberries sliced ¾ of the way to hull and fan out

CAKE: In a medium saucepan over medium-low heat, melt the chocolate and butter. Stir constantly until combined and melted. Remove from heat.

In the bowl of a mixer, fitted with a flat beater, combine flour, sugar and salt on medium speed. Add eggs, 1 at a time, beating until a pale yellow color and dissolving ribbons are formed when batter is lifted, about 5 minutes. Fold batter into chocolate mixture. Refrigerate for 30 minutes.

Grease ramekins very well with butter and sprinkle generously with sugar.

Preheat oven to 375°F/190°C.

15 minutes before serving time, divide chilled batter between the 6 ramekins. Bake for 15 minutes or until top is set and tester comes out wet.

TOPPING: Invert individual hot cakes onto dessert plates. Place chocolate square on top of each cake. Place strawberry on top of chocolate. Serve immediately.

Preparation Time: 15 minutes
Chill Time: 30 minutes
Cook Time: 20 minutes
Experience Level: Intermediate

CHOCOLATE CREAM PIE

PARVE   SERVES 8

¾ cup sugar

3 tablespoons flour

1 tablespoon cornstarch

⅛ teaspoon salt

1½ cups soy milk or non-dairy creamer

3 egg yolks, lightly beaten

¼ cup unsweetened chocolate, melted

2 tablespoons margarine

1 teaspoon vanilla

1 teaspoon chocolate or coffee liqueur, optional

Graham cracker crust or prebaked pie crust

Sweetened whipped cream, optional garnish

In a medium saucepan over medium heat, combine sugar, flour, cornstarch and salt. Stir in soy milk, egg yolks and melted chocolate. Add margarine and stir constantly, until mixture is thick and bubbling. Remove from heat and mix in vanilla and liqueur. Pour into prepared crust. Cool to room temperature. Refrigerate at least 2 hours.

Garnish with sweetened whipped cream.

Preparation Time: 10 minutes
Cook Time: 10 minutes
Chill Time: 2 hours
Experience Level: Beginner

HIDDEN TREASURE CUPS

PARVE   SERVES 6

The hidden treasure is a molten chocolate center. Keep the custard cups warm on a warming plate or blech on Friday night for a hot dessert.

8 ounces semi-sweet chocolate

½ cup margarine

4 eggs

½ cup sugar

3 tablespoons prepared coffee or water

2 tablespoons flour

Confectioners' sugar

Preheat oven to 400°F/200°C.

Prepare 6 greased and lightly floured custard cups.

Melt chocolate with margarine in microwave for 2 minutes on high power. Stir and set aside.

In the bowl of a mixer fitted with a flat beater, beat eggs, sugar and coffee at high speed until thick, about 6 minutes. Add flour and chocolate mixture. Beat until just combined. Pour into prepared custard cups. Place on a jelly-roll pan.

Bake for 11 to 15 minutes or until puffed and crusted, but soft in center. Cool 7 minutes. Sprinkle with confectioners' sugar and serve.

Preparation Time: 10 minutes
Cook Time: 11 to 15 minutes
Experience Level: Beginner

Chocolate Covered Peanut Butter Pie

PARVE   SERVES 16

- 1½ cups crushed chocolate sandwich cookies
- 1 cup peanut butter, divided, spray measuring cups with non-stick cooking spray for easy release
- 4 ounces non-dairy cream cheese
- ¾ cup confectioners' sugar
- 2 tablespoons non-dairy creamer
- 2 tablespoons chopped peanuts
- 3 (8-ounce) cartons non-dairy whipping cream, divided
- 6 ounces semi-sweet chocolate chips

Preheat oven to 350°F/180°C. Prepare a greased (9-inch) springform pan.

In a medium bowl combine cookie crumbs with ¼ cup peanut butter. Press into prepared pan. Bake for 8 to 10 minutes.

In the bowl of a mixer fitted with a flat beater, whip cream cheese and confectioners' sugar until smooth. Add remaining ¾ cup peanut butter, non-dairy creamer and nuts, whip for 1 minute on medium speed. Set aside.

Whip 2 cartons plus ¼ cup of whipping cream. Fold into peanut butter mixture. Pour into prepared crust. Refrigerate for at least 2 hours or until pie is set.

In a small saucepan over medium heat, melt chocolate chips with ¾ cup of whipping cream to make ganache. Remove from heat and cool for 2 minutes, stirring constantly.

When pie is set remove springform ring. Place pie on a wire rack, over a baking sheet lined with wax or parchment paper. Pour chocolate ganache over pie covering top and sides completely. Refrigerate 2 hours until chocolate is set.

Preparation Time: 35 minutes
Cook Time: 8 to 10 minutes
Chill Time: 4 hours
Experience Level: Intermediate

Ceramic teapots date back to the nineteenth century and are available in a wide variety of shapes, patterns and styles. They are a design inspiration for objects from ceramic trivets to textiles.

DEEP CHOCOLATE DECADENT TORTE

PARVE   SERVES 12

This is a very rich and dense chocolate torte. No frosting is needed but if one desires, the Death by Chocolate Pudding on page 317 works well. Just let the pudding set for 4 to 6 hours and frost.

To make this a 2 layer torte double the recipe and bake in 2 (9-inch) springform pans. Cool completely and frost with the pudding. Use optional raspberry mixture as a topping beneath the frosting or as a glaze between the layers of the 2 tortes.

TORTE

12 ounces good quality semi-sweet chocolate chips	1½ cups sugar
1 cup margarine	¼ cup flour
5 eggs	1 teaspoon baking powder
	6 to 8 ounces semi-sweet chocolate chips

RASPBERRY MIXTURE, OPTIONAL FOR UNDER FROSTING FOR 2 LAYER TORTE

¼ cup raspberry jam	1 tablespoon brandy

TORTE: Preheat oven to 350°F/180°C.

Prepare a 9-inch springform pan lined with parchment paper and grease bottom and sides of pan.

In a medium saucepan over medium-low heat melt chocolate and margarine together. Remove from heat, set aside.

In the bowl of a mixer fitted with a flat beater, beat eggs and sugar on medium speed. In a small bowl stir together flour and baking powder. Add to the egg and sugar mixture. Add melted chocolate and mix on slow speed until well combined. Add remaining chocolate chips and pour into greased pan.

Bake for 30 minutes or until toothpick inserted into torte approximately 1-inch from side of pan, not in center, comes out clean. Remove from oven. Cool on a wire rack for at least 30 minutes before releasing from pan.

If glazing or frosting, peel off upper crust and discard i.e. eat. Flip over, remove parchment paper and use top as bottom.

RASPBERRY MIXTURE FOR 2 LAYER OPTION: In a small saucepan, over low heat, mix raspberry jam with brandy and bring to a simmer. Remove from heat and cool for about 5 minutes. Brush over both layers and let stand 10 minutes. Frost with cooled Death by Chocolate Pudding.

Preparation Time: 15 minutes
Cook Time: 30 minutes
Experience Level: Intermediate

Tiny Chocolate Tarts
with Cocoa Crusts

DAIRY OR PARVE

YIELD 20 PIECES

COCOA CRUSTS
1 cup flour

3 tablespoons unsweetened cocoa

3 tablespoons confectioners' sugar

⅓ cup cold butter or margarine

1 egg

1½ teaspoons water

½ teaspoon vanilla

FILLING
¼ cup fancy seedless raspberry jam or preserves

4 ounces semi-sweet chocolate chips

2 tablespoons vanilla sugar

2 tablespoons butter or margarine

½ cup whipping cream or non-dairy whipping cream

GARNISH, OPTIONAL
Whipped cream

20 fresh raspberries

COCOA CRUSTS: Preheat oven to 350°F/180°C.

In a medium bowl combine flour, cocoa and confectioners' sugar. Using a pastry blender or 2 knives cut butter into mixture until it resembles coarse crumbs. In a small bowl, beat together egg with water and vanilla until well blended. Pour egg mixture into flour mixture, stirring with a fork until dough clings together. Using hands, knead dough into a smooth ball. Do not overwork dough.

Roll dough into a log and divide into 4 equal pieces. Divide each into 5 (1-inch) balls. Press down and up sides of 20 ungreased (1¾-inch) mini muffin pans. Bake until lightly browned and firm to touch, about 10 to 15 minutes.

Cool in pans on wire racks. Remove shells from muffin pans.

FILLING: Spoon a scant ½ teaspoon of jam into each tart.

In a small saucepan over low heat, combine chocolate, vanilla sugar and butter. Heat, stirring until chocolate and butter melt and sugar is dissolved. Add whipping cream, raise heat to medium and stir until mixture is hot to the touch, about 2 to 3 minutes. Remove from heat. Let stand until cooled to room temperature, about 20 minutes.

Spoon about ½ tablespoon of chocolate filling into each tart shell. Let stand at room temperature until filling is set.

GARNISH: This optional garnish gives chocolate tarts a professional look. Top each mini tart with a dollop of whipped cream and a fresh raspberry.

Preparation Time: 30 minutes
Cook Time: 15 minutes
Chill Time: 1 hour
Experience Level: Intermediate

Death by Chocolate Pudding

DAIRY OR PARVE   **YIELD 8 TO 12 SMALL DESSERTS**

A very intense dessert, a few ounces can satisfy even the most die hard chocoholic. Recipe can easily be doubled to serve a large crowd. Heavy cream or non-dairy whipping cream yield a more dense pudding then soy milk, but all are useable. Can be topped with strawberries, blueberries and whipped cream for a patriotic look or just blueberries and whipped cream for the Israeli look. The taste contrast goes very well with the intense flavor of the chocolate.

- 12 ounces heavy cream or non-dairy whipping cream or high fat soy milk,
- 12 ounces good quality semi-sweet chocolate chips
- 2 egg yolks slightly beaten
- 4 tablespoons butter or margarine, cut into pieces, at room temperature
- 1½ tablespoons brandy or to taste

In a medium saucepan over medium flame, heat cream to just before boiling. Remove from heat. Add chocolate chips and let sit for 1 minute before stirring. Stir until chocolate melts.

Temper egg yolks by mixing 2 to 3 tablespoons of hot chocolate mixture into egg yolks. Pour egg yolks into chocolate and stir well. Add margarine stirring until dissolved. Add brandy and stir until combined.

Pour into small dessert cups and chill for 4 to 6 hours or overnight.

Preparation Time: 5 minutes
Cook Time: 5 minutes
Chill Time: 4 to 6 hours or overnight
Experience Level: Beginner

Milky Way Tarts

DAIRY OR PARVE   **SERVES 6**

These tarts are out of this world. Set aside time to make them. Only 40 minutes of preparation time is needed, but it is divided by several hours of chill time.

CHOCOLATE GANACHE FILLING
- 6 ounces milk or semi-sweet chocolate chips
- 12 ounces heavy cream or non-dairy whipping cream

SUGAR DOUGH SHELL
- 1 cup flour
- 1 teaspoon baking powder
- ¼ cup cocoa
- ½ cup butter or margarine softened
- ½ cup confectioners' sugar
- 1 extra large egg

CARAMEL

½ cup sugar

¼ cup heavy cream or non-dairy whipping cream

¼ cup butter or margarine

CHOCOLATE GANACHE FILLING: Place chocolate chips in a medium heat proof bowl. In a small saucepan over low heat, bring cream to just under a boil. Pour over chocolate chips and let sit for one minute. Gently stir until chocolate is melted and smooth. Refrigerate for 2 to 3 hours until cool and firm.

SUGAR DOUGH SHELL: Prepare 6 (4-inch) parchment lined tartlet pans, set aside. Make a template by cutting a paper circle ½-inch larger than tartlet pan. Use as a pattern to cut dough into circles for crust.

In a medium bowl combine flour, baking powder and cocoa, set aside.

In the bowl of a mixer fitted with a metal whisk, cream together butter and confectioners' sugar on medium speed. Scrape down the sides of bowl and beaters until sugar is well incorporated. Add egg and beat for 1 to 2 minutes. The batter will look like scrambled eggs. Slowly add the flour and cocoa mixture and mix at medium speed until a soft dough is formed, approximately 2 minutes. Form into a ball, wrap in plastic wrap and refrigerate for 15 minutes.

On a lightly floured work surface using a rolling pin, quickly roll out dough to form a 15x9-inch rectangle. Dough should be ⅛-inch thick or slightly thinner. Using paper template cut 6 circles out of dough. If dough seems difficult to work with, refrigerate for an additional 15 minutes. Gently press each circle of dough into bottom and up the sides of prepared tartlet pans. Using a fork, poke a few holes in the bottom of each shell. Freeze for about 10 minutes or refrigerate for 1 hour.

Preheat oven to 350°F/180°C.

Place tartlet pans on a baking sheet and bake for 10 to 12 minutes. Remove and cool completely on wire racks. When cool remove dough from tartlet pans and set aside.

CARAMEL: In a small saucepan over medium-low flame, heat sugar until melted, mixing occasionally with a wooden spoon. It should take about 5 minutes to dissolve and become a caramel liquid. In a small saucepan over medium heat, melt butter and cream together. When sugar caramelizes, slowly add melted cream and butter and cook for 2 minutes, stirring occasionally with a wooden spoon. If there are clumps of sugar break up as it dissolves. Pour into a heat-proof bowl and refrigerate for 30 minutes or until semi soft. If caramel hardens simply microwave on high for 30 seconds and stir until re-dissolved.

ASSEMBLY: Place tart shells on a baking pan. Stir the caramel a few times. Spoon 2 tablespoons of caramel into each tart pan to coat bottoms and sides tilting the shells as necessary. Mix the chocolate ganache to loosen a bit, spoon 2 to 3 tablespoons into each tart shell being careful not to disturb the caramel. Refrigerate for about 15 minutes.

Preparation Time: 40 minutes
Cook Time: 20 minutes
Chill Time: 3 to 4 hours
Experience Level: Advanced

Peanut Butter Fudge

DAIRY OR PARVE   **SERVES 12**

PEANUT BUTTER LAYER

½ cup creamy peanut butter

3 tablespoons margarine

¼ cup light corn syrup

2 tablespoons water

2 teaspoons vanilla

4 cups confectioners' sugar

CHOCOLATE LAYER

⅔ cup whipping cream or non-dairy
   whipping cream

6 ounces semi-sweet chocolate, chopped

GLAZE

¾ to 1 cup confectioners' sugar

1 tablespoon margarine, melted

2 teaspoons milk or non-dairy creamer

GARNISH

Unsalted peanuts, optional

Line and grease an (8x8-inch) baking pan, set aside.

PEANUT BUTTER LAYER: In a medium saucepan over low heat, combine peanut butter and margarine until melted. Stir in corn syrup, water and vanilla. Remove from heat. Gradually stir in confectioners' sugar until blended. Knead mixture together, about 2 minutes until well combined. Turn into prepared pan. Level mixture to cover pan evenly. Let cool. Score top with a fork.

CHOCOLATE LAYER: In a small saucepan over low flame, heat cream just until tiny bubbles appear around edge of pan. Remove from heat. Add chocolate and let stand for 30 seconds. Stir until smooth. Pour chocolate over peanut butter layer, spreading to cover. Sprinkle evenly with peanuts if desired. Refrigerate until just firm, about 1 hour. Can be kept refrigerated, covered for up to 2 weeks.

Preparation Time: 25 minutes
Cook Time: 10 minutes
Experience Level: Beginner

Praline Truffles

PARVE   **YIELD APPROXIMATELY 72 (1-INCH) TRUFFLES**

12 ounces ground hazelnuts

4 (3½-ounce) bars truffle filled Swiss dark
   or bittersweet chocolate

1 cup confectioners' sugar

Place hazelnuts in the bowl of a food processor, process for 5 minutes until a paste is formed.

In the top of a double boiler melt chocolate. Remove from heat. Add nuts and sugar, mix well. Place in pastry bag without a tip or place in a large ziploc bag. Snip off end of bag and squeeze into chocolate molds. Allow to set. Pop out and store in an airtight container.

Preparation Time: 15 minutes
Cook Time: 5 minutes
Experience Level: Beginner

Mini Chocolate Bon Bons

PARVE   **YIELD 36 PIECES**

BON BONS

6 ounces semi-sweet chocolate, chopped

5 tablespoons margarine

½ cup sugar

2 eggs

½ cup flour

½ teaspoon baking powder

1 teaspoon vanilla

1 cup ground almonds or hazelnuts

FROSTING

½ cup non-dairy whipping cream

¾ cup sugar

3 ounces unsweetened chocolate, chopped

1 egg yolk

2 tablespoons margarine

1 teaspoon vanilla

Sliced almonds, optional garnish

BON BONS: Preheat oven to 375°F/190°C.

Prepare 36 mini muffin tins with liners.

In a medium saucepan over medium heat, combine chocolate with margarine. Stir until melted. Remove from heat. Add sugar, eggs, flour, baking powder, vanilla and almonds. Spoon halfway up mini muffin liners. Bake for 8 minutes.

FROSTING: In a medium saucepan over medium heat, bring whipping cream and sugar to a boil. Boil for 5 minutes, stir in chocolate. Remove from heat. In a small bowl, beat egg yolk with a little of the mixture from saucepan. Add to saucepan with margarine and vanilla. Stir until combined.

Frost bon bons and place sliced almonds on top for garnish.

Preparation Time: 20 minutes
Cook Time: 15 minutes
Experience Level: Intermediate

MAYAN HOT CHOCOLATE WITH CHILI PEPPERS

DAIRY OR PARVE   SERVES 16

A pleasure on a cold winter's night served in a demitasse cup with dessert. This South American hot chocolate drink has a balance of sweet chocolate with the heat of chili water. Adjust the heat level to your taste by using more or less of the pepper infused liquid.

1 fresh Hungarian Hot chili pepper, halved and seeded

2 cups water

5 cups milk or high fat soy milk

1 vanilla bean, split lengthwise or 1 teaspoon pure vanilla extract

2 cinnamon sticks

8 ounces good quality bittersweet chocolate, chopped

2 tablespoons sugar or honey, to taste

1 tablespoon finely ground almonds or hazelnuts

In a medium saucepan over medium heat, place chili pepper and water. Bring to a boil. Cook until liquid has been reduced to 1 cup, approximately 15 minutes. Strain chili pepper and seeds, reserve liquid.

In medium saucepan combine milk, vanilla bean and cinnamon sticks. Cook over medium heat until bubbles appear around edge of pan. Reduce heat to low. Add chocolate and sugar. Whisk oceasionally until chocolate is melted and sugar dissolves, about 5 minutes. Continue to simmer over a low flame for an additional 10 minutes.

Turn off heat, remove vanilla bean and cinnamon sticks. Stir in ground nuts. Add chili pepper liquid a little at a time until desired heat is reached.

Serve hot.

Preparation Time: 20 minutes
Cook Time: 15 minutes
Experience Level: Intermediate

PEACH APRICOT COBBLER WITH SPICED WHIPPED CREAM

PARVE OR DAIRY   **SERVES 8**

This is a dessert you'll find yourself making mid-winter when craving fresh summer fruits. Canned peaches and apricots make this a year round favorite.

COBBLER
½ cup sugar
2 tablespoons cornstarch
1 (1-pound 13-ounce) can sliced peaches, drained, ½ cup juice reserved

1 (10½-ounce) can apricot halves, drained, ½ cup juice reserved
1 tablespoon margarine
½ teaspoon cinnamon
¼ teaspoon nutmeg

TOPPING
½ cup flour
½ cup sugar
¾ teaspoon baking powder

½ teaspoon salt
2 tablespoons margarine, softened
1 large egg

WHIPPED CREAM
1 cup non-dairy whipping cream or heavy whipping cream

2 tablespoons honey
½ teaspoon cinnamon

COBBLER: Preheat oven to 400°F/200°C.

In a medium saucepan over medium heat, combine sugar and cornstarch. Stir in reserved peach and apricot juices. Cook over medium heat, stirring constantly until mixture boils and thickens, about 2 minutes. Remove from heat. Stir in margarine, cinnamon and nutmeg. Add peaches and apricots. Spoon mixture into a (1½-quart) casserole dish.

TOPPING: In a small bowl combine flour, sugar, baking powder, salt, margarine and egg. Spoon topping over fruit mixture in casserole.

Bake cobbler until topping is lightly golden, about 30 minutes. Place on a wire rack to cool slightly.

WHIPPED CREAM: In the bowl of a mixer fitted with whisk attachment, on medium speed, beat together cream, honey and cinnamon until soft peaks form.

Serve cobbler warm, topped with spiced whipped cream.

Preparation Time: 15 minutes
Cook Time: 35 minutes
Experience Level: Beginner

STRAWBERRY FILLED ALMOND PUFFS

DAIRY   **SERVES 12**

PUFFS
1 cup water
½ cup butter or margarine
½ cup almond paste

¼ teaspoon salt
1 cup flour
4 eggs

FILLING
1 cup whipping cream
2 tablespoons confectioners' sugar
¼ teaspoon almond extract or 2 tablespoons
   amaretto

½ cup sour cream
3 cups strawberries, sliced
Confectioners' sugar, optional

PUFFS: In a medium saucepan, combine water, butter, almond paste and salt. Bring mixture to a boil. Stir until butter melts. Add flour all at once, stirring vigorously. Cook until mixture forms a ball that doesn't separate. Remove from heat and cool for 10 minutes.

Preheat oven to 400°F/200°C.

Prepare a greased (15x10-inch) jelly-roll pan.

Add eggs to dough, one at a time, beating with a wooden spoon after each addition for 1 to 2 minutes until smooth. Drop dough into 12 mounds 3-inches apart on prepared pan. Bake for 25 to 30 minutes or until golden and firm. Remove from pan and cool on wire rack.

FILLING: In the bowl of a mixer fitted with a whisk, combine whipping cream, confectioners' sugar and almond extract. Beat until stiff peaks form. Fold in sour cream. Cover and refrigerate.

To serve, cut off top quarter of each puff, reserve. Remove any soft dough from middle with a fork. Place a heaping tablespoon of cream into each puff. Top each with about ¼ cup of strawberries. Replace tops of puffs. If desired cover and chill for 2 hours before serving. Sift confectioners' sugar over tops before serving, if desired.

Preparation Time: 30 minutes
Cook Time: 25 minutes
Chill Time: 2 hours
Experience Level: Intermediate

Poached Pears Stuffed with Chocolate Sauce

DAIRY OR PARVE   **SERVES 6**

Choose pears with pleasing shapes for this beautiful and elegant dessert.

POACHED PEARS

1 lemon, zest and juice	6 cups water
2 cups sugar	2 teaspoons vanilla
1½ cups dry white wine	6 large, firm, ripe Bartlett pears

CHOCOLATE SAUCE

16 ounces good quality semi-sweet chocolate, coarsely chopped or chocolate chips	Approximately ½ cup cream or Soy milk with a high fat content

TO SERVE

6 slices prepared pound cake (optional)

POACHED PEARS: Using a vegetable peeler, peel 5 to 6 (1-inch) strips of zest, from lemon. Juice lemon.

In an 8-quart stock pot over medium high-heat place the sugar, wine and water. Mix well. Add zest, lemon juice and vanilla. Stir well to combine ingredients. Cook for 2 minutes to dissolve sugar. Turn off heat.

Slice ⅛-inch off bottom of each pear in order for pears to stand upright. Peel pears leaving stems and a ½-inch diameter around stem intact.

Using a melon baller or zucchini scooper, scoop out core of pears through flat bottom end, leave stem intact.

Place pears in stock pot with hot poaching syrup. Syrup must cover pears completely. Lay a few plain, white paper towels over pears. Place an inverted plate on top of paper towels, this is to keep pears submerged and to prevent discoloring.

Over medium high heat, bring syrup to a boil. Reduce heat to maintain a gentle boil. Poach until a knife can pierce pears easily, about 30 minutes. Remove from heat. Let pears cool for at least 3 hours or refrigerate overnight, submerged in poaching syrup.

CHOCOLATE SAUCE: In a small saucepan over a low flame, melt chocolate. Add cream or Soy milk one tablespoon at a time until it thickens, similar to a mayonnaise like consistency. Remove from flame.

SYRUP: Remove pears from cooking liquid, set aside. Over high heat, uncovered, reduce cooking liquid to about 1 cup, stirring occasionally. Remove from heat, let cool to room temperature.

TO SERVE: Cut a 3-inch diameter circle out of each slice of pound cake. Place on dessert plates.

Fill each pear cavity with chocolate sauce. Place on pound cake circles. Spoon syrup over each pear.

Preparation Time: 30 minutes
Cook Time: 45 minutes
Chill Time: 3 hours
Experience Level: Advanced

APPLE SCOTCH PIE

PARVE   **SERVES 8**

Cooking the apples with brown sugar gives this pie a butterscotch flavor. Serve warm with a scoop of vanilla ice cream for a comforting dessert.

PIE

5 large green apples, peeled and thinly sliced	2 tablespoons sugar
1 cup brown sugar	1 teaspoon vanilla
¼ cup water	3 tablespoons margarine
1 tablespoon lemon juice	1 deep dish pie crust
¼ cup flour	

TOPPING

1¼ cups flour	½ cup margarine, melted
½ cup plus 2 tablespoons sugar	Cinnamon
½ cup plus 2 tablespoons brown sugar	

PIE: In a large saucepan over medium heat place the apples, brown sugar, water and lemon juice. Bring to a boil. Lower heat and simmer for 8 minutes or until apples are tender. Push apples to side of saucepan. Add flour 1 tablespoon at a time, mixing with a fork to avoid lumps. Stir together. Add sugar and cook, stirring over medium-high heat until thickened and boiling. Stir for 1 minute more. Remove from heat, add vanilla and margarine, mix well. Let cool.

Preheat oven to 325°F/160°C.

Pour apple mixture into crust.

TOPPING: In a medium bowl combine flour, sugar, brown sugar and margarine. Sprinkle topping onto apples. Sprinkle with cinnamon. Bake for 45 minutes.

Preparation Time: 20 minutes
Cook Time: 1 hour
Experience Level: Beginner

Apricot Cherry Slab Pie

PARVE   SERVES 25

CRUST
3¼ cups flour
1 teaspoon salt
1 cup shortening

1 egg yolk, lightly beaten
Non-dairy creamer

FILLING
½ cup sugar
3 tablespoons cornstarch
3 (15¼-ounce) cans apricot halves, drained and quartered

1 (16-ounce) can pitted, tart, red cherries, drained

GLAZE
1¼ cups confectioners' sugar
½ teaspoon vanilla

5 to 6 teaspoons non-dairy creamer

CRUST: In a large mixing bowl, stir together flour and salt. Using a pastry blender, cut shortening into flour until mixture resembles coarse crumbs. In a measuring cup, add enough non-dairy creamer to egg yolk to make a total of ¾ cup of liquid. Mix well. Stir egg yolk mixture into flour mixture, mixing well. Set aside ⅓ of the dough.

On a lightly floured surface, or between 2 sheets of plastic wrap, using a rolling pin, roll remaining ⅔ of dough into an 18-inch by 13-inch rectangle. Carefully wrap dough around rolling pin. Unroll into a (15x10-inch) jelly-roll pan. Dough will hang over sides of pan.

Preheat oven to 375°F/190°C.

FILLING: In a large bowl combine sugar and cornstarch. Stir in apricots and cherries to combine. Spoon into prepared crust. Roll remaining dough into a (16x11-inch) rectangle. Carefully place over fruit. Bring dough from lower edges of crust up and over top edges of crust. Seal by pressing down with tines of a fork.

Prick top with a fork all over in a pleasing pattern.

Bake for 40 minutes or until golden brown. Cool in pan on a wire rack.

GLAZE: In a small bowl combine confectioners' sugar, vanilla and enough creamer to make a drizzling consistency. Drizzle over pie. Cut into 2 by 3-inch bars. Serve warm or cool.

Preparation Time: 20 minutes
Cook Time: 40 minutes
Experience Level: Intermediate

Sherry Glazed Grape Tart with Pecan Crust

PARVE   SERVES 8

This picture perfect tart is made with a pecan crust. The dough is simply pushed into a fluted tart pan, ideal for those who prefer not to roll out dough.

CRUST
¼ cup pecans, lightly toasted at 350°F/180°C
    for 5 minutes, cooled
¼ cup brown sugar
1 cup flour

FILLING
½ cup sherry
1 cup grape jelly
½ teaspoon lemon juice

½ cup margarine cut into ½-inch slices
½ teaspoon cinnamon
½ teaspoon ground ginger
¼ teaspoon salt

2 to 3 pounds small red seedless grapes,
    washed, dried and stems discarded

CRUST: Grease a (10-inch) round, fluted tart pan, with a removable bottom.

In the bowl of a food processor, process together the pecans and brown sugar. Pulse until finely ground but not a paste. Add flour, margarine, cinnamon, ginger and salt. Pulse until combined with large clumps.

Turn mixture out onto a clean work surface. Knead for 2 minutes to form a dough. Press dough into tart pan, on bottom and up the sides. Chill for 30 minutes.

Preheat oven to 350°F/180°C. Locate oven rack to lower third of oven.

Bake crust until golden brown, about 25 minutes. Cool completely on a wire rack. When cooled carefully remove sides of pan.

FILLING: In a small saucepan over medium heat, combine sherry and jelly. Stir occasionally. Reduce to 1 cup, about 25 minutes. Remove from heat and stir in lemon juice. Reserve 2 tablespoons of glaze for drizzling over completed tart.

In a large bowl combine sherry mixture, minus 2 tablespoons, with grapes until grapes are well coated. Pour coated grapes into prepared shell.

Before serving drizzle tart with reserved glaze.

Preparation Time: 30 minutes
Cook Time: 45 minutes
Chill Time: 30 minutes
Experience Level: Beginner

Lemon Pudding Cake

DAIRY OR PARVE   **SERVES 9**

During the cooking process this separates into 2 layers. A light and fluffy layer adorns a creamy, rich lemon pudding. The combination is everything you would wish for in a light dessert.

1 cup buttermilk or 1 cup non-dairy creamer
    mixed with 1 tablespoon vinegar
3 eggs, separated
4 tablespoons margarine, melted
⅓ cup lemon juice

1 tablespoon lemon rind
¾ cup sugar, divided
¼ cup flour
⅛ teaspoon salt

Preheat oven to 350°F/180°C.

Prepare a greased (8x8-inch) glass baking dish and a roasting pan large enough to hold baking dish. Prepare boiling water to pour into roasting pan.

In the bowl of a mixer fitted with a flat beater, beat buttermilk, egg yolks, margarine, lemon juice, lemon rind and ½ cup of sugar. Beat in flour and salt until blended.

In the bowl of a mixer fitted with a whisk, beat egg whites until foamy. Slowly add ¼ cup sugar until soft peaks form. Fold whites into lemon mixture ⅓ at a time, until just combined. Pour into prepared baking dish in roasting pan. Place into preheated oven. Carefully pour boiling water into metal pan to come halfway up sides of baking dish. Bake for 35 to 40 minutes, or until top is golden and set. Allow to cool 10 minutes. Serve warm.

Preparation Time: 15 minutes
Cook Time: 35 to 40 minutes
Experience Level: Intermediate

Lemon Freeze

PARVE   SERVES 16

PIE CRUST
1½ cups graham cracker crumbs   ⅓ cup margarine, melted
¼ cup sugar

FILLING
4 pasteurized eggs, separated, at room   ½ cup lemon juice
   temperature   8 ounces non-dairy whipping cream,
1 cup sugar   whipped

PIE CRUST: In a medium bowl combine graham cracker crumbs, sugar and margarine. Push into 2 (8-inch) pie pans or one large loaf pan, to form crust.

FILLING: In the bowl of a mixer fitted with a whisk, beat egg whites until stiff peaks form. In a large bowl combine sugar, egg yolks and lemon juice. Fold in whipped cream. Fold in beaten egg whites. Pour into prepared pie crust. Cover and freeze until hard, about 4 hours.

Preparation Time: 10 minutes
Chill Time: 4 hours
Experience Level: Beginner

Layered Chocolate and Butterscotch Parfait Pie

DAIRY OR PARVE   **SERVES 20**

The ultimate in a dessert maker's repertoire. The butterscotch and mousse layers are outstanding on their own. Divide among parfait glasses or use as filling for a wonderful cream pie.

CRUST
3¼ cups chocolate graham cracker crumbs, about 25 crackers

¼ cup brown sugar
¾ cup butter, melted

CHOCOLATE GANACHE LAYER
6 ounces good quality semi-sweet chocolate, chopped

½ cup heavy cream
2 tablespoons butter

BUTTERSCOTCH LAYER
5 tablespoons butter
¾ cup dark brown sugar
¾ cup heavy cream
2¼ cups milk
⅛ teaspoon salt

¼ cup cornstarch
4 tablespoons water
1 package unflavored gelatin
2 tablespoons boiling water
2 teaspoons vanilla

CHOCOLATE MOUSSE LAYER
8 ounces semi-sweet chocolate, chopped
2 cups heavy cream, divided
2 tablespoons brandy, optional

1 teaspoon vanilla
¼ cup confectioners' sugar

CREAM LAYER
1 cup heavy cream

2 tablespoons brandy, optional

GARNISH
Dark chocolate curls

CRUST: Preheat oven to 350°F/180°C.

Prepare a greased (9-inch) springform pan.

In a medium bowl, mix together graham cracker crumbs and brown sugar. Stir in butter until just combined. Press evenly onto bottom and sides of prepared pan. Bake for 15 minutes in preheated oven until crust browns. Cool and refrigerate.

CHOCOLATE GANACHE: Place chocolate in a medium bowl. In a small saucepan over high heat bring heavy cream and butter to a boil. Pour cream mixture over chocolate. Set aside for 5 minutes. Whisk until smooth. Pour chocolate ganache into prepared crust. Swirl pan to ensure even coverage on sides and bottom. Set aside at room temperature

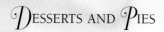

BUTTERSCOTCH LAYER: In a medium saucepan over medium heat, melt butter. Whisk in brown sugar, stirring until melted and bubbly. Lower heat. Gradually add heavy cream and stir until butterscotch is dissolved. Whisk in milk and salt.

In a small bowl, whisk together cornstarch and water. Stir cornstarch mixture into butterscotch mixture. Cook for about 3 to 5 minutes over medium-high heat until mixture thickens. Reduce heat to low, stir briskly and simmer for 1 minute.

In a small bowl combine gelatin and boiling water. Whisk into butterscotch mixture until boiling. Remove from heat and add vanilla, whisk until smooth. Immediately pour over chocolate ganache in pan. Cool until set.

CHOCOLATE MOUSSE: Place chocolate in a medium bowl. In a small saucepan over medium heat, bring ½ cup heavy cream, brandy and vanilla just to a boil. Pour cream mixture over chocolate. Set aside for 5 minutes. Whisk smooth. Cool to room temperature, whisking occasionally.

In the bowl of a mixer fitted with a whisk, beat remaining cream until it holds a soft peak. Sift sugar over whipped cream and continue beating until slightly thicker. Do not over whip cream. Fold ⅓ of cream into chocolate mixture to lighten. Fold in remaining cream. Spread over butterscotch mixture

CREAM: In a clean bowl of a mixer fitted with a clean whisk, beat heavy cream with brandy until it forms soft peaks. Spoon dollops of whipped cream over chocolate mousse layer to cover. Refrigerate until set, about 6 hours.

Decorate with chocolate shavings. Carefully remove springform ring and transfer pie to cake stand.

To make Layered Chocolate and Butterscotch Parfait Pie parve, substitute equal amounts:

margarine for butter

non-dairy whipping cream for heavy cream

soy milk with a high fat content or non-dairy creamer for milk

Does not freeze well.

Preparation Time: 1 hour and 30 minutes
Cook Time: 35 minutes
Chill Time: 7 hours
Experience Level: Advanced

PUMPKIN CUSTARD

DAIRY OR PARVE   SERVES 8

When the children are home for Thanksgiving vacation this is a fun and simple custard to prepare. Use pure maple syrup to enhance the flavor of the pumpkin.

WHIPPED CREAM

1 cup whipping cream or non-dairy   2 tablespoons pure maple syrup
   whipping cream

CUSTARD

1 (15-ounce) can pumpkin   2 heaping teaspoons pumpkin pie spice
6 eggs   2 cups vanilla rice milk
1 cup sugar   8 tablespoons pure maple syrup
1 teaspoon vanilla

WHIPPED CREAM: In the bowl of a mixer fitted with a whisk, beat whipping cream with maple syrup to form stiff peaks. Cover and refrigerate until needed.

CUSTARD: Preheat oven to 325°F/160°C. Place 8 custard cups or ramekins in a roasting pan just large enough to hold ramekins without touching. Prepare boiling water to pour into roasting pan.

In a large bowl whisk together pumpkin, eggs, sugar, vanilla and pumpkin pie spice. Whisk in rice milk. Divide among custard cups. Place in preheated oven. Fill roasting pan with enough water to come half way up the side of custard cups. Bake until custard is softly set in middle, 45 to 50 minutes.

Chill uncovered at least 4 hours. Drizzle each custard with 1 tablespoon pure maple syrup and top with a dollop of whipped cream.

Preparation Time: 20 minutes
Cook Time: 45 to 50 minutes
Chill Time: 4 hours
Experience Level: Beginner

WHITE CHOCOLATE MOUSSE WITH CHOCOLATE SAUCE

DAIRY   SERVES 6 TO 8

Grandmothers will be tickled knowing that their treasured teacups are adored and well used. A collection of magnificent teacups need not match. Pass a different set to each of your guests to spark a conversation about the lovely china patterns and markings.

MOUSSE
7 ounces white chocolate, chopped
2 eggs, separated
¼ cup sugar
1¼ cups heavy cream

1 envelope unflavored gelatin
⅔ cup plain yogurt
2 teaspoons vanilla

SAUCE
2 ounces semi-sweet chocolate, chopped
2 tablespoons rum

¼ cup light cream

MOUSSE: Line a 4 cup loaf pan with wax or parchment paper.

In the top of a double boiler over medium heat, melt chocolate. Remove from heat.

In the bowl of a mixer using a whisk, beat yolks and sugar until pale and thick. Add melted chocolate and beat until combined.

In a small saucepan, heat cream until almost boiling, turn off heat. Sprinkle gelatin into cream and stir until completely dissolved. Pour cream mixture into chocolate mixture, whisking until smooth. Whisk in yogurt and vanilla.

In a clean bowl with clean beater, beat egg whites until stiff, fold into chocolate mixture. Pour into prepared pan. Chill for 4 hours.

SAUCE: In the top of a double boiler melt chocolate with rum and cream. Remove from heat and let cool.

TO SERVE: Spoon a large dollop of mousse into dessert cups. Drizzle sauce over mousse.

Preparation Time: 25 minutes
Cook Time: 10 minutes
Chill Time: 4 hours
Experience Level: Intermediate

Chocolate Crème Brûlée

DAIRY   SERVES 6

½ cup whole milk
1½ cups heavy cream
½ cup sugar, divided
4 ounces good quality semi-sweet chocolate, finely chopped

4 egg yolks
1 teaspoon vanilla
6 teaspoons turbinado sugar, or granulated sugar, optional

Preheat oven to 325°F/160°C.

Prepare 6 (6-ounce) ramekins in a roasting pan just large enough to hold the ramekins without touching. Prepare boiling water to pour into roasting pan.

In a medium saucepan over medium heat, bring milk, cream and ¼ cup of sugar to a boil. Remove from heat and whisk in chocolate until melted.

In a bowl with a spout, or 4 cup measuring cup, combine egg yolks, remaining ¼ cup of sugar and vanilla. Slowly whisk in about ½ of the warm chocolate mixture, stirring constantly. Pour egg mixture into remaining warm chocolate mixture in saucepan. Pour mixture through a fine mesh strainer back into bowl with spout. Pour into ramekins.

Place roasting pan in preheated oven and pour hot water ⅔ the way up the sides of ramekins.

Bake until custards are softly set in center, about 45 minutes. Remove from water bath and let cool. Serve warm or at room temperature.

At serving time sprinkle each custard with 1 teaspoon turbinado sugar, if desired. Using a propane torch, torch until sugar is melted and browned or carefully broil until melted and browned.

Preparation Time: 30 minutes
Cook Time: 45 minutes
Experience Level: Intermediate

Quick Lime and Berry Tart

DAIRY   SERVES 8

1 sheet puff pastry dough, thawed
1 egg white, slightly beaten
Sugar
1 (14-ounce) can sweetened condensed milk

⅓ cup lime juice
⅓ cup sour cream
3 cups fresh raspberries, blueberries and/or quartered strawberries

Preheat oven to 375°F/190°C.

On a lightly floured work surface, using a rolling pin, roll pastry into a 7x12-inch rectangle. Cut a ¾-inch strip from each side of rectangle. Set strips aside. Place pastry rectangle on an ungreased (15x10-inch) jelly-roll pan. Brush with egg white. Lay pastry strips on edges of rectangle, aligning outer edges of the strips to fit. Brush strips with egg white. Sprinkle pastry with sugar. Prick bottom with a fork several times.

Bake 15 to 20 minutes or until light brown. Let cool.

In a medium sized bowl, combine sweetened condensed milk, lime juice and sour cream. Spoon into the cooled pastry. Cover and chill up to 4 hours. Arrange berries on top of tart before serving.

Preparation Time: 10 minutes
Cook Time: 15 to 20 minutes
Chill Time: 1 to 4 hours
Experience Level: Beginner

Apple Tart Cheesecake

DAIRY   **SERVES 8**

The apples layered atop this tart create a beautiful presentation. It is a perfect dessert for a brunch buffet.

CRUST
1 cup flour
⅓ cup sugar

½ cup margarine
¼ teaspoon vanilla

TART
8 ounces cream cheese
¼ cup sugar

1 egg
½ teaspoon vanilla

TOPPING
3 McIntosh apples
⅛ cup sugar

¼ cup sliced almonds, optional

Preheat oven to 450°F/230°C.

CRUST: In the bowl of a mixer fitted with a flat beater, combine flour, sugar, margarine and vanilla on medium speed for 2 minutes. Knead by hand for 1 minute to incorporate small pieces. With fingers, press dough into bottom and up the sides of (9-inch) tart pan.

TART: In a clean bowl, using a whisk, mix cream cheese, sugar, egg and vanilla on medium speed for 2 minutes. Pour into unbaked crust.

TOPPING: Peel, core and thinly slice apples. Place in a large bowl, sprinkle with sugar and toss to coat. Arrange apples on top of cream cheese mixture in spoke fashion. Sprinkle almonds on top if desired.

Bake tart for 10 minutes. Lower heat to 400°F/200°C. Bake tart for an additional 25 minutes. Remove from oven and let cool on a wire rack.

Preparation Time: 20 minutes
Cook Time: 35 minutes
Experience Level: Beginner

Cheesecake Fruit Tart

DAIRY   **SERVES 8**

TART SHELL
1⅓ cups graham cracker crumbs
¼ cup sugar
¼ teaspoon nutmeg
¼ teaspoon cinnamon
½ cup butter, melted

TART FILLING AND TOPPING
8 ounces cream cheese, softened
½ cup sugar
1 tablespoon light cream
1 egg
1 teaspoon vanilla
1 tablespoon flour
2½ cups fresh fruit, blueberries, bananas
   and peaches
¼ cup blueberry preserves
1 tablespoon boiling water

TART SHELL: Prepare a (9-inch) greased tart pan.

In a medium bowl, combine graham cracker crumbs, sugar, nutmeg, cinnamon and melted butter. Press evenly over prepared pan. Roll a rolling pin over edge of pan to create a neat edge. Refrigerate.

Preheat oven to 350°F/180°C.

TART FILLING AND TOPPING: In the bowl of a mixer fitted with a flat beater, cream the cream cheese, sugar, cream, egg and vanilla until smooth. Add flour and combine until fully incorporated. Pour into prepared tart shell. Bake for 15 to 18 minutes or until filling is set and slightly browned. Cool on wire rack.

Arrange fruit in spoke fashion on top of cooled pie.

In a small bowl, beat preserves with boiling water. Gently brush top of tart with preserve mixture.

Preparation Time: 20 minutes
Cook Time: 15 to 18 minutes
Experience Level: Beginner

RHUBARB RASPBERRY GÂTEAU

DAIRY OR PARVE   SERVES 10

MERINGUE LAYERS
4 egg whites
¼ teaspoon cream of tartar

Pinch of salt
1 cup sugar

RHUBARB PURÉE
1 pound fresh rhubarb, cut into ½-inch pieces
½ cup sugar

2 teaspoons cornstarch
1 tablespoon water

CREAM FILLING AND RASPBERRIES
1 cup chilled whipping cream or non-dairy
   whipping cream

2½ cups fresh raspberries

MERINGUE: Preheat oven to 225°F/105°C.

Prepare 2 parchment lined jelly-roll pans. Draw 3 (10x4½-inch) rectangles onto parchment paper. Turn paper over.

In the bowl of a mixer fitted with a whisk, beat egg whites with cream of tartar and pinch of salt until soft peaks form. Gradually add sugar, beating until stiff, glossy peaks form. Transfer to a pastry bag fitted with a ½-inch fluted tip. Pipe meringue evenly onto rectangles, filling them in. If a pastry bag is unavailable divide meringue evenly between rectangles, spread with a spatula.

Bake for 1 hour until crisp and firm. Cool completely. Carefully peel off parchment paper. Meringue may be made 1 day in advance and stored in an airtight container.

RHUBARB PURÉE: In a medium saucepan over medium heat combine rhubarb with sugar. Simmer, stirring occasionally until rhubarb is softened, about 12 minutes. In a small bowl dissolve cornstarch in water. Add to softened rhubarb, stirring continuously. Simmer for 2 to 3 minutes or until rhubarb is thickened. Cool slightly. Place in the bowl of a blender or food processor and process until smooth. Transfer to a large bowl to cool. Purée may be made 2 days in advance covered and chilled. Bring to room temperature before using.

CREAM FILLING: In a clean bowl using a clean whisk, whip cream until soft peaks form. Reserve ½ cup whipped cream.

ASSEMBLY: Place 1 meringue layer on cake stand. Spread ½ cup of rhubarb purée on meringue layer. Spread half of whipped cream evenly over purée and top with ¾ cup raspberries. Repeat with second meringue layer. Top with remaining meringue layer. Decoratively spread reserved ½ cup whipped cream on top layer. Garnish with remaining raspberries.

Preparation Time: 30 minutes
Cook Time: 1 hour 15 minutes
Experience Level: Intermediate

Raspberry Meringue Gâteau

DAIRY OR PARVE   **SERVES 8**

Gâteau is simply the French term for cake. Here the meringues form the structure of the "gâteau". Choose brightly colored, plump berries to ensure sweetness. Raspberries are very fragile, rinse lightly just before using.

MERINGUE
4 egg whites
1 cup sugar
½ teaspoon vanilla

1 teaspoon malt vinegar
1 cup hazelnuts, roasted and ground

SAUCE
1⅓ cups fresh raspberries
3 to 4 tablespoons confectioners' sugar

1 tablespoon orange liqueur

CREAM
1¼ cups whipping cream or non-dairy
   whipping cream
3 tablespoons confectioners' sugar

2 cups fresh raspberries
Confectioners' sugar

MERINGUE: Preheat oven to 350°F/180°C.

Grease 2 (8-inch) round cake pans and line bottoms with wax paper.

In the bowl of a mixer fitted with a whisk, beat egg whites on medium-high speed until soft peaks form. Gradually beat in sugar until mixture becomes very stiff. Fold in vanilla, vinegar and ground hazelnuts. Divide mixture between the two pans and spread the tops level.

Bake 50 to 60 minutes or until crisp.

Turn meringues out onto wire racks to cool.

SAUCE: In the bowl of a blender or a food processor, purée raspberries, confectioners' sugar and liqueur until smooth. Press the purée through a fine strainer or a sieve to remove seeds. Chill until ready to serve.

CREAM: In a clean bowl of a mixer, with a clean whisk, beat cream on medium-high speed until it just begins to hold its shape. Gradually add the confectioners' sugar beating until stiff peaks form. Gently fold in raspberries.

Spread cream on one meringue round. Top with second round. Dust with confectioners' sugar. To serve plate a slice and drizzle with sauce.

Preparation Time: 30 minutes
Cook Time: 50 minutes
Experience Level: Intermediate

COOKIES AND BARS

DARK CHOCOLATE BROWNIES WITH FROZEN COFFEE WHIPPED CREAM

DAIRY OR PARVE   SERVES 12

Our version of brownies à la mode. The traditional vanilla ice cream is replaced by frozen coffee whipped cream.

COFFEE WHIPPED CREAM

⅔ cup dairy or non-dairy whipping cream
4 teaspoons sugar

4 teaspoons brewed black coffee, cooled
½ teaspoon vanilla

BROWNIES

7 ounces unsweetened chocolate, coarsely chopped
¾ cup butter or margarine
¼ cup water
1 cup sugar
¾ cup light brown sugar

2 eggs
1 teaspoon vanilla
1⅓ cups flour
⅛ teaspoon salt
⅛ teaspoon cinnamon

COFFEE WHIPPED CREAM: In the bowl of a mixer fitted with a whisk, combine whipping cream, sugar, cooled coffee and vanilla. Beat on high speed until soft peaks form. Place in a freezer safe container, cover and freeze for 2 to 3 hours or until firm.

BROWNIES: In a small saucepan, combine chocolate, butter and water. Place saucepan over low heat and stir until chocolate is melted.

Preheat oven to 350°F/180°C.

Grease an (8x8-inch) baking pan, set aside.

Transfer chocolate mixture to the bowl of a mixer fitted with a flat beater. Add sugar and brown sugar. Beat on low speed until combined. Add eggs and vanilla, beating on medium speed for 2 minutes. Scrape sides of bowl with a spatula, as necessary. Add flour, salt and cinnamon. Beat until combined. Spread batter evenly into prepared pan. Bake for 25 minutes.

Remove frozen coffee whipped cream from freezer and let stand 10 minutes.

To serve, place a warm brownie on a dessert plate. Top with a scoop of frozen coffee whipped cream.

Preparation Time 30 minutes
Cook Time: 25 minutes
Chill Time: 2 to 3 hours
Experience Level: Intermediate

Chocolate Pecan Bars

PARVE   YIELD 24 TO 30 BARS

CRUST LAYER
1½ cups flour   ¼ cup brown sugar
½ cup margarine, softened

PECAN LAYER
3 eggs   1 teaspoon vanilla
¾ cup light corn syrup   1¾ cups semi-sweet chocolate chips
2 tablespoons margarine   1½ cups pecan halves

CRUST LAYER: Preheat oven to 350°F/180°C.

Prepare a greased (9x13-inch) baking pan.

In a medium bowl using a wooden spoon, mix flour, margarine and brown sugar together. Press evenly into bottom of prepared pan. Bake until lightly brown, about 12 to 15 minutes.

PECAN LAYER: In a large bowl using a wooden spoon, combine eggs, corn syrup, margarine and vanilla. Stir in chocolate chips and pecans. Pour over prepared crust. Bake for 25 to 30 minutes or until set. Cool before cutting into squares.

Preparation Time: 15 minutes
Cook Time: 40 minutes
Experience Level: Beginner

Sweet Nut Bars

PARVE   YIELD 48 BARS

24 graham cracker squares   1 cup flaked coconut
1 cup margarine   1 cup chopped nuts, optional
1 cup firmly packed brown sugar   2 cups light corn syrup or honey

Preheat oven to 375°F/190°C.

Grease a (15x10-inch) jelly-roll pan.

Arrange graham cracker squares in pan side by side in a single layer.

In a medium saucepan over medium heat, combine margarine, brown sugar, coconut, nuts and corn syrup. Stir constantly until mixture comes to a boil. Remove from heat. Pour over graham crackers and quickly, thinly and evenly spread over graham crackers.

Bake until lightly browned, about 10 minutes. Cut into 48 bars.

Preparation Time: 15 minutes
Cook Time: 10 minutes
Experience Level: Beginner

Pecan Brittle Bars

PARVE

YIELD 24 PIECES

Making candy takes a little effort but the results are well worth the time invested. Here a nut filled candy tops fudgy brownies.

CAKE LAYER

4 ounces semi-sweet chocolate

¾ cup margarine

1¾ cups brown sugar

½ teaspoon salt

2 teaspoons vanilla

2 eggs

1¼ cups flour

TOPPING

1¾ cups brown sugar

¾ cup non-dairy whipping cream

½ cup margarine

⅛ teaspoon salt

2 teaspoons vanilla

1½ cups chopped toasted pecans

CAKE LAYER: Preheat oven to 350°F/180°C.

Prepare a greased (9x13-inch) baking pan.

In a small saucepan over low heat, melt chocolate with margarine. Remove from heat, set aside.

In a large bowl using a wooden spoon combine brown sugar, salt, vanilla and eggs. Stir in chocolate mixture. Add flour ½ cup at a time until incorporated. Pour into prepared pan.

Bake for 25 to 30 minutes or until set. Cool for 1 hour.

TOPPING: In a medium saucepan, over medium heat, combine sugar, whipping cream, margarine and salt. Bring to a boil. Boil for approximately 20 minutes, stirring occasionally until mixture reaches the soft ball stage 234°F to 238°F/112°C to 116°C on a candy thermometer. Remove from heat. Stir in vanilla and pecans. Pour on top of chocolate layer. Chill.

To serve bring to room temperature and cut into bars.

Preparation Time: 20 minutes
Cook Time: 45 to 50 minutes
Experience Level: Intermediate

TRUFFLE BROWNIES

PARVE   YIELD 16 BROWNIES

1 (8-ounce) package semi-sweet chocolate squares, chopped
2 tablespoons margarine
¾ cup sugar, divided

3 eggs
1 cup flour
⅔ cup non-dairy whipping cream
Confectioners' sugar for dusting

Preheat oven to 350°F/180°C.

Line an (8x8-inch) baking pan with aluminum foil extending over edges. Grease foil.

In a medium bowl microwave 2 (2-ounce) squares of chocolate with margarine on high for 1 to 1½ minutes. Stir chocolate until melted. Using a wooden spoon, stir in ½ cup sugar. Add 1 egg, mixing until well blended. Mix in flour until combined. Press into bottom of prepared pan.

In a small bowl microwave remaining chocolate and cream until chocolate is melted, about 1 minute.

In the bowl of a mixer fitted with whisk, beat ¼ cup of sugar and 2 eggs on medium speed for 1 minute, until thick and lemon colored. Beat in chocolate and cream mixture. Pour over batter in prepared pan. Bake for 35 to 40 minutes or until truffle topping is set and edges begin to pull away from sides of pan.

Cool in pan. Dust with confectioners' sugar when cooled and cut into 16 squares.

Preparation Time: 25 minutes
Cook Time: 35 to 40 minutes
Experience Level: Beginner

PARTY SQUARES

PARVE   YIELD 48 SQUARES

These squares are refreshing served as a frozen dessert in the summertime. The shortbread crust, chocolate filling and meringue topping will satisfy every craving your sweet tooth may have.

BOTTOM LAYER
1 cup margarine
1 cup sugar
2 egg yolks

1 teaspoon vanilla
½ teaspoon salt
2½ cups flour

MIDDLE LAYER
2 cups semi-sweet chocolate chips

TOP LAYER
3 egg whites   ⅔ cup sugar

Preheat oven to 375°F/190°C.

In the bowl of a mixer fitted with a flat beater, on medium speed, cream together margarine and sugar. Add egg yolks, vanilla and salt. Mix to combine. Add flour and mix to form a stiff dough. Press evenly into bottom of prepared pan. Bake for 15 minutes.

Remove from oven. While still hot, pour chocolate chips over bottom layer. Spread evenly. Return to oven and bake for 3 minutes to melt chocolate. Using a spatula evenly spread melted chocolate over bottom layer.

In a clean, dry bowl of a mixer fitted with a whisk, beat egg whites at high speed until foamy. Gradually add sugar, beating until stiff peaks form. Spread egg whites over chocolate. Bake for 10 minutes.

Cut immediately, dipping knife in hot water between cuts. Store in an airtight container.

Preparation Time: 20 minutes
Cook Time: 28 minutes
Experience Level: Beginner

Coconut Chews

PARVE   YIELD 24 PIECES

¾ cup margarine
3 tablespoons sugar
1 cup flour
2¼ cups dark brown sugar

3 eggs, separated
1 cup chopped pecans
¾ cup sweetened coconut flakes
Confectioners' sugar, optional

Preheat oven to 350°F/180°C.

Prepare a greased (9x13-inch) baking dish.

In the bowl of a mixer fitted with a flat beater cream margarine and sugar at medium speed. Stir in flour to form a thick dough. Press dough into prepared pan. Bake for 12 to 15 minutes or until light brown around edges.

In the bowl of a mixer fitted with a flat beater, at low speed, combine brown sugar and egg yolks. Mix in pecans and coconut, set aside.

In a clean dry bowl of a mixer fitted with whisk attachment, beat egg whites on high speed until thick and frothy but not stiff, about 4 minutes. Gently fold whites into nut mixture. Spread over baked layer.

Bake for 30 minutes or until set. Cool for about 45 minutes before cutting into squares. Sprinkle with confectioners' sugar if desired.

Preparation Time: 30 minutes
Cook Time: 45 minutes
Experience Level: Intermediate

Syrian Baklava

DAIRY OR PARVE   YIELD 24 PIECES

Rose water adds a unique flavor to this sticky sweet treat. Rose water is a distillation of rose petals that has the intensely perfumy flavor and fragrance of its source. It has been a popular flavoring for centuries in the cuisines of the Middle East.

ROSE WATER SYRUP

¾ cup water

2 cups sugar

1 tablespoon plus 2 teaspoons rose water

1 tablespoon fresh lemon juice

BAKLAVA

1 pound phyllo dough, thawed according to package directions

3½ cups shelled, raw pistachio nuts, finely chopped

¼ cup sugar

3 tablespoons rose water

2½ teaspoons cinnamon

1 cup butter or margarine, melted, divided

½ recipe cold rose water syrup

ROSE WATER SYRUP: In a medium saucepan over medium heat, combine water and sugar. Bring to a simmer. Reduce heat to medium-low and cook uncovered for 12 to 15 minutes, stirring occasionally. Liquid will thicken slightly. Remove from heat. Immediately stir in rose water and lemon juice. Cool slightly. Refrigerate for 5 to 6 hours or overnight. Syrup will remain fresh, kept covered in refrigerator for several months.

BAKLAVA: Preheat oven to 350°F/180°C.

Prepare a well greased (9x13-inch) baking pan.

In a medium bowl, combine nuts, sugar, rose water, cinnamon and 3 tablespoons of melted butter. Set aside.

Place remaining melted butter in a small bowl, ready with a pastry brush.

Unroll phyllo dough onto a clean dry work surface and gently smooth out with dry hands. With kitchen scissors or a very sharp knife cut phyllo dough in half widthwise. Cover 1 section with plastic wrap and a damp towel.

Working quickly, lift 2 sheets of phyllo dough and spread over bottom of baking pan. Using a pastry brush, cover the entire surface of phyllo in pan with melted butter. Continue to layer and butter every two sheets until half of dough is used.

Distribute nut mixture evenly over the buttered phyllo sheets, pressing down gently with hands.

Uncover remaining phyllo and working in same fashion as bottom half, brush and layer remaining dough. Brush the top sheet generously with melted butter.

Using a sharp knife, cut unbaked baklava lengthwise at 1½-inch intervals, cutting ¾ of the way down. Starting 1-inch from the upper left hand corner, cut diagonally through the entire pastry in 1-inch intervals to the lower right hand corner.

Bake until top of phyllo is golden brown and crispy, 20 to 30 minutes.

Remove from oven and immediately drizzle cold rose water syrup over top of entire baklava. Allow the syrup to soak in for 5 to 6 hours. Do not cover and seal it or it will get soggy. Serve at room temperature. Best eaten within 1 or 2 days. Store in refrigerator loosely covered for up to 7 days.

Preparation Time: 40 minutes
Cook Time: 25 to 45 minutes
Chill Time: 5 hours to overnight
Experience Level: Intermediate

White Chocolate Meringue Bars

DAIRY   YIELD 24 BARS

A brown sugar meringue topping adds a caramel flavor to these bars. The preparation is quick and simple, making these a good choice for a last minute dessert.

CRUST
2 cups flour   1 cup margarine, softened
½ cup confectioners' sugar

TOPPING
2 cups white chocolate chips   3 egg whites
1¼ cups sliced almonds, divided   1 cup packed brown sugar

CRUST: Preheat oven to 375°F/190°C.

Prepare a greased (9x13-inch) baking pan.

In a medium bowl, combine flour and confectioners' sugar. Cut in margarine with a pastry blender until mixture resembles coarse crumbs. Press into prepared baking pan. Bake for 10 to 12 minutes or until set.

Sprinkle hot crust with white chocolate chips and 1 cup of nuts.

In the bowl of a mixer fitted with a whisk, beat egg whites until frothy. Gradually add brown sugar and beat until stiff peaks form. Gently spread meringue over chips and nuts. Sprinkle with remaining nuts.

Bake for 15 to 20 minutes or until golden brown. Cut into bars when cooled.

Preparation Time: 10 minutes
Cook Time: 15 to 20 minutes
Experience Level: Beginner

Persian Baklava

PARVE OR DAIRY **YIELD 24 PIECES**

SYRUP
2 cups sugar

1½ cups water

2 teaspoons lemon juice

BAKLAVA
1 pound phyllo dough, thawed according to
    package directions

1 cup margarine or butter, melted

1 cup sugar

1½ cups chopped walnuts or pecans, divided

3 teaspoons cinnamon

SYRUP: In a medium saucepan over medium heat, combine sugar and water. Bring to a boil. Simmer until a thin syrup forms, about 10 minutes. Remove from heat. Immediately stir in lemon juice. Set aside to cool.

BAKLAVA: Preheat oven to 375°F/190°C.

Place melted margarine in a small bowl, ready with a pastry brush.

Prepare a greased (15x10-inch) jelly-roll pan.

In a medium bowl combine sugar, walnuts and cinnamon.

Unroll phyllo dough onto a clean dry work surface. Gently smooth out with dry hands. With kitchen scissors or a very sharp knife cut phyllo dough in half widthwise. Cover 1 section with plastic wrap and a damp towel. Sheets should now measure approximately 9x13-inches.

Place a sheet of phyllo dough on bottom of prepared pan. Brush with margarine. Repeat for 8 layers. Spread half of nut mixture evenly over phyllo dough. Top with 8 more layers of phyllo dough and margarine. Sprinkle remaining nuts evenly over dough. Top with remaining 8 layers of dough and margarine. Brush top layer generously with margarine. Using a sharp knife cut top layers of dough into squares or diamonds. Do not cut all the way through to pan.

Bake for 20 minutes. Reduce temperature to 250°F/120°C. Bake for an additional hour. Remove from oven. Pour off margarine that has not been absorbed by pastry. Pour syrup over all. Allow to cool at least 2 hours. Pour off excess syrup. Cut through to bottom and serve.

Preparation Time: 45 minutes
Cook Time: 1 hour 40 minutes
Chill Time: 2 hours
Experience Level: Intermediate

Sweet Raspberry Scones

DAIRY   YIELD 30 SCONES

Grab a plate and curl up with a good book. Buttery scones will melt in your mouth. Warm the scones and top with a pat of butter for a special treat.

3 cups flour	1 cup milk
1/3 cup sugar	1 tablespoon lemon juice
2½ teaspoons baking powder	1 tablespoon lemon zest
½ teaspoon baking soda	2 tablespoons butter, melted
¾ teaspoon salt	2 teaspoons sugar, divided
¼ cup cold butter, cut into ½-inch pieces	½ to 2/3 cup raspberry or strawberry preserves

In the bowl of a mixer fitted with a flat beater, combine flour, sugar, baking powder, baking soda and salt. Add cold butter, using fingers to combine. Stir in milk, lemon juice and zest, mixing on medium speed for 1 minute until combined.

Preheat oven to 425°F/220°C.

Prepare 2 greased, parchment lined (15x10-inch) jelly-roll pans.

Place dough on a lightly floured work surface. Knead dough until it is soft and workable, about 2 minutes. Cut dough in half. Working with 1 half, using a rolling pin, roll dough into a 12x16-inch rectangle. Brush with butter, sprinkle with a teaspoon of sugar. Spoon half of preserves over all but 1-inch along edge of length of dough. Roll up tightly, jelly-roll style beginning at edge with preserves. Seal by pinching length of log along edge without preserves.

Using a sharp serrated knife, cut log evenly into 1-inch thick rounds. Place cut side down, onto prepared pans. Bake for 10 minutes. Let stand 1 minute. Transfer to cooling racks.

Repeat with remaining dough. May be eaten warm. Can be frozen in an airtight container for up to 1 month.

Preparation Time: 40 minutes
Cook Time: 10 minutes in 2 batches
Experience Level: Intermediate

Summer Fruit Cookies

The presentation of this cookie makes it a perfect choice for a dessert buffet. Adjust the fruits in the toppings to coordinate with your party's color scheme.

COOKIES

½ cup butter
½ cup confectioners' sugar
¼ cup sugar
1 egg yolk
¼ teaspoon vanilla

¼ teaspoon almond extract
1¼ cups flour
1 teaspoon baking soda
1 teaspoon cream of tartar

EDGING

1 cup chopped pistachio nuts

1 tablespoon corn syrup

GLAZE

2 teaspoons cornstarch
½ cup orange juice, divided

1 tablespoon fresh lemon juice
¼ cup sugar

FROSTING

8 ounces cream cheese, softened
½ cup confectioners' sugar
¼ teaspoon orange zest

¼ teaspoon lemon zest
¼ teaspoon vanilla

TOPPING

3½ cups fresh fruit i.e. blueberries,
    quartered strawberries, raspberries,
    kiwi's sliced in eighths, green grapes

COOKIES: In the bowl of a mixer fitted with a flat beater, on low speed, beat butter, confectioners' sugar and sugar until light and fluffy. Add egg yolk, vanilla and almond extract. Beat well.

In a small bowl combine flour, baking soda and cream of tartar. Mix with butter mixture until combined. Shape into 4 1-inch diameter logs, rolling so edges are neat. Wrap in plastic wrap and refrigerate until firm, about 2 hours. May be frozen at this point.

Preheat oven to 350°F/180°C.

Prepare 2 (15x10-inch) parchment lined jelly-roll pans.

EDGING: Place chopped pistachio nuts on a piece of plastic wrap or wax paper. Unwrap logs and brush sides of logs with corn syrup. Roll logs into pistachio nuts until well coated. Cut logs into ¼-inch slices. Place cut side down 2-inches apart on prepared pans. Bake cookies for 10 minutes, or until edges are slightly browned. Transfer to wire racks to cool.

GLAZE: In a small bowl, combine cornstarch with 1 tablespoon of orange juice. Set aside.

In a small saucepan over medium heat, bring remaining orange juice, lemon juice and sugar to a boil. Stir in orange juice and cornstarch mixture. Continue cooking until mixture thickens, about 2 minutes. Remove from heat. Set aside.

Frosting: In the bowl of a mixer fitted with a flat beater, combine cream cheese, powdered sugar, orange zest, lemon zest and vanilla. Mix on medium speed until light and fluffy.

ASSEMBLY: Spread 1 teaspoon of frosting on each cookie. Arrange fruit on top of frosting in an assembly line fashion i.e. all the strawberries, then all the grapes etc. Brush glaze over each cookie with a pastry brush. Cover and place in refrigerator until 15 minutes before serving.

Preparation Time: 45 minutes
Cook Time: 15 minutes
Chill Time: 2 hours
Experience Level: Intermediate

Date Nut Rolls

PARVE   YIELD 72 PIECES

4 tablespoons margarine	4 cups Rice Krispies
2 cups sugar	½ cup chopped almonds
4 eggs	2 teaspoons vanilla
12 ounces pitted pressed dates	1 (8-ounce) package shredded coconut

In a medium saucepan over low heat, melt margarine. Remove from heat. Stir in eggs, sugar and dates. Return to heat and cook, stirring occasionally, until mixture begins to pull away from pan, about 20 minutes. It may take a few minutes longer if dates are hard. Remove from heat.

Add Rice Krispies, almonds and vanilla. Mix well with a wooden spoon. Shape into 1-inch balls. Roll in coconut. Freeze in a covered container, serve frozen.

Preparation Time: 1 hour
Cook Time: 25 minutes
Experience Level: Beginner

Pecan Miniatures

DAIRY OR PARVE

YIELD 36 PIECES

DOUGH
½ cup butter or margarine
½ cup plus 2 tablespoons sugar
1 egg

½ teaspoon almond extract
1¾ cups flour

FILLING
1 cup confectioners' sugar
½ cup butter or margarine

⅓ cup dark corn syrup
1 cup chopped pecans

TOPPING
36 pecan halves

⅓ cup dark corn syrup

DOUGH: Preheat oven to 400°F/200°C.

Grease a mini muffin pan for 36 muffins.

In the bowl of a mixer fitted with a flat beater, cream together butter and sugar. Add egg and almond extract. Mix to combine. Add flour and mix to form a dough. Roll dough into 36 (1-inch) balls. Push into bottom and up sides of mini muffin tin. Shape so edges are even with edge of tin. Bake for 7 to 10 minutes.

Let cool 2 minutes. Remove dough shells and place on large jelly-roll pan or cookie sheet.

Reduce oven temperature to 350°F/180°C.

FILLING: In a medium saucepan over low heat, combine confectioners' sugar, butter and corn syrup. Bring to a boil. Remove from heat. Stir in chopped pecans.

Carefully pour into prepared shells and bake for 5 minutes.

TOPPING: Dip pecan halves into dark corn syrup and place in center of each miniature.

Preparation Time: 45 minutes
Cook Time: 18 minutes
Experience Level: Intermediate

A small floral arrangement adds charm when placed upon a serving tray. Choose flowers with a subtle sweet scent to add to the ambiance of your meal.

PECAN AND CHEESE TARTLETS

DAIRY OR PARVE   **YIELD 48 TARTLETS**

CRUST

1 cup butter or margarine, softened
6 ounces cream cheese, or parve cream cheese

2 cups flour

FILLING

1½ cups pecans
2 eggs
1½ cups light brown sugar
2 tablespoons vanilla
3 tablespoons butter or margarine

2 tablespoons bourbon, brandy or amaretto, or to taste
½ teaspoon salt
48 pecan halves

TOPPING, OPTIONAL

½ cup semi-sweet chocolate, melted

CRUST: In the bowl of a mixer fitted with a flat beater, beat butter and cream cheese on medium speed until light and fluffy, about 3 minutes. Stir in flour with a wooden spoon, until just incorporated. Divide dough into 4 equal portions. Shape each into a 6-inch log. Wrap in plastic wrap and refrigerate for 1 hour or more.

Prepare greased mini muffin pans, enough for 48 mini muffins.

Divide each log into 12 equal pieces. Press dough into bottom and up sides of each mini muffin tin.

Preheat oven to 325°F/160°C.

FILLING: Divide pecans using ⅓ cup for each dozen. In the bowl of a mixer fitted with a flat beater beat pecans, eggs, brown sugar, vanilla, butter, bourbon and salt on medium speed. Fill each crust ¾ full with filling. Top each with a pecan half.

Bake in preheated oven for 25 minutes or until filling is set. Cool for 20 minutes. Remove from pans.

TOPPING: Place melted chocolate in a squeeze bottle and drizzle back and forth over each tartlet.

Preparation Time: 40 minutes
Cook Time: 25 minutes
Chill Time: 1 hour
Experience Level: Intermediate

ALMOND MANDEL BREAD

PARVE · YIELD 72 COOKIES

Almond extract and chopped almonds give this traditional cookie a delicate and sweet almond flavor throughout.

COOKIE

4 cups flour
1½ cups sugar
3 eggs
¾ cup oil

1 teaspoon vanilla
1 teaspoon almond extract
2 teaspoons baking powder
Dash of salt

TOPPING

⅛ cup sugar

½ cup chopped almonds

COOKIE: Preheat oven to 350°F/180°C.

Prepare 2 (15x10-inch) greased jelly-roll pans.

In the bowl of a mixer fitted with a flat beater combine 2 cups flour with sugar, eggs, oil, vanilla and almond extract. Slowly add baking powder, salt and remaining 2 cups of flour. Mix to combine.

TOPPING: Combine sugar and almonds on a piece of plastic wrap or waxed paper.

Form dough into 4 logs. Roll each log into topping. Place onto prepared pans. Bake for 12 to 15 minutes. Remove from oven, cut into ½-inch slices. Lie down each slice and return to oven for an additional 10 minutes. Transfer to wire racks to cool.

Preparation Time: 20 minutes
Cook Time: 25 minutes in 2 batches, if necessary
Experience Level: Beginner

Double Chocolate Mocha Biscotti

DAIRY

YIELD 36 COOKIES

COOKIES

½ cup margarine

⅔ cup sugar

2 teaspoons baking powder

2 teaspoons instant coffee granules

1½ cups semi-sweet chocolate chips, melted

2 eggs

1 teaspoon vanilla

2 cups flour

½ cup mini semi-sweet chocolate chips

FOR DIPPING

1 cup or 6 ounces white chocolate baking pieces

1 teaspoon shortening

COOKIES: In the bowl of a mixer fitted with a whisk, cream margarine and sugar. Add baking powder and instant coffee, beating until combined. Mix in melted chocolate, eggs and vanilla. Scrape sides of bowl with a rubber spatula, as necessary. Add flour mixing until incorporated. Stir in miniature chocolate chips. Divide dough in half.

Preheat oven to 375°F/200°C.

Prepare a lightly greased (15x10-inch) jelly-roll pan.

Lightly flour hands. Shape each half into an 8-inch log. Place logs 5-inches apart on prepared pan. Flatten logs so they are 2½-inches wide. Bake for 25 to 30 minutes or until toothpick inserted in center comes out clean. Cool on pan for 1 hour.

Preheat oven to 375°F/190°C.

Carefully transfer logs to a cutting board. Cut each loaf diagonally into ½-inch slices. Lay slices on pan cut side down. Bake for 10 minutes. Turn slices over and bake an additional 10 to 15 minutes or until dry and crisp. Transfer to wire racks to cool.

FOR DIPPING: In a small saucepan over low heat, melt white chocolate pieces together with shortening, stirring occasionally. Dip one corner of each cookie into melted white chocolate mixture. Place on wax paper to harden.

Preparation Time: 30 minutes
Cook Time: 35 to 45 minutes
Experience Level: Intermediate

PECAN OR CHOCOLATE CHIP BISCOTTI

PARVE   **YIELD 96 COOKIES**

This is a twist on the Italian cookie. The batter is spread onto a cookie sheet to bake, then it is sliced and rebaked. The result is a crisp cookie that is a perfect choice for your cookie jar. Try pecans or chocolate chips to discover which is your favorite.

4 eggs
¾ cup canola oil
1 teaspoon vanilla
1 cup sugar
3 cups flour
1⅛ teaspoons baking powder

⅛ teaspoon salt
1 cup chopped pecans or mini, semi-sweet
    chocolate chips
2 tablespoons orange juice
Cinnamon, if preparing with pecans
Sugar, if preparing with pecans

Preheat oven to 375°F/190°C.

Prepare a greased jelly-roll pan.

In the bowl of a mixer fitted with a flat beater, combine eggs, oil, vanilla, sugar, flour, baking powder, salt, pecans or chocolate chips and orange juice. Mix on medium speed until combined. Spread evenly onto prepared pan. Sprinkle with sugar. If using pecans, sprinkle with sugar and cinnamon.

Bake for 25 to 30 minutes or until browned.

Slice lengthwise into thirds then in ¾-inch slices widthwise. Turn pieces on their sides. Sprinkle with sugar or cinnamon and sugar if using pecans. Return to oven and bake for an additional 10 minutes. Allow biscotti to cool completely in oven, with door ajar, for one hour.

Preparation Time: 20 minutes
Cook Time: 30 minutes
Experience Level: Beginner

SWEET KAAK

PARVE   YIELD 60 COOKIES

This is a traditional Syrian cookie which is sweet with hints of orange and lemon flavors. It is perfect paired with a steamy cup of tea steeped with peppermint leaves.

COOKIE

4 eggs

1 cup canola oil

1¼ cups sugar

1 teaspoon vanilla

1 tablespoon lemon zest

1½ tablespoons orange zest

1 tablespoon lemon juice

1 tablespoon baking powder

5 cups flour

GLAZE

1 egg

¾ cup water

5 teaspoons sugar

COOKIE: In the bowl of a mixer fitted with a flat beater, beat eggs for 1 minute. Add oil, sugar, vanilla, lemon zest, orange zest and lemon juice. Mix until combined. Add baking powder then flour, ½ cup at a time, combining with each addition. Form dough into a ball. Refrigerate uncovered for 30 minutes.

Preheat oven to 325°F/160°C. Prepare several greased cookie sheets.

Using about 1½ teaspoons of dough for each cookie, on an unfloured work surface, roll dough into a thin log about 8-inches long. Fold in half and twist to form a rope shape. Place on prepared cookie sheets.

GLAZE: In a small bowl, combine egg with water and sugar. Before cookies are baked, brush with glaze.

Bake for 15 to 18 minutes or until lightly colored, not golden or brown.

Store in an airtight container at room temperature. May be frozen up to 2 months.

Preparation Time: 1 hour
Cook Time: 15 to 18 minutes
Chill Time: 30 minutes
Experience Level: Intermediate

Churgays

PARVE   YIELD 48 COOKIES

This recipe was published many years ago in a Columbus, Ohio community newspaper. The daughter-in-law of the author of this recipe proudly shares these cookies, once again, with the public.

This deliciously sweet, impressive looking cookie is fried. Making it a perfect choice for a Chanukah treat.

½ cup shortening	3½ cups flour
⅔ cup sugar	¼ cup orange juice
3 eggs	Canola oil for deep frying
1 teaspoon vanilla	Confectioners' sugar

In the bowl of a mixer fitted with a flat beater, cream shortening and sugar until light and fluffy. Beat in eggs and vanilla until smooth. Add flour and orange juice alternately, beginning and ending with flour. Beat until smooth. Divide dough in half.

On a well floured work surface, using a rolling pin, roll out half of dough as thin as possible, about ¹⁄₁₆-inch If dough is too soft to roll, add more flour. Using a pizza wheel or sharp knife cut dough into 1½-inch strips. Cut diagonally into 4-inch long diamond shapes. Cut a 1-inch slit in center of each diamond (photo 1). Pull one end through slit (photo 2), then back toward its original direction (photo 3). Repeat with remaining dough.

Prepare a paper towel lined jelly-roll pan to place cookies on after frying.

In a medium saucepan, heat oil for deep frying to 375°F/190°C. Fry cookies a few at a time, until crisp and golden on both sides. Remove with a slotted spoon.

Store in an airtight container. When ready to serve, sprinkle with confectioners' sugar.

Preparation Time: 40 minutes
Cook Time: 30 minutes
Experience Level: Intermediate

❧

CINNAMON BOW TIES

PARVE   YIELD 72 COOKIES

DOUGH

1 cup non-dairy creamer   4 cups flour
2 tablespoons white vinegar   1 cup margarine, melted
¼ cup warm water   2 eggs
2¼ teaspoons active dry yeast   1 teaspoon vanilla

TOPPING

1 cup sugar   2 teaspoons cinnamon

DOUGH: In a small bowl combine non-dairy creamer and vinegar, set aside.

In a small bowl combine water with yeast, set aside for 5 minutes.

Place the flour into the bowl of a mixer fitted with a dough hook. Make a well in the center of flour, pour in creamer, yeast mixture, margarine, eggs and vanilla. Mix on medium speed for 5 minutes to form dough. Cover and refrigerate for 6 to 24 hours.

TOPPING: In a small bowl, combine sugar and cinnamon.

Preheat oven to 350°F/180°C.

Prepare 2 ungreased, aluminum foil lined cookie sheets.

On a lightly floured work surface, using a rolling pin, roll out dough into a large rectangle about ³/₁₆-inch thick. Generously sprinkle all of topping over dough. Fold dough in thirds, being careful not to spill out topping. Roll out again to ³/₁₆-inch thick. Using a sharp knife or a pizza wheel cut dough into 2x½-inch strips, twist and place on prepared cookie sheets. Bake for 17 minutes.

Preparation Time: 45 minutes
Cook Time: 17 minutes per pan, 3 pans
Chill Time: 6 to 24 hours
Experience Level: Intermediate

An elegant creamer and sugar bowl can set the mood for teatime. Share a charming afternoon with friends enjoying a luxurious cup of herbal tea with treats infused with home baked goodness.

Orange Bow Knots

PARVE   YIELD 48 COOKIES

DOUGH

4 to 4½ cups flour

4½ teaspoons active dry yeast

¾ cup sugar

½ cup non-dairy creamer

⅓ cup margarine

½ teaspoon salt

2 eggs

2 tablespoons finely shredded orange peel

½ cup orange juice

ICING

1½ cups confectioners' sugar

1 teaspoon finely shredded orange rind

1 tablespoon orange juice

DOUGH: In the bowl of a mixer combine flour and yeast, set aside.

In a small saucepan over medium-low heat, combine sugar, non-dairy creamer, margarine and salt until warm and margarine almost melts. Add contents of saucepan to flour mixture. Add eggs and orange juice. Beat on medium speed for 30 seconds, scraping down sides of bowl. Beat on high speed for 3 minutes. Using a wooden spoon, stir in orange peel.

Turn dough out onto a lightly floured work surface. Knead in as much of remaining flour as you can to make a dough that is smooth and elastic. Place dough in an oiled bowl, turn to coat. Cover and let rise for 1 hour or until doubled in size.

Punch down dough. Turn out onto a lightly floured work surface. Divide in half. Cover and let rest for an additional 10 minutes.

Prepare 2 greased cookie sheets.

Using a rolling pin, roll each half of dough into a 10x12-inch rectangle. Cut each into 24 (5x1-inch) strips. Tie each strip into a loose knot. Place 3-inches apart on prepared cookie sheets. Cover and let rise for about 30 minutes or until nearly doubled in size.

Preheat oven to 375°F/190°C.

Bake for 8 to 10 minutes or until lightly browned. Transfer to wire racks to cool.

ICING: In a medium bowl mix together confectioners' sugar, orange rind and orange juice. Mix to create an icing that is easy to drizzle. Drizzle icing over knots. Place cooled knots in a single layer in an airtight container at room temperature for up to 3 days.

Preparation Time: 25 minutes
Cook Time: 12 minutes
Rising Time: 1 hour 40 minutes
Experience Level: Intermediate

Chocolate Wows

PARVE   **YIELD 48 TO 60 COOKIES**

The name says it all. These chocolate cookies have a melt in your mouth appeal. The batter is very sticky, until you stir in the nuts and chocolate chips, so do not be alarmed by its consistency.

⅓ cup flour	2 cups semi-sweet chocolate chips, divided
¼ cup cocoa	2 eggs
1 teaspoon baking powder	¾ cup sugar
¼ teaspoon salt	1 teaspoon vanilla
½ cup margarine	2 cups chopped pecans

Preheat oven to 325°F/160°C. Prepare greased cookie sheets.

In a medium bowl combine flour, cocoa, baking powder and salt. Set aside.

In a small saucepan over low heat, melt margarine and 1 cup of semi-sweet chocolate chips, stirring until smooth.

In the bowl of a mixer fitted with a flat beater, beat sugar and eggs at medium speed until lemon colored, about 2 minutes. Reduce speed, add chocolate mixture, flour mixture and vanilla. Beat until just blended. Increase to medium speed, beat 2 minutes. Add pecans and remaining cup of chocolate chips, using a wooden spoon, stir to combine.

Drop by teaspoonfuls 2-inches apart onto prepared pans. Bake for 15 minutes or until tops are shiny and cracked.

Preparation Time: 30 minutes
Cook Time: 10 minutes per batch
Experience Level: Beginner

Chewy Chocolate Chip Cookies

PARVE   **YIELD 36 COOKIES**

A cookie jar favorite. Our version has a chewy texture that children love. The cookies are large, making them a great choice for ice cream sandwiches.

¾ cup canola oil
1¼ cups light brown sugar
2 tablespoons orange juice
1 egg
1 teaspoon vanilla

1 teaspoon salt
¾ teaspoon baking soda
2 cups flour
1 cup semi-sweet chocolate chips

Preheat oven to 375°F/200°C.

In the bowl of a mixer fitted with a flat beater, combine oil, brown sugar, orange juice, egg, vanilla, salt, baking soda and flour. Mix together, add chocolate chips mixing to combine. Cookie dough may also be done in a mixing bowl with a wooden spoon.

Drop by rounded tablespoonfuls onto ungreased cookie sheets. Bake for 12 to 15 minutes.

Preparation Time: 15 minutes
Cook Time: 12 to 15 minutes per batch
Experience Level: Beginner

Rosemarie Praline Cookies

PARVE   **YIELD 36 COOKIES**

1¼ cups flour
½ cup margarine
½ cup brown sugar
¼ cup white sugar
1 teaspoon vanilla

1 egg
2 (3½-ounce) bars truffle filled Swiss dark or
   bittersweet chocolate, coarsely chopped
1 cup pecans, chopped

Preheat oven to 350°F/180°C. Prepare greased cookie sheets.

In the bowl of a mixer fitted with a flat beater, combine flour, margarine, brown sugar, white sugar, vanilla and egg. With a wooden spoon, mix in chocolate and pecans. Wet hands and roll dough into walnut sized balls, place onto greased cookie sheets 2-inches apart. Using a damp flat bottomed glass, press down each of the balls to flatten cookies. Bake for 12 minutes.

Preparation Time: 15 minutes
Cook Time: 12 minutes
Experience Level: Beginner

CRISP CHOCOLATE CHIP COOKIES

PARVE   YIELD 36 COOKIES

The author of this recipe always bakes a batch of these cookies and delivers them wrapped in a basket to newcomers to the neighborhood. What an inviting welcome.

¾ cup brown sugar
¾ cup white sugar
¾ cup margarine
2 eggs
1 teaspoon vanilla
2¼ cups flour

1 teaspoon baking soda
1 teaspoon salt
⅓ cup honey crunch wheat germ
1 (10 or 12-ounce) package semi-sweet chocolate chips
½ cup chopped pecans or walnuts, optional

Preheat oven to 320°F/155°C.

In the bowl of a mixer fitted with a flat beater, mix together brown and white sugar. Add margarine and cream together. Add eggs and vanilla, mix to combine.

In a medium bowl, combine flour, baking soda, salt and wheat germ. Gradually add to bowl of mixer. Add chocolate chips and nuts, if desired. Mix to combine.

Drop by teaspoonfuls onto ungreased cookie sheets. Bake for 12 to 15 minutes or until golden brown. Transfer to wire racks to cool.

Preparation Time: 20 minutes
Cook Time: 12 to 15 minutes
Experience Level: Beginner

Chewy Graham Cookies

PARVE OR DAIRY   **YIELD 42 COOKIES**

2 cups graham cracker crumbs
1½ cups flour
1 teaspoon baking powder
½ teaspoon salt
1 cup margarine or butter

¾ cup brown sugar
¾ cup white sugar
2 eggs
1½ teaspoons vanilla

In a large bowl combine graham cracker crumbs, flour, baking powder and salt.

In the bowl of a mixer fitted with a flat beater, cream margarine with brown and white sugars. Add eggs one at a time, add vanilla. Gradually beat in flour mixture.

Refrigerate for 10 minutes for easily handling.

Preheat oven to 350°F/180°C.

Shape dough into balls, using about 1 tablespoon per cookie. Place on ungreased cookie sheets.

Bake for 7 to 10 minutes or until lightly browned. Edges will brown before cookies are done. Cool for 3 minutes before removing from cookie sheets.

Preparation Time: 20 minutes
Cook Time: 7 to 10 minutes per batch, 3 batches
Chill Time: 10 minutes
Experience Level: Beginner

ROLLED NUT COOKIES

PARVE   YIELD 36 COOKIES

Chopped nuts create a chunky cookie. Ground nuts create a cookie that will melt in your mouth. Both versions are scrumptious.

2 cups flour

¼ cup sugar

½ teaspoon salt

1 cup margarine

2 teaspoons vanilla

2 cups finely chopped or ground walnuts

Confectioners' sugar

Preheat oven to 350°F/180°C.

Prepare 2 lightly greased cookie sheets.

In a large mixing bowl, mix together flour, sugar, salt, margarine, vanilla and nuts to form a dough. Roll into 1-inch balls. Place on prepared cookie sheets 1½-inches apart.

Bake for 15 to 17 minutes. Cool for 5 minutes. Place confectioners' sugar in a small bowl. Roll cookies in confectioners' sugar. Cool completely. Store in an airtight container.

Preparation Time: 20 minutes
Cook Time: 15 to 17 minutes
Experience Level: Beginner

RICE KRISPIE COOKIES

PARVE   YIELD 96 COOKIES

Everything but the kitchen sink goes into these moist cookies. The recipe makes plenty of cookies, but they go so fast, you will find yourself having to make another batch.

1 cup margarine

2 cups sugar

2 eggs

1 teaspoon vanilla

1 teaspoon baking soda

½ teaspoon salt

2½ cups flour

2 cups Rice Krispies

2 single serving packets instant oatmeal or ⅔ cup oatmeal

1 cup white chocolate chips

¾ cup semi-sweet chocolate chips

Preheat oven to 350°F/180°C.

In the bowl of a mixer fitted with a flat beater, cream together margarine and sugar. Add eggs one at a time until combined. Add vanilla, baking soda, salt and flour, mix well. Add Rice Krispies and oatmeal, mixing until combined and Rice Krispies are slightly crushed. Stir in white and semi-sweet chocolate chips.

Drop by teaspoonfuls onto ungreased cookie sheets. Bake in preheated oven for 8 to 10 minutes. Cookies will look raw, remove anyway. Let cool on cookie sheets.

Preparation Time: 10 minutes
Cook Time: 8 to 10 minutes per batch
Experience Level: Beginner

Sesame Almond Cookies

PARVE OR DAIRY   **YIELD 36 COOKIES**

Sucanut and spelt flour are available in the natural section of most supermarkets. The use of spelt flour instead of flour derived from wheat makes this recipe the perfect choice for those with wheat allergies.

¼ cup raw sesame seeds	½ teaspoon baking soda
¼ cup margarine or butter, softened	1½ to 2 cups spelt flour
¼ cup raw almond butter	2 eggs
1 tablespoon raw tahini	1 teaspoon vanilla
1 cup sucanut	1 teaspoon real almond extract

Preheat oven to 375°F/190°F.

Place sesame seeds on a parchment lined jelly-roll pan. Place in preheated oven until toasted, about 10 minutes. Set aside.

In the bowl of a mixer fitted with a flat beater, cream margarine, almond butter, tahini and sucanut until well mixed. Mixture will not be smooth. Add toasted sesame seeds, baking soda, spelt flour, eggs, vanilla and almond extract, using enough flour to form a somewhat firm mixture. Mixture will be slightly sticky and may be refrigerated for easier handling.

Drop by teaspoonfuls 1½-inches apart onto parchment lined cookie sheets.

Bake in preheated oven for 8 to 10 minutes or until lightly golden. Remove from oven and let stand 5 minutes, transfer to wire racks to cool completely.

Preparation Time: 25 minutes
Cook Time: 20 minutes
Experience Level: Intermediate

POTATO CHIP COOKIES

DAIRY OR PARVE   YIELD 24 COOKIES

Potato chips in a cookie? You will love the taste of these cookies, which benefit from the crunch of the chips, but taste nothing like the salty snack.

½ cup butter or margarine
⅓ cup sugar
¾ teaspoon vanilla
1 cup flour

⅓ cup crushed potato chips
⅓ cup chopped walnuts
1 tablespoon sugar
Confectioners' sugar

Preheat oven to 350°F/180°C.

In the bowl of a mixer fitted with a flat beater, cream together butter with sugar and vanilla until light and fluffy. Add flour, beating until well blended. Using a wooden spoon stir in potato chips and nuts. Shape into 1-inch balls. Place 3-inches apart on ungreased baking sheets. Using a flat bottomed glass dipped in sugar, flatten cookies.

Bake for 12 to 15 minutes or until edges are lightly brown. Sift confectioners' sugar over cookies while warm.

Preparation Time: 20 minutes
Cook Time: 12 to 15 minutes
Experience Level: Beginner

JELLY RAISIN NUT COOKIES

PARVE   YIELD 36 COOKIES

DOUGH
1 cup margarine
1 cup sugar
4 cups flour

FILLING
Strawberry jelly
Chopped walnuts

½ cup water
1 teaspoon baking powder
1 teaspoon vanilla

Raisins

DOUGH: Preheat oven to 350°F/180°C.

Prepare 2 parchment lined (15x10-inch) jelly-roll pans.

In the bowl of a mixer fitted with a flat beater, cream together margarine and sugar. Add flour, water, baking powder and vanilla. Mix until well combined.

Divide dough into thirds. Using a rolling pin, thinly roll out each piece of dough. Spread a thin layer of strawberry jelly over dough. Sprinkle with walnuts and raisins to cover, avoiding edges. Roll up each jelly-roll style. Cut into ½-inch slices and place on prepared pans. Bake for 10 minutes or until lightly brown.

Preparation Time: 20 minutes
Cook Time: 10 minutes
Experience Level: Intermediate

Menu Suggestions

These menus are for the experienced cook whose desire is to go all out for company or a holiday meal. Here are samples of foods that complement and enhance each other's flavors and textures. From the first course to the finale join your company in their appreciation of an elegant culinary experience.

AUTUMN SHABBOS OR YOM TOV

Wine Suggestions: Bartenura Soave 2001,
Tishbi Estate 1999 Cabernet Sauvignon or Layla Vinyards Malbec

Seven Grain Challah

Roasted Asparagus Soup

Sparkling Kumquat Salad

Quick Marinated Salmon with Arugula

Spinach and Herb Stuffed Chicken

Tongue with Mushrooms and Artichokes

Pastallim

Fragrant Persian Rice

Ratatouille

Poached Pears Stuffed with Chocolate on Pound Cake with Syrup

Nut Cookies

AUTUMN SHABBOS OR YOM TOV

Wine Suggestion: Baron Herzog White Zinfendel

Sweet Potato Soup

Stuffed Whitefish

Caramelized Apple and Sautéed Mushroom Salad

Homemade Corned Beef

Honey Pecan Crusted Chicken

Vegetable Stuffed Zucchini

Sweet Stuffed Acorn Squash

Song of India Rice

Chickpea Stew

Blackberry Jam Cake with Brown Sugar Frosting

Chocolate Wows

Rice Krispie Cookies

WINTER SHABBOS

Wine Suggestions: Herzog Selection French Cabernet Sauvignon 1999,
Gamla Chardonnay

Sweet Honey Challah

Spicy Gefilte Fish in Tomato Sauce

Persian Meatball Soup

Stir-Fried Salad on Radicchio Spoons

Harvest Leg of Lamb

Pungent Sweet Chicken

Savory Roasted Baby Eggplants with Tomatoes and Onions

Zucchini Creole

Fava Bean and Chickpea Salad

Peach Apricot Cobbler with Spiced Whipped Cream

Persian Baklava

Sweet Kaak

THANKSGIVING DINNER

Wine Suggestion: Yarden Sauvignon Blanc 1999

Pumpkin Rolls with Streusel Filling

Magnificent Crown Herb Bread

Root Vegetable Soup

Mixed Greens with Portobello Mushrooms and Honey
Glazed Almonds

Classic Roasted Turkey

Crispy Sautéed Rosemary

Tri Color Meat Roll

Carrot Soufflé

Scrumptious Sage Stuffing

Marinated Asparagus

Chickpea Salad with Oven Dried Tomatoes

Sherry Glazed Grape Tart

Hazelnut Torte

Pumpkin Custard

ORIENTAL DINNER

Apricot Chicken Pot Stickers

Asian Chicken Salad

Hong Kong Orange Chicken

Egg Rolls

Bite Size Spinach Egg Foo Yong

Oriental Green Beans

Cantonese Fried Rice

Sesame Almond Cookies

Churgays

SHEVA BRACHOS

Wine Suggestions: Gamala Sauvignon Blanc 2000,
Alfasi Sauvignon Blac

Herbed Dinner Rolls

Shallot Butter

Sweet Stuffed Mini Peppers

Braised Stuffed Veal Breast

Roast Chicken with Rosemary and Roasted Garlic

Caramelized Onion and Beef Tartlets

Stuffed Mushrooms

Garlic Green Beans

Baked Rice and Vegetable Medley

Chocolate Indulgence

Mayan Hot Chocolate with Chili Peppers

SUMMER BARBECUE

Wine Suggestion: Herzog Selection Syrah

French Baguettes

Cuban Salsa

Cumin and Lime Grilled Skirt Steaks

Pulled Chicken Sandwiches

Salami Stuffing

Herb Marinated Grilled Vegetables

Wild Rice and Bean Salad

Apricot Cherry Slab Pie

Crisp Chocolate Chip Cookies

WEEKNIGHT MEAT

Oasis Nan Bread

Spinach, Orange and Pomegranate Salad

Chicken with Olives and Dates

Mediterranean Pasta Salad

Garlic Green Beans

Coconut Chews

DAIRY YOM TOV

Wine Suggestion: Gan Eden Gewürztraminer,
Golan Chardonnay

Caramelized Onion Braids

Baby Romaine and Watercress Salad

Fettuccini with Mushrooms and Cream

Salmon with Sun-Dried Tomato Crust

Striped Zucchini Stuffed with Chickpeas and Rice

Mango Salad

Fila with Cheese

Lorraine's Cheesecake

Raspberry Scones

BREAK THE FAST MEAL

Crescent Rolls

Kaak

Celery Garlic Soup

Tapenade

5 Color Summer Salad

Halibut with Apricot Sauce

Sweet Cheese Casserole

Spanek U Giben

Tabouli Salad

Key Lime Pie

Sour Cream Pound Cake

WEEKNIGHT DAIRY

Wine Suggestion: Alef Chianti Classico 2000,
Abarbanel Selection

French Bread with Olives

Dairy Vegetable Soup

Fresh Ravioli with Spinach Ricotta Filling and Tomato Sauce

Roasted Zucchini with Red Peppers and Scallions

Garlic Croutons over Tossed Salad
with Oven Dried Tomatoes

Apple Tart Cheesecake

List of Recipes 15 Minutes or Less Preparation Time

Index

Metric Conversions

WEIGHT EQUIVALENTS

These are not exact weight equivalents, but have been rounded up or down slightly to make measuring easier.

AMERICAN	METRIC	AMERICAN	METRIC	AMERICAN	METRIC	AMERICAN	METRIC
¼ ounce	7 grams	5 ounces	150 grams	11 ounces	325 grams	1 pound 2 ounces	500 grams
½ ounce	15 grams	6 ounces	175 grams	12 ounces	350 grams	1½ pounds	750 grams
1 ounce	30 grams	7 ounces	200 grams	13 ounces	375 grams	2 pounds	900 grams
2 ounces	60 grams	8 ounces (½ pound)	225 grams	14 ounces	400 grams	2¼ pounds	1 kilogram
3 ounces	90 grams	9 ounces	250 grams	15 ounces	425 grams	3 pounds	1.4 kilgrams
4 ounces	115 grams	10 ounces	300 grams	16 ounces (1 pound)	450 grams	4 pounds	1.8 kilograms
						4½ pounds	2 kilograms

VOLUME EQUIVALENTS

These are not exact volume equivalents, but have been rounded up or down slightly to make measuring easier.

AMERICAN	METRIC	AMERICAN	METRIC
¼ teaspoon	1.25 milliliters	⅔ cup (10 tablespoons)	150 milliliters
½ teaspoon	2.5 milliliters	¾ cup (12 tablespoons)	175 milliliters
1 teaspoon	5 milliliters	1 cup (16 tablespoons)	250 milliliters
½ tablespoon (1½ teaspoons)	7.5 milliliters	1¼ cups	300 milliliters
1 tablespoon (3 teaspoons)	15 milliliters	1½ cups	350 milliliters
¼ cup (4 tablespoons)	60 milliliters	1 pint (2 cups)	500 milliliters
⅓ cup (5 tablespoons)	75 milliliters	2½ cups	625 milliliters
½ cup (8 tablespoons)	125 milliliters	1 quart (4 cups)	1 litre

OVEN TEMPERATURE EQUIVALENTS

OVEN	°FAHRENHEIT	°CELSIUS	GAS MARK
very cool	250–275	130–140	½–1
cool	300	150	2
warm	325	170	3
moderate	350	180	4
moderately hot	375	190	5
moderately hot	400	200	6
hot	425	220	7
very hot	450	230	8
very hot	475	250	9